1 ⁰⁰
8/22

D0722407

Tupperware Unsealed

Florida A&M University, Tallahassee
Florida Atlantic University, Boca Raton
Florida Gulf Coast University, Ft. Myers
Florida International University, Miami
Florida State University, Tallahassee
New College of Florida, Sarasota
University of Central Florida, Orlando
University of Florida, Gainesville
University of North Florida, Jacksonville
University of South Florida, Tampa
University of West Florida, Pensacola

University Press of Florida

Gainesville·Tallahassee·Tampa

Boca Raton·Pensacola·Orlando

Miami·Jacksonville·Ft. Myers

Sarasota

TUPPERWARE

Unsealed

Brownie Wise, Earl Tupper,

and the Home Party Pioneers

Bob Kealing

Copyright 2008 by Bob Kealing

13   12   11   10   09   08   6   5   4   3   2   1

Library of Congress Cataloging-in-Publication Data
Kealing, Bob.
Tupperware, unsealed : the inside story of Brownie Wise,
Earl Tupper, and the home party pioneers / Bob Kealing.
p. cm.
Includes bibliographical references and index.
ISBN 978-0-8130-3227-6 (alk. paper)
1. Tupperware Corporation—History. 2. Tupperware Home
Parties—History. 3. Wise, Brownie. 4. Tupper, Earl Silas.
5. Home parties (Marketing)—United States—History.
6. Plastic container industry—United States—History.
7. Plastic tableware—United States—History. I. Title.
HD9662.C664T865 2008
338.7′668497092273—dc22   2007047539

Photographs on pages ii, vi, viii, 4, 8, 13, 24, 37, 41, 57, 72,
77, 84, 87, 94, 95, 104, 109, 115, 121, 124, 139, 162, 165, 206
are used by permission of the Smithsonian Institution.
The photograph on page 3 is courtesy of Orange County
Regional History Center.
The photographs on pages 207, 208, 209, 210, 217, and 218
were taken by the author.

The University Press of Florida is the scholarly publishing
agency for the State University System of Florida, compris-
ing Florida A&M University, Florida Atlantic University,
Florida Gulf Coast University, Florida International
University, Florida State University, New College of
Florida, University of Central Florida, University of
Florida, University of North Florida, University of South
Florida, and University of West Florida.

University Press of Florida
15 Northwest 15th Street
Gainesville, FL 32611-2079
www.upf.com

In memory of
James L. Kealing
and Donna Ross

CONTENTS

Acknowledgments   ix

One   The Brownie Wise Problem   1

Two   Going It Alone   6

Three   The Product and the Plan   17

Four   Filling In the Gaps   28

Five   A Turbulent New Home   35

Six   The Confluence of Genius   51

Seven   Permanent Roots   64

Eight   Groundwork for a Revolution   82

Nine   Success and Jubilation   97

Ten   Explosive Growth   112

Eleven   A Revolt from Within   118

Twelve   New Players in Place   136

Thirteen   The Foundations Shaken   143

Fourteen   Hibiscus, the Sunshine Cinderella   158

Fifteen   Jubilee Nightmare   169

Sixteen   The Breaking Point   179

Seventeen   Pictures of Despair   188

Eighteen   Moving On, Selling Out   198

Nineteen   Legacies   205

Notes   221

Selected Bibliography   245

Index   247

Acknowledgments

This project would not have been possible without the availability of the Brownie Wise and Earl Tupper collections at the Smithsonian Institution's National Museum of American History, Behring Center. Through what in many instances was hundreds of pages of their own writings, it was possible for Wise and Tupper, their families and close associates, to tell their own stories. They were the road map and timeline for this project.

I would also like to thank the many people who were willing to share their time and stories with me: Gary McDonald, Elsie Mortland, the late Jerry Wise, Tony Ponticelli, Don Hinton, Pat Jordan, Glenn Tupper, Brenda Ansley, Jack McCollum, Esther Dulger, Fred DeWitt, and the late Marilyn Mennello; a special thanks to Melissa Bancroft for helping lay some of the groundwork. Thanks also to the clerks at the Osceola County Courthouse for pulling so many court files. From decades-old depositions came the words of Hamer Wilson, Glen Bump, Dave Seraphine, Gerald and Thelma Croxton, and Bill Boyd. Florida Sunshine laws have been crucial in helping to tell so much of this history.

Thanks to my editor, John Byram, at the University Press of Florida for his immediate faith in this book and his long-term guidance.

Thanks to my wife, Karen Kealing, and our children, William and Kristen Kealing, for their constant love and support. Special thanks to my brother Jeff Kealing for the title work. Thanks also to Jane Kealing, John K. Kealing, William L. Kealing, and Mr. John Ross.

Thanks to my friends at the Jack Kerouac Writer-in-Residence Project of Orlando. Our grassroots effort has grown beyond imagination, and writers worldwide continue to benefit from everyone's efforts and dedication. Thanks also to Susan Albury at University Press of Florida and to Bonnie Fesmire.

Two works have been instrumental in piquing my interest in the great American success story of Tupperware and its home-party pioneers: Alison Clarke's groundbreaking 1999 book, *Tupperware: The Promise of Plastic in 1950s America*, and filmmaker Laurie Kahn-Leavitt's Peabody Award–winning PBS documentary, *Tupperware!*

Tupperware Unsealed

One

THE BROWNIE WISE PROBLEM

I don't need any hobbies.
I have everything I want
right here. I hope it
never ends.
—Brownie Wise

Earl Tupper never made grand entrances. The eccentric Yankee inventor who brought Tupperware to the world seemed to blow in and out of central Florida like afternoon thunderstorms sparked by a July sea breeze. Tupper never went in for all the razzle-dazzle of his Home Party Division, the company's sales arm that had helped him rake in millions. He wasn't one for the high-octane dealer pep rallies known as the annual Tupperware Jubilee. The only picture Tupperware photographer Jack McCollum remembered getting of Tupper, the boss, was of him sliding in the company's back door. People around Earl Silas Tupper knew the cloak-and-dagger stuff was just his way.

It was January 1958. The phone rang at the homes of two top Tupperware executives: Hamer Wilson and Gary McDonald. Tupper told them he was in town and ordered them to an unscheduled meeting the next morning at the Angebilt Hotel in downtown Orlando. Must be good news, McDonald thought; maybe Tupper had a new idea or, better yet, a bold new invention and he wanted to share the secret with them. McDonald had no inkling of the bomb Tupper was about to drop.

The last week in January had that kind of chamber-of-commerce weather people around most other parts of the county could only envy. Tupper had left behind gale warnings and heavy snows in the Northeast for balmy Orlando temperatures near seventy. With these clear skies and light winds, you could sneak in a game of golf at Sanford's Mayfair Country Club. On a cloudless January morning, you could run a Carolina-rigged finesse worm along the Kissimmee grass in Lake Tohopekaliga, Toho for short, and with any luck snag one of the best bass in the state. The central Florida of 1958 was still very much the outdoorsman's paradise. On some of the plentiful rangelands near Tupperware's Orange Blossom Trail headquarters, cowboys could ride by the compass for miles and not see a lick of paved road.

To the east along the sweeping expanse of sand, swamp, and sunning alligators, bedeviled navy scientists on the fledgling Space Coast had been frustrated yet again in their attempts to send a tiny earth satellite into space. This time the Martin Vanguard rocket developed mechanical faults. The month previous, another version had barely cleared the launch pad when it burst into a million fiery bits. The explosion, reflected in the sunglasses of spectators, made for a classic photo in *Life* magazine.

In its heyday, the Angebilt Hotel hosted wealthy rooster owners from across the world. In the 1920s and 1930s, Orlando gained international recognition as North America's cockfighting capital. Built in 1923 for $1 million, Joseph Fenner Ange's eleven-story creation was about the only building Orlandoans could call a skyscraper. A massive wrought-iron framed canopy with scrolled brackets made for an impressive front entrance to one of the city's few grand hotels, located at 37 North Orange Avenue. In the mezzanine, WLOF blasted 250 watts of top-40 radio. With that kind of power, you could hear the number-one hit that week, "At the Hop" by Danny and the Juniors, all the way down to Kissimmee.

Still in his late twenties, the confident, redheaded wunderkind Gary McDonald already had more than a decade of direct-selling know-how under his belt. He'd worked his way up selling mops and cleaning products to suburban housewives. Now he was an up-and-coming executive at one of the most celebrated direct-selling companies in America. He knew how to whip up a crowd, instill dealer loyalty, and come up with new ways to recognize their successes.

Sales counselor Hamer Wilson was older and had a wider array of real-world business experience. He had spent most of his three years with Tupperware on the road building relationships with those crucial to the company's home-party business: the dealers, managers, and distributors. He had a gift for remembering not just their names but also those of their spouses and children. Wilson's low-key approach, sense of humor, and friendly smile had gotten him considerable notice in the short time he'd spent with the company.

The Angebilt Hotel in downtown Orlando, site of the fateful January 1958 meeting between Earl Tupper, Hamer Wilson, and Gary McDonald.

As ordered, Wilson and McDonald made their way to Tupper's hotel room. Greeting them was the prematurely bald but imposing inventor. Never one for small talk that exceeded "Good morning," the boss showed great loyalty to obedient and competent employees and a swift, iron hand to anyone who crossed him. The taskmaster had a thing for used foreign sports cars. His mind never stopped analyzing the way things worked. Never in a million years did the people who gave Tupper a smelly, dark waste product imagine that one day he would turn it into plastic gold. It took tireless experimenting, determination, and creativity. That was Earl Tupper's genius. He was direct, even to the point of being harsh. There wasn't much funny business or fraternizing. But you knew darn well where you stood with Earl Tupper.

When Tupper convened the meeting in his hotel room, it was obvious one key player was missing, Brownie Wise. For seven years she'd been the head of Tupper's Home Party Division, guided it through explosive growth, millions of dollars in sales, and national notoriety. Brownie Wise felt at home on a horse, played violin, and once served dead rattlesnakes as a joke to shocked dinner guests. She could burp bowls at a Tupperware party and go head to head with

Earl Silas Tupper, inventor
of Tupperware.

strong-minded male underlings. Brownie Wise was a loving if often absentee
mother and a long-suffering divorcée whose alcoholic and abusive ex-husband
was like a dark cloud of shame that never left the horizon.

A master motivator and communicator, Wise refined and feminized home-
demonstration selling. She was the yin to Tupper's yang. Where he was fussy
and reclusive, Wise lived to mingle with and inspire the dealer workforce. She
was one of the few people who felt confident enough to speak her mind with
Earl Tupper, even to dress him down if she felt it necessary. If one of his products seemed like it would be a natural sell, fine. But not all of his ideas were
Wonder Bowls. When it came to something impractical like the Wigloo, the
job often fell to Wise and McDonald to do the unsell.

Decades before female tycoons Martha Stewart and Oprah Winfrey, Wise
stoked the fires of dealer loyalty with a kind of religious devotion to her work.
Like a ubiquitous fairy godmother, she seemed to cast a magic spell over many
of her Tupperware dealers. They adored Wise to the point of competing to
win her clothing, even if it meant dropping significant pounds to fit into an
actual Brownie Wise dress. The stories of trailblazing executive Brownie Wise
had been carefully crafted by the top Tupperware brass, then churned off their
remarkable public relations assembly line. The adoring press loved to write
about the coquettish charm girl, doting single mother, and strong-willed chief

executive all molded into one. Some of it was true, other parts pure puffery. But it didn't matter. In just seven years, with Brownie Wise on the public relations pedestal, Tupperware expanded its dealer force by thousands and reaped millions in profits. Brownie Wise was a direct-selling legend, instrumental in making Tupperware an American revolution.

"I need to talk to you guys about something that's gonna happen and it's gonna happen today and it's gonna involve the two of you," Tupper told his executives. "I have had enough of Brownie Wise, and I'm going down there to headquarters and I'm going to tell her this is her last day. She's fired."[1]

The revelation met with stunned silence from McDonald and Wilson. "That was a bombshell," McDonald remembered. "We were shocked beyond saying anything."[2]

Millions of dollars were at stake. Before Tupper could make the moves he felt necessary, he had to clean up the Brownie Wise problem, lest anyone forget that his baby was the real star of this food-storage revolution. Not Tupper himself, mind you, but the plastic products that bore his name and burped up cash as well as they sealed in freshness. From a long, comfortable distance, and usually over the telephone, the odd couple of Earl Silas Tupper and Brownie Humphrey Wise together had built something far bigger than both of their formidable personalities. A writer once called Wise and Tupper "a pair of geniuses always on the brink."[3] It was an apt description. Only this time their unlikely business relationship had fractured beyond repair.

Tupper would reap the fortune, Wise would fade into obscurity with a pittance, and soon both would be done with Tupperware forever. Tupper was the president. Tupperware was his product. He owned the stock and held all the cards. In 1958 corporate America, that's just how things were.

Two

Going It
Alone

The Fruits of life fall
into the hands of
those who climb the
tree and pick them.
—Earl Tupper

There's one word in the groundbreaking 1967 film *The Graduate* that came to represent the emerging counterculture's rejection of adult America. Dustin Hoffman's character, Benjamin Braddock, is wandering like a stranger at his own college graduation party. The camera follows in claustrophobic close-up as martini-swilling, chain-smoking adult strangers bombard him with unwanted advice and unnerving questions about his future.

At the climax of this scene, one self-assured bore takes the befuddled young man by the shoulder and glares at him, obviously intending to resolve all of the graduate's uncertainty. His answer to what's haunting Hoffman's disaffected character boils down to one thing: "Plastics."[1]

At the time the film was playing to overflow crowds of empathetic youngsters facing civil unrest at home and Vietnam overseas, the word *plastics* brought howls of derisive laughter. Finally, a filmmaker dared to see things from the younger generation's antiestablishment point of view, dared to expose the phoniness and materialism of those on the other side of the growing generational divide—the "plastics" society.

"Plastics" may well have been code for Tupperware, the ever-present product line that in the 1950s swept across America like a flash fire. The Bell Tumblers, Wonder Bowls, and two-ounce Midget containers became as common in American households as television, telephones, and hula hoops. Like the boring adult preaching plastics to Hoffman, Tupperware dealers extolled the virtues of the Tupperware party. Those gatherings of suburban housewives playing games and exchanging gossip were key to the product's combustible growth and popularity. Spread the gospel of Tupperware everywhere—burp it and they will come. To some, the "Tupperware Lady" in her hose, hat, heels, and gloves seemed to personify the female stereotype of the plastic, *Father Knows Best* 1950s.

In a very pragmatic and nonthreatening way, the Tupperware phenomenon was having just the opposite effect. One sale at a time, housewives were finding an economic niche outside the household. Tupperware executives had the shrewd notion—untried in any organization before them—that women would power the engine of this home-selling revolution.

Tupperware wasn't the first direct-sale product, but it was arguably the best. The airtight seal meant food stayed fresh much longer than with the old-fashioned trick of using a limp shower cap. That meant Tupperware saved money. The company didn't invent home-party selling, but arguably its pioneering early executives perfected it. The spread of Tupperware transformed the lives of a legion of dealers, managers, and distributors, none of whom actually drew a paycheck from Tupperware. The achievers took their cut from the goods they sold, grew their businesses, and transformed their lives. The genius was in the company's knack for inspiring people to be more successful than they ever thought possible, while encouraging them to help friends do the very same thing.

The confluence of this revolutionary product and perfection of the home-based sales technique began with a bankrupted tree surgeon who fancied himself a modern-day Leonardo da Vinci and a young Detroit divorcée without much in the way of real business experience. Long before these two would seal the nation's devotion in pastel-colored containers, they had to go about reversing their own fortunes, dusting themselves off from failure, and finding their way to each other.

On her own twenty-fifth birthday, May 25, 1938, Brownie Wise was about to become a mother. In Depression-era Detroit, General Motors created a sensation with its Cadillac "Sixty Special" sedan. The Detroit Tigers superstar first baseman Hank Greenberg was already on his way to challenging Babe Ruth's home-run record. He ended up with fifty-eight, just two shy of the Bambino.

Brownie Wise in Detroit, ca. 1945.

Childbirth proved difficult for Brownie Wise. Doctors used forceps to facilitate bringing Jerry Wise into the world on his mother's birthday. The instrument took off the tip of the baby's left ear and gave him a permanent scar just above his left eyebrow. But none of that in any way dimmed or diminished his mother's love. Giving birth seemed to infuse Brownie Wise with a new sense of wonder and responsibility.

"Having a child is like being given a second life to live—we see so much and feel so much and learn so much through their eyes and hearts," Wise wrote. "Nothing is quite so awesome as watching tiny hands reach out from the bassinet to first grasp this strangely, beautifuly [*sic*] and inexplicable mixture of life and love and want and achievement we mortals call Life. The blessing of having my own boy I shall never take for granted."[2]

The birth of baby Jerry was one bright spot in the turbulent marriage of Brownie and Robert Wise. The two met in 1936 at the Texas centennial celebration in Dallas. The Ford building with its fifty-five thousand square feet of sprawling exhibit space enthralled guests with a look at the first car Henry Ford ever built, one of the first circa 1905 Model As, and a view of Fords of the future. Guests could see examples of all the roads Americans had traveled to that time. Twenty-three-year-old Brownie Humphrey and her husband-to-be were so impressed with the future of Ford that they decided to make Detroit their home. On December 15, 1936, less than a month after the end of the centennial celebration, they were married.

Robert Wise took a job as an engineer for Ford. When times were good, the short, stocky, and clean-shaven Wise was known to his friends as the ultimate "Good-time Charlie." At one of his parties, everyone was welcome. With his wife and baby at home, Wise often stayed out drinking until the good-time side of him was gone. His mean streaks sometimes included violence. One of the most disturbing episodes was when he threw a bottle of acid at his mother-in-law, Rosabelle Humphrey. Although he missed, the acid hit her 1939 Plymouth sedan, eating a hole through the upholstery and chassis.[3] Brownie Wise knew this was no environment in which to raise her son. Less than five years into her marriage, she filed for divorce.

In a child-support agreement dated September 17, 1941, in the district court of Wayne County, Michigan, Brownie Wise was awarded custody of her three year-old son. The judge granted Robert Wise one visit per week. On Sundays at 3 p.m., he could "take said child for outing not to exceed five hours."[4] For the rest of his life, Robert Wise would make intermittent attempts to regain a place in his ex-wife's and son's lives. He would see considerable success in business, have more wives and children, even become a minister. Yet his struggle with alcohol undermined everything he did for the rest of his life, reducing Robert Wise to a pariah among those who had loved him. Three months after the divorce, the Japanese bombed Pearl Harbor, and the United States entered World War II. Brownie and Jerry Wise became like many women and children in wartime America, doing without husbands and fathers.

○ ○ ○

Like Brownie Wise, Earl Silas Tupper wasn't long on formal education, barely graduating from Fitchburg Massachusetts High School in 1925. Born to agrarian New Englander parents in 1907, Tupper showed a knack for invention and innovation early on. Ever the tinkerer, Tupper developed means for improving work life on his family's farm. His first known patent of the scores to follow was a frame that made cleaning chickens easier. At ten years old, Tupper decided he could sell more of the family's produce by peddling it directly to customers, door-to-door. What he lacked in formal education, Tupper more than compensated for in ambition, making it his goal to become a millionaire by age thirty. He held down other jobs as a young man at the post office and laboring in the rail yards.

In 1928, Tupper founded his first business, Tupper Tree Doctors. Through the Depression years, his landscaping and nursery business grew. In 1931 he married Marie Whitcomb. While his business and personal lives were taking shape, Tupper poured much of his passion into a notebook he used to sketch new ideas for inventions. Below a cartoon of another inventive genius, Thomas Jefferson, Tupper wrote: "DaVinci and Jefferson, Edison and a host of others are proof that an inventive, intuitive, enthusiastic and trained mind continues to experiment, study, search and develop along an entire line of human endeavor, conceiving developments in every field to which it turns."[5]

Long before Tupperware, the young inventor drew up "No Drip" ice-cream cones equipped with a gutter to catch the drippings and funnel them back in to the cone. The "Dagger Comb" came with a clip to fit nicely on bathing suits. Tupper even devised a way to perform an appendectomy without leaving a scar. None of these inventions had the kind of mass appeal that could earn Earl Tupper a living, but he kept on. Always with pencil and notebook nearby, Earl Tupper looked at how things worked and tried to devise a way to make them work better.[6]

The deepening depression chipped away at people's spirits and their enterprises. The malaise took a toll in Tupper's hometown of Shirley, Massachusetts. People didn't have the disposable income to spend on trees and landscaping. After a positive start, in 1936 the slow economic war of attrition forced Tupper Tree Doctors into bankruptcy. With his wife and young sons, Ronald and Myles, to support, Tupper decided to pursue his fortune in nearby Leominster, Massachusetts. The town's proximity was serendipitous. It was already known as America's "Pioneer Plastics City."

The year before, Tupper had been introduced to a man named Bernard Doyle, founder of DuPont's plastics manufacturing division known as Viscoloid. Accepting a job there in 1937, Tupper started small, making sixty cents an hour in the company's experiment and development department. From small wages came great ideas and education. The experience and know-how he acquired from seasoned pros in the plastics business was invaluable. "That's when my education really began," he reflected.[7]

Tupper designed and built his own home on Horse Pond Road in the town of

Shirley. Tupper loved the beauty of reflecting ponds on his property. The home evoked the Spartan rural lifestyle he'd come to know as a New Hampshire farm boy. In 1938, he became a father for the third time. When the doctor was too drunk to make it to their home, Earl Tupper brought his breech baby daughter, Starr, into the world, following instructions from his wife, Marie.[8] The same year, Tupper started work with molding machines, renting at first, then buying a surplus unit from Commonwealth Plastics.

Around that time, Tupper broke away from Viscoloid and founded his own industrial plastics company. Tupper's old boss, Bernard Doyle, farmed out some work to him. To say the young entrepreneur was dedicated to the work is an understatement. In an unpublished biographical sketch among Tupper's papers, Neil Osterweil reported that Tupper "would often stay at the molding machine 22 hours per day, 2–5 days at a time, breaking only to eat and to sleep on a cot next to the machine." During one stretch, Tupper suffered a serious injury that almost cost him sight in one eye. "He ignored the doctor and followed his own course of treatment," Osterweil wrote, "and the eye healed safely."[9]

With the onset of World War II, Tupper expanded the business and opened his first plant in Farnumsville, Massachusetts. In the plant's sprawling forty-five thousand square feet, Tupper Plastics churned out parts for an array of wartime materials: jeeps, gas masks, and navy signal lamps. Three shifts of workers kept the molding machines humming away. It was a time of supply shortages, self-sacrifice, and Rosie the Riveter. As men streamed to war by the millions, American women entered the workforce out of necessity.

○ ○ ○

With Robert Wise out of the picture, Brownie Wise, son Jerry, and mother Rose made their home at 845 N. Melborn Street in Dearborn, Michigan, the Detroit suburb best known as the home of Henry Ford. The family's two-story house stood five blocks off Telegraph Road just west of the Dearborn Country Club. A carpenter finished the attic so Brownie could use it as a combination bedroom and sewing room. She and her mother made all their own clothes. Rose liked to tend the large garden they planted in the lot next door. She turned the rhubarb crop into wine. Young Jerry hated the smell, but during the war Rose could trade it for something they didn't have, like butter, which was in short supply. Jerry passed the time in the basement, playing with the big train set he had situated on top of nine sheets of plywood.

According to Jerry Wise, in wartime the family got rid of the sewing machines and turned the attic into bedrooms for airmen who needed a place to live. During the worst part of the war, their basement became a first-aid center for wounded soldiers. The home next door was converted into a hospital. Brownie Wise had taken a job as an executive secretary to the general manager at Bendix, the company manufacturing brakes and struts for the *Avenger,* a navy torpedo plane. Wise and other employees were asked to volunteer their homes, time, and talents for the war effort. Chauvinism of the day had to give way to ambitious minds, even if they happened to belong to women. Now on her own, the executive secretary was stretching her wings in many ways. "She was always doing something," her son remembered.[10]

Draftsmen were also in short supply so Wise studied drafting at Detroit City College. In a matter of weeks, she was proficient in mechanical drawing. Jerry enjoyed all the tools that came with the job. As a child, Brownie learned violin and later took up the sax. Theirs was a musical household, and songs with patriotic themes were always favorites. Pat, their homely but intelligent Boston bull terrier, liked to plop himself down and snore next to Brownie's favorite chair. At night, Wise enjoyed indulging in a more creative passion, writing.

In a notebook from the 1940s: "I was searching for a basic premise on which to plan my life. I was trying to piece together some of the many lessons I learned from my mother, my teachers, my ministers, old friends," Wise wrote. "Sum up and weed out and establish a set of maxims. I wanted to work and expected to work hard to build a successful life. Not just money—but to be a success in dealing with people, bringing Jerry up and to find an inner sense of accomplishment. I was fiercely determined to draw a blueprint for this as I had done for my home. I wanted to be a *successful human being*."[11]

Her correspondence didn't end with letters or personal journals. Wise developed a pen name under which she wrote an advice column in a local newspaper. She named her alter ego Hibiscus, after a favorite flower often found in the sunny reaches of Florida. She often referred to son Jerry as "Tiny Hands." With "something lovely on the radio awfully late," Wise wrote, "I feel a writing jag coming to life."[12] As snow "the size of silver dollars" drifted past her Melborn Street window, Hibiscus blossomed:

> The earth holds its breath when it's snowing as it is tonight—death could be no more quiet than this night. Nor more beautiful, either. Even the swish of auto tires on the streets is muted, and people pass to and fro under the warm circle of street-light without making a sound. The evergreens, especially the long needled Scotch and Austrian pines, are already coated heavily—they look as though some giant hand had picked them up, and dipped them upside down in marshmallow frosting. I love walking in the new snow, before the dirge of snow shovels sets in—a form of conceit, I suppose, if you look deeply enough into it, to want to make tracks where none have been made before.[13]

As Hibiscus, Wise commented on wartime strife: "I have despaired at each new war bulletin and prayed to God for something better for his children; I have watched the sun go down in a riot of breathless color, and seen the moon rise over the crest of a little hill, like a benediction to a day. I have done many things lately; life is full and rich and beautiful to your Hibiscus."[14]

In her fictional world, Wise created a devoted husband she named "Coeur" and a great palace of a home called Lovehaven. The Hibiscus letters foreshadow many of the techniques Wise would later use to inspire the Tupperware faithful, creating a kind of idealized, shared existence with her readers:

I thought, as I swung open the door, of what a grave responsibility Coeur had placed upon us who will live in this house. A haven of love it must always be. I stood a moment in the wide reception hall, thinking of the many feet that will tread those tiles, of the friends who would come bringing us cheer and gaiety, and a corner of my heart hoped that if any came in search of encouragement or happiness they would never fail to find it. I paused before the white marble fireplace in the living room, and my heart's eye saw the gracious glow and warmth of the flames that will dance in its arms on long winter evenings to come.[15]

Brownie Wise in her early days as a divorced executive secretary at Bendix, ca. 1947.

In real life, Wise had held a torch for a South Carolina doctor named Wade C. Marshall. On a mid-July night, with Pat snoring at her side, she sat down at the typewriter. "Wade Dearest, a waning moon is caught in the tops of little elms down in the lower corner of my garden now," Wise observed. "Is it the inference of the train whistle, I wonder, that brings you so close tonight? You might be sitting in that big chair over there by the window, with a pipe in your hand, for all the closeness I feel about you—and yet time and distance have taken away the certainty of what your smile is actually like."[16]

In the same letter, Wise praises her long-distance love as someone who will never have a "satisfied" life. "You'll always be seeking the bit of life that's just around the next curve in the road, and that's how it should be," Wise observed. "You not only dream but you seek—and consequently life will be very rich for you."[17] It was with that mixture of curiosity and the need to support her family that Wise began to seek a change in her own life. A lack of formal education and prevailing stereotypes about women could have tempered her ambition, but not Brownie Wise. She had a young son to support. "I'm going to be making a change in jobs in the first of the year," Wise reported in one of her Hibiscus letters. "And I think I feel more enthusiastic about it than I have about anything."[18] Brownie Wise stood on the precipice of a life-changing career move, and making history in the business world.

○ ○ ○

It was the winter of 1945. Thirty-eight-year-old Earl Tupper was carrying a large briefcase into the Worcester, Massachusetts, office of a CPA he had never met. It was tax time, and the subject always seemed to make him a little edgy.

During the war there were shortages of all kinds of raw materials. Many small manufacturers like Tupper who wanted to stay in business participated in a thriving black market. These were off-the-books cash transactions.[19] The 1944 taxes were due, Tupper had an overage, and he wanted to know what this tax man would advise him to declare—if anything.

Ed Creiger wanted to know how Tupper chose him. Tupper said he was following a business associate's recommendation.

"If Ed Creiger is good enough for that smart ass," Tupper declared, "he ought to be good enough for me."[20]

Creiger found out later that Tupper had already done a considerable amount of checking his background. "Earl did not make impulsive decisions," Creiger wrote, "but he seemed to delight in giving the impression that he was."[21] Tupper said one of the reasons he'd come to Creiger's office was to find a new accountant. The ones he had at present were good enough, but he wondered if they had the amount of talent necessary to take care of his proposed growth and resulting needs. "This from a man who had a total of four molding machines and with no proprietary product!" Creiger marveled.

That was true, but the wily businessman had amassed the capital necessary to go to the next level. That's why he needed Creiger's help. "There are $35,000.00 in this brief case that I don't know what to do about," Tupper declared, "and I need your advice and opinion."[22] He also explained that the money had come from the sale of basic plastic raw material, the cash had not been entered into the company books for 1944, and everyone was doing it.

"What should I do?" the intense bald man asked.

Creiger knew instinctively this was a make-or-break moment. "Here I was new to the public field of accounting and anxious to become a professional and financial success," Creiger wrote. "How does this stranger put me to the test so early in my new career?"[23] If he told Tupper to do the right thing, he might get up and take a potentially lucrative new account right out the door. If he helped Tupper hide the loot, Creiger knew he'd be just as big a crook.

"I took a deep breath, crossed my fingers, and told Earl to play it straight, deposit the funds enter the sales on the books and report them for tax purposes," Creiger said. "I got the expected response."

"Why should I?" Tupper protested. "Everyone is doing it and getting rich. I cannot buy the raw materials I need to carry on my business, everyone tells me to keep the money. Why do you advise otherwise?"[24]

"He was not angry or belligerent, but truly interested in my response," Creiger remembered. "Although I did not know it at the time, Earl was really putting me to the test. Many years later he told me so." What Earl Tupper wanted was an honest tax guy who could keep him clear of legal snares. "It looked like Earl was waiting for someone to tell him to do what he had already decided to do on his own," Creiger wrote. "His response was most gratifying."

"How soon can you get started as my accountant?" the ever-direct Tupper asked.[25]

Wartime and the shortages of other materials gave people in the plastics business a chance to expand. The end of wartime gave Tupper an opportunity to sink his money into all sorts of surplus at fire-sale rates. The military no longer had a need for much of its nationwide infrastructure. Tupper bought up air bases and a staggering amount of hardware that came with them: buildings, jeeps, trucks, busses, office equipment. All things easy to make liquid if need be.

The nagging shortage of raw materials did not subside as quickly. Plastic resins—one of the cornerstone materials Tupper needed for manufacturing—

was still hard to come by or subject to a steep markup. "Sorry, there's just not enough to go around and there's nothing we can do about it," a Bakelite representative told him. "Well, in that case, what else have you got?" Tupper asked. "You must have something kicking around."

"As a matter of fact, we do," the rep conceded. What he handed Tupper was a smelly glob of greasy, rubbery, black slag. "We have tons of this stuff sitting around and we don't know what to do with it," the rep told Tupper. "You can have all of it you want."[26]

The substance was polyethylene, a smelting waste product. During the war, both the British and the United States used it in radar installations and to protect weapons from the elements. In peacetime, companies like DuPont and Bakelite had no use for it. Enter the inventor side of Earl Silas Tupper. This was the material he needed to come up with his first proprietary product.

From this worthless glob of waste product, this smelly slag, Earl Tupper mined translucent gold.

Three

THE PRODUCT AND THE PLAN

If you are *roosting* instead of *boosting* you ARE our problem! This business is not for those who loiter by the way and "wish." It's for those who hit the road and *work*!
—Brownie Wise

In the spring of 1947, the dramatic life change for Brownie Wise arrived at the front door of her Dearborn home. A sales rep for Stanley Home Products gave Wise a pitch fumbling enough that it led her to remark later, "I could do better than that."[1] The introduction of Brownie Wise to Stanley Home Products created the historic bridge in home-based selling between Wise and the company founded by Frank Stanley Beveridge, the man credited with being the first to incorporate the home-party plan as his foremost sales strategy.

Beveridge had been sales director of the Fuller Brush Company, the name synonymous with door-to-door selling in the early part of the twentieth century. In 1933, fifty-four-year-old Beveridge founded Stanley Home Products, in part to create jobs for friends stuck in the throes of the Depression. The Stanley line included the Brown Beauty mop and an array of cleaners, detergents, and floor waxes—utilitarian products that appealed mainly to the American housewife. The first person to use home parties was a New Hampshire Stanley salesman who set up a card table and invited women to come over and watch his demonstration. The simple concept brought the business to him, and it also appealed to homemakers who cherished some time away from children and chores. When Beveridge saw firsthand that the salesman's home parties were the reason for such formidable sales numbers, he went back and told his underlings, "we have to change."[2] At first, many salesmen resisted the idea of putting on parties. They recruited their wives to help in that end of the business.[3]

For Wise, the timing of her career change could not have been better. The years of rationing and doing without during World War II had given way to a new American consumer culture. Across the land soldiers streamed home, settled down, and started building suburban neighborhoods and families. Rosie the Riveter, celebrated during the war, was now expected to resume her feminine role and let the men handle the heavy lifting. But in many cases, that quintessential American wartime woman had gotten a taste of what it was like to be out on her own, earning a little money and enjoying a few of the finer things it bought. In 1947, this was an apt description of the thirty-four-year-old divorcée Brownie Wise.

At first, Wise saw Stanley as a way to supplement her secretarial income on evenings and weekends. In June 1947, she received her first Stanley Speaker's kit and an outline of an effective-speaking course. "The voice exercise has practical value if you use it," Stanley's director of education advised.[4] Wise already had some experience when it came to public speaking. When she was just a teenager, Wise had given speeches at union rallies in the Deep South organized by her mother, Rose. The job carried enough danger that the women would often travel in a team with a guard. Despite that, Wise awed people, who were surprised that someone so young could deliver a speech like a pastor. After all that, Brownie Wise would have no trepidation as an adult about getting up and talking to women about how Stanley products could make their homes more spic-and-span. Her drive and sales moxie soon brought enough financial success that she could say good-bye to her wartime Bendix job.

Stanley dealers were expected to fill out a daily report, including delivery-day Saturdays, that started at 8:30 each morning and ended "6 p.m. or later." During specified blocks of time, dealers were asked: "Did you go prospecting? Did you put on a party? If so, how many did you book? Did you verify your parties? Anything else for Stanley?"[5] Beveridge told his sales force that there are only two types of salesmen: "The man who plods along and by his own force gains mediocre success, and the man who keeps every channel for new ideas open, welcomes all suggestions from his own organization and other fields, and then profits from the other fellow's experience. To which class do you belong?"[6] Wise was no plodder; by 1948, she had risen through the ranks of the Michigan area, becoming manager of the so-called Triangle Unit.

Wise continued to learn the Frank Stanley Beveridge sales mantra and to correspond with the company's director of education, Elmer Nyberg. He wrote back on letterhead from Stanley's "Little Red School House." "If you and I learn to fill each sixty seconds of the passing minutes with purposeful work," Nyberg opined, "we will succeed beyond our dreams."[7] Extra effort, he told her, combined with a strong personality is the key to success. Many of these concepts Wise internalized and expanded upon at Tupperware. These are Nyberg's five characteristics of a strong-willed person:

He has a *Love of Humanity* = He loves people.

He has *Warmth* = He is not a "cold fish."

He is *Friendly* = He is a friend. He gives out kindness. The way to have a friend is to be one.

He has *Courage* = He stands on his own feet. He works terribly hard and he keeps his mouth shut.

He is *Genuine* = He doesn't deal in tricks. He is genuine in his dealings with people.[8]

Nyberg also included seven ways "to make people like you."

1. Make it a habit of being interested in other people
2. Smile. A true smile comes from within. Smile with your eyes.
3. Pronounce a man's name as though it is the most important sound in the language.
4. Be a sympathetic, enthusiastic listener. Stimulate the other person to talk about himself.
5. Talk in terms of the other man's interest and he will listen to you.
6. Make the other person feel important, not as a trick but sincerely.
7. Treat every person you meet as though he is a messenger from heaven.[9]

The company had a Stanley prayer and, as a way to develop resourcefulness, encouraged employees to use their Sundays to "reproduce at home the central thought of the morning sermon."[10]

With the zeal of someone who had found a new and true religion, Brownie Wise soaked it all in and applied these lessons to motivate her own sales force. In another practice she would amplify at Tupperware, Wise started producing a regular newsletter entitled the *Go-Getter*. "Anybody who works in the Triangle Unit is going to be a Go-Getter, who gets what he goes after," Wise wrote to her team of dealers. "As a unit, we're out for first place again; as a dealer you're out for more parties, bigger weeks, fatter profits . . . or you're part of the problem."[11] One quote she used often in her newsletters came from J. G. Holland, "God gives every bird his food, but He does not throw it into the nest."[12] Wise wrote to Nyberg at Stanley that she felt she had hit upon a key principle to motivating her sales force, "The secret of education lies in respecting the pupil."[13]

Wise lavished attention on big earners and high achievers and found a way to give recognition to new recruits. "Ray Arsenault and his Stanley case went to a party the other nite . . . his Michigan debut and they rang the bell with a quality party! Swell."[14] Wise punctuated many passages with a kind of calculated corniness. "Florence's sales this week averaged almost $8.00 per person!" Wise gushed. "*That's* real, honest-to-goodness sizzlemanship."[15] Between the swells and sizzles, Brownie Wise was beginning to harness a concept that would bring her the devotion of thousands of Americans, women especially. The profits coming in from all the evening parties, Saturday deliveries, and Monday morning sales meetings were good, but for housewives used to assuming an invisible role behind their breadwinning husbands, the recognition was even better. Wise seemed to have an intuitive balance of praise, motivation, and discipline, the carrot and the stick.

"One half of knowing what you want is knowing what you must give up before you get it."[16] Wise told her go-getters, "40 hours a week will give you success: if you want a new fur coat, another room added to your house, a new car . . . the next step is filling a 40-hour week out on your yellow sheet, and following through."[17] Like a mother bird waiting in the nest, at the beginning of each week Wise would decide who was go-getting and who was part of the problem. "Monday morning—9:30 here at my house. . . .See Grace with your fines if you're late."[18] Wise always used a ruler so her signature at the bottom of the page was spot-on straight.

Across Detroit, some of the others who would go on to be major players with Tupperware matriculated by selling Stanley: Rose Humphrey, Florence Zewicky, Peter and Elsie Block, Dorothy Shannon, and her nephew Gary McDonald. For McDonald, the Stanley job provided a way to make money while he was still in school. He helped his aunt fill orders and delivered them to the homes of party hostesses. Shannon would collect the money paid by party guests, then go home and count the take into two piles. One, covering the cost of acquiring the goods, would go into her business account. Shannon took what was left of the profits and deposited those into her personal account. The industrious teen McDonald saw his aunt do this week in and week out and asked if he could be a dealer. "Sure," she told him, "there are no age requirements, but you'll have to book [arrange] your own parties."[19]

A month shy of his sixteenth birthday, Gary McDonald held his first Stanley party in suburban Detroit. In time, McDonald saw success as a Stanley dealer, selling the complete Stanley line to homemakers all over town, who took to calling him "Mister Stanley."[20] With McDonald as a dealer and his aunt Dorothy Shannon as a manager, both eventually took their place on the roster of star Stanley manager Brownie Wise. Now that all were educated in the field of home selling, fully indoctrinated in how to put on successful home parties and motivate others to do the same, the stage was set for a new home-sale product to come in and transform their lives, sweep across the nation, and take its place among the American icons of the 1950s.

○ ○ ○

Earl Tupper wrote to one of his early admen, J. C. Healy, about why polyethylene had so much potential. "Polyethylene served its time in the war," Tupper told him; "With the end of the war it was another young veteran that had accelerated from childhood to a fighting job. It had done its job well, but like all young vets returning from the wars it had never had civilian adult experience."[21] Tupper saw the economic potential of developing polyethylene "as a civilian." But transforming that potential into something new and revolutionary would take a great deal of time, dedication, and know-how. "We experimented, we developed and tested," Tupper wrote.[22] That was an understatement.

As a manufacturer of plastic products, Tupper was looking for something that would hold up better than the generally brittle products formed from molding transparent styrene. He thought polyethylene had the greatest potential for food storage. During wartime, polyethylene had shown it did not give off odors or other chemicals harmful to food. It could hold up even when exposed to highly acidic agents like lemon juice or vinegar. But in its wartime form, the dark clump would hardly appeal to homemakers. It would take months of experimentation, patience, and refinement before Earl Tupper found his solution.

Early tests placing polyethylene in the injection molding machines had proved disastrous. Tupper would have to go back and strip the polyethylene down to its purest form, then subject it to different temperatures to see which was the right one to give it "flowability."[23] Tupper took numerous samples to his home on Horse Pond Road and enlisted the help of his son Myles.

"Just about every night he'd bring home a dozen or so," Myles Tupper remembered, "and my job was to put all the samples into boiling water at the same time, and then after a specified time remove one piece and set it aside, then wait for a specified time and remove the next sample and so on. I'd take the last one out when it was no longer recognizable."[24] Sometimes a sample would be blended with other additives; other times it was pure polyethylene.

This went on for months, until Tupper hit on what he thought was the ideal formula: the correct balance of temperature and pressure. Now the polyethylene could be flowed into a variety of shapes and sizes with the appropriate thickness; unlike other, more brittle, plastics of the day, it was flexible and didn't break or chip. Tupper also devised a precise system of adding colored dyes to give his new translucent product attractive pastel tones. This was something new and different, a polished, waxy, upscale plastic that needed a name to reflect its inventor's swagger. Tupper called it "Poly-T: Material of the Future."

By itself, Poly-T would still not solve the problem of how to keep food fresh longer. In the 1940s, it was common for women to put a shower cap or tin foil over leftovers to try to slow their quick spoiling in the icebox.[25] Tupper got the idea for his next great invention from a paint-can lid. He could take the flexible Poly-T material and manufacture covers that fit tightly on top of metal cans. But finding a way to make the lids fit on top of his narrow-lipped, flexible, Poly-T plastic bowls took more work. On June 2, 1947, Tupper filed a patent application for the "E. S. Tupper Open Mouth Container and Nonsnap type of Closure Therefor."[26] In a series of eight now-classic drawings, Tupper outlined the noiseless and nonsnapping cover that fit snuggly over the top of his Poly-T food and beverage containers. The "simple hand manipulation"[27] to expel air as the cover is placed over the container created an airtight, spill-proof vacuum seal, even if the container were dropped on the floor. For the first time, Earl Tupper burped his multimillion-dollar baby. He christened his line of Poly-T products "Tupperware."

In a September 8, 1947, article on Tupper and his new invention, *Time* magazine called him a "one-man boom" and raved that Tupper's "all important contribution is a process which overcomes the material's tendency to split, makes it tough enough to withstand almost anything except knife cuts and near-boiling water."[28] Tupper had given his World War II veteran polyethylene a mettle tough enough to withstand almost any of the slings and arrows of a typical American household, and he had done something more. Tupper raised the reputation of plastic in the eyes of the middle-class American consumer. *House Beautiful* called Tupperware, "Fine Art for 39 cents." The plastic bowls you squeezed to pour and seal recovered their normal shape and appearance. This was a new American aesthetic. *House Beautiful*'s editor Elizabeth Gordon gushed that the bowls look "as good as a piece of sculpture."[29] Like a proud father, Earl Tupper was thrilled to see his new Poly-T bowls included in a housewares exhibit at the Museum of Modern Art in New York City.

Tupper called the original output of fourteen Tupperware products produced behind the big windows of his Farnumsville plant the "Millionaire Line." As a youngster, Tupper predicted he'd be a millionaire by the age of thirty. As a manufacturer and inventor, he believed each product in his first Tupperware line would bring in a million dollars. Tupper's instincts were right again, although his prediction came true a few years after he hit thirty. Camel ordered three hundred thousand Tupperware cigarette cases, Canada Dry Ginger Ale bought fifty thousand bowls to sell with beverages, and fifty thousand of Tupper's Bell Tumblers went to the Tek Corporation to market alongside toothbrushes.[30] "A Massachusetts mental institution found Tupperware an almost ideal replacement for its noisy, easily battered aluminum cups and plates." As *Time* reported, "Patients could damage Tupperware only by persistent chewing."[31]

After the initial flood of positive publicity and brisk wholesale orders, a problem started to develop for Tupper in the marketing of his new Poly-T products. "We always try to remember," Tupper wrote, "that a product is not exactly what you make it in the factory, but it is also and more so what you make it when you sell it."[32] He turned down offers to develop a line of flexible dog-feeding dishes for fear that "such a thing could have made our job more difficult to sell our dishes as appropriate for any table."[33] To counter preconceived notions about plastic being cheap or flimsy, Tupperware ads implored housewives to "think of it as having taken its rightful place with other fine table furnishings . . . silver, linen, china. Tupperware is here in a most substantial way. . . . its position is assured."[34]

In 1948 that was not yet quite true. Tupperware retail sales were flat, and the issue was more than perception. People didn't know the proper way to "lock in freshness" with Tupper's new airtight seal. Some sent back the containers explaining that "the tops don't fit."[35] In big department stores across America, Tupperware languished on shelves; the revolutionary product was waiting for someone to figure out an innovative way to sell it. One of the first people to do that was the redheaded, suburban Detroit teenager with the beaming smile nicknamed "Mister Stanley."

○ ○ ○

In the late 1940s, people regarded the J. L Hudson Department Store as the heart of downtown Detroit. Established in 1911 by Joseph Lowthian Hudson, the soaring twenty-five-story behemoth occupied the old Detroit Opera House. Located on the corner of Woodward and Gratiot avenues, people came from all over the city to marvel at the massive American flag—seven stories high and weighing 1,600 pounds—that hung on the side of J. L. Hudson's. Twelve

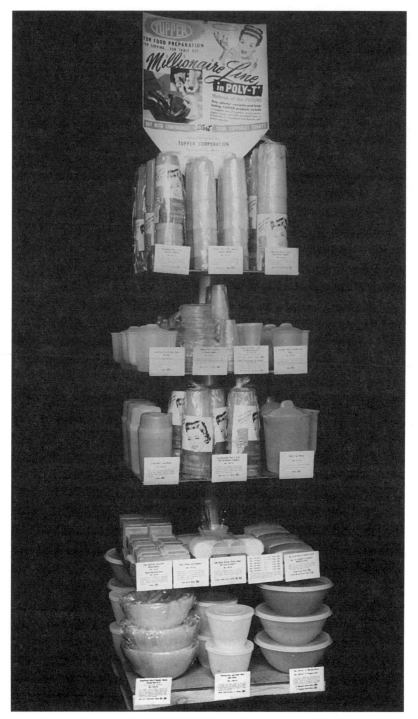

Earl Tupper's early Tupperware "Millionaire Line" languished in department stores.

thousand employees rang up one hundred thousand sales a day, and patrons feasted on Hudson's famous Maurice salad.[36] In the days before racial unrest exploded in downtown Detroit, young Diana Ross was the first black busgirl in the store's basement cafeteria.[37] One of the world's largest fireworks displays wowed customers on Independence Day, and towers of festive lights twinkled at Christmas.

It's no wonder a place so bustling would attract the attention of an ambitious sixteen-year-old kid like Gary McDonald. J. L. Hudson carried all fourteen items of the original Tupperware Millionaire Line. On a trip through the store one day after high school, the Wonder Bowl caught his eye, and McDonald also spied the Bell Tumbler on sale for a dollar. But these so-called products of the future were hardly flying off the shelves. Usually they just sat there until a store employee showed customers how to apply the Tupper seal. Then containers could be turned upside down or even dropped without the contents inside being spilled or otherwise ruined. People had to be *told* the bowls and canisters were specially designed for the refrigerator or pantry shelf, to stretch the life of leftovers and the family budget. After all that, customers were much more enthusiastic and bought the new product. Immediately, McDonald told himself, "Man, *that* could be a great home-demonstration product!"[38]

McDonald was not the only member of the Stanley family starting to get excited about the potential of Tupperware. In suburban Boston, husband and wife dealers Ann and Tom Damigella also discovered the Wonder Bowl and all the things they could do with it. Ann brought the first one to their home in Melrose, an upscale bedroom community north of Boston. "Tommy," she exclaimed, "look at this! It's made of plastic!"[39] Yet that plastic was soft to the touch and appeared to be very functional. Where most Americans would see a simple bowl or canister, Ann and Tom Damigella immediately saw dollar signs. "This is why we were fascinated," Tom Damigella reflected decades later in Tupperware's *Our World* publication, "and then, why we got so excited. You see, we realized what a great sales opportunity this new product called Tupper Plastics could be." The Damigellas did some searching and found a Tupperware wholesaler in Boston's South Shore; they started selling the product separately from their Stanley line.

In Detroit, Gary McDonald had a feeling Tupperware would be a big seller on the party plan and wanted to get an expert opinion. "I showed it to my aunt with whom I was living because my Mom had died and I was only sixteen," McDonald said. "She was excited too."[40] He looked on the bottom of the product, where it said, "Tupper Corporation, Poly-T, Farnumsville, Massachusetts." McDonald got on the phone, called the company, and with money he borrowed from his father, placed his first-ever order for Tupperware. His aunt did the same thing. The only problem with Tupperware was the scarcity and lack of variety. Where the Stanley line featured more than sixty items, Tupperware had just the first fourteen. McDonald knew he had to share his discovery with their dynamic manager—the woman who would forever claim a place in the history of Tupperware.

At one of the regular Monday morning Stanley sales meetings, McDonald brought Tupperware to the Dearborn home of Brownie Wise. She, like most other Tupperware novices, wasn't quite sure what to do with it. "Who ever heard of a bowl you could squeeze?" Wise reflected many years later. "And in the beginning, I really struggled to get that seal on right. Then I accidentally knocked the bowl off the table and it bounced. I was so surprised I called out to my mother, 'Why, this bowl actually bounces.' We ended up using that line in our promotion: 'It bounces instead of breaks!'" As Wise struggled with the seal, she finally came to the conclusion, "you had to burp it just like a baby."[41]

Brownie Wise was a successful, star manager with Stanley, pulling down a decent income and providing a good home for ten-year-old Jerry. Gary McDonald became like a big brother, helping the boy set up a new electric train set in the basement. Wise vacationed in Florida and built a roster of motivated dealers who helped make their branch one of the Michigan's largest. She had no reason to walk away from that success even if the new Tupperware line did seem to hold so much potential. It wasn't until her esteemed mentor in Stanley Home Products, Frank Stanley Beveridge, gave Brownie Wise the inspiration—and consternation—to do so.

Part of Stanley's primer to educate and motivate the sales force—from which Tupperware executives like Brownie Wise would borrow extensively in the coming decade—was the idea of an annual pilgrimage to the company's home base. On Sunday, August 22, 1948, Wise and a contingent of her Detroit West Side dealers arrived by train at Stanley's Westfield, Massachusetts, headquarters. "You come here to Westfield to learn, to get inspiration," Beveridge told the assembled throngs in his welcome address. "Those of you who bring the greatest spirit of service, of kindness and helpfulness, will take the most home."[42] At the Monday morning breakfast kickoff rally, Stanley's regional sales manager, Hubert L. Worrell, told the Michigan group, "You're a bunch of builders and a fine group of people." They responded with a standing ovation and sang back to him, "We Think You're Wonderful."[43]

That spirit of camaraderie carried over the North to Stanley's factory in Easthampton. Traveling past a big, red-lettered sign that said, "Welcome Michigan Area," Wise and her sales force toured Stanley's manufacturing operation. Five thousand feet of gravity and power-driven belts moved the merchandise, eliminating the need for any unnecessary handling. "Oh look! They put the bristles out in a long row, and when they whirl them, they all go up in the brush!" one dealer exclaimed.[44] Inspectors passed or trashed clothes brushes; dealers marveled at how the new Cel-O-Sorb mops were made. "They think this little factory can supply what we can sell," said a brash young dealer named Jack Marshall. "But we'll show 'em!"[45]

Brownie Wise had an agenda beyond brushes and mops for this pilgrimage; it also provided an opportunity to put in some face time with the Stanley big shots. Wise had ingrained in her character the idea of never being stagnant or satisfied, and her ambitions far exceeded Detroit's West Side branch. "Remember," she once advised her dealers, "if you don't grow, someone else will."[46] It seemingly never occurred to Wise that her growth potential could be forever stunted in a company because of one factor that had nothing to do with her ability to move merchandise or coach her dealers to book more parties. It was still the late 1940s, and Brownie Wise was a woman.

"I remember how mad she was when she came back from Stanley Home Parties' convention in Massachusetts," Jerry Wise recalled. Frank Stanley Beveridge told Wise she shouldn't waste her time hoping to own Stanley stock or ascend to an executive position within the company. Wise recounted to her son that she'd been told that the halls of Stanley's top executives were "no place for a woman."[47]

By 1949, the U.S. Census Bureau found that women made up a respectable 31 percent of America's workforce. But that percentage in no way reflected the paltry number of women who'd risen to top management positions. After the long train ride home to Dearborn, Brownie Wise still fumed about what Beveridge had said. She vowed to her son, "I'll show him!"[48]

Four

Filling In the Gaps

Workers who will be successful always speak pleasantly to others . . . thus proving broad minded. The right to gossip, be catty and gripe is the priviledge [*sic*] only of those who pay the price of failure.

—Earl Tupper

On March 8, 1949, Earl Tupper addressed the emerging role of women in the professional workforce through a page-long dress-down memo to his advertising manager, J. C. Healy. In a letter that Tupper considered to be just the latest example of Healy's bombast regarding the idea of women in business, Healy had taken it upon himself to disparage "Lady" copy writers and "Lady" editors.[1] Tupper's response to Healy's letter showed broad-mindedness about the issue and foreshadowed his willingness to entrust the success or failure of his treasured inventions into the hands of one woman.

"I'm sure all of the ladies with whom this corporation deals will be big enough to not be angered by your expressions," Tupper wrote Healy, "but I'm afraid they wouldn't be human if they neglected an opportunity to make things a little hard for you."[2] Tupper went on to show how his visionary nature applied to more than just plastics. "Look closely at the roster of top publishers and other business firms in this country," Tupper suggested, "who with obviously good reason have seen fit to staff their top jobs with women who are giving top performance in any man's language." In the homespun, father-to-child tone typical of Tupper, he ended the memo by chiding his top adman. "You have delivered yourself of expressions best reserved for banter amongst the office small frye [*sic*]."[3]

Starting in September 1949, countries worldwide granted Tupper Seals the affirmation and patent protection their inventor craved. From Belgium to Italy, Switzerland to South Africa, countries bestowed upon Tupper Corporation the right to have what amounted to a monopoly on manufacturing Tupperware. The United States followed on November 9, 1949, granting Tupper Corporation patent #2,487,400.[4] In a full-page ad in *Modern Plastics* magazine, Tupper puffed out his chest to all would-be competitors, shysters, and copycats. "The Tupper Corporation further has anticipated the inevitable attacks to which leadership is subject," the ad blustered, "and has taken measures provided by law to preserve the creative rights to its products, methods, and design by patent protection both in the United States and abroad."[5] In an interesting twist, Tupperware wasn't introduced to most of the global markets for which Tupper requested patent protection until after he had washed his hands of the company entirely.

In 1949, Tupper had expanded his operation west, establishing a manufacturing facility and lab at a former air base in Cuero, a town that barely registered a dot on the sweeping southeast Texas landscape. Cuero, whose name is Spanish for "rawhide," is situated ninety minutes from Austin and San Antonio. Where young airmen had once learned navigation and meteorology and practiced on an early flight simulator called the Link Trainer, Tupper envisioned a manufacturing hub. Texas seemed to have clear advantages for his business: it was a warm-weather state experiencing population growth and the unions didn't have the kind of stranglehold they enjoyed in the Northeast.[6] Before he could make the expansion plan reality, however, he had to solve the problem of how to sell Tupperware to the average consumer. Former Los Angeles distributor Elsie Block summed up the marketing problem: "Everybody seemed to love the products, but nobody seemed to be buying them."[7]

Tupper sought to solve that problem by publishing his first mail-order catalogue, complete with illustrations and instructions on how to put the full range of the now twenty-two Tupperware items to use. By putting Tupperware on display in a New York City showroom on Fifth Avenue, he underscored attempts to differentiate his wonder product from the cheap plastics of the past. Tupper resisted criticism from buyers who said, "Our colors were not gaudy enough, that our dishes were too flexible, that it would be impossible to hold such a flexible tumbler filled with water."[8] As far back as 1947, Tupper made notes to himself toying with the idea of Tupperware parties and a Tupper theme song, but he failed until years later to put those proven Stanley strategies into his own playbook. Tupper's lack of marketing know-how left him in need of outside help.

Fortunately for Tupper, the foundation of all the riches and success that the 1950s would bring had already started to take shape. Door-to-door salespeople, direct sellers, had already begun to take notice of Tupperware's potential to freshen their product line. It was bright, clean, colorful and innovative, and easy to carry and demonstrate. Where Tupperware sat idly on department and hardware store shelves, the tactile, in-home demonstrations brought it alive to the people Tupper had largely failed to reach. Motivated salespeople across the United States, like the Damigellas and Gary McDonald, had already started to fill in the gaps in Tupper's marketing strategy. Tupper took notice of these dealers' steady stream of mail orders and embarked on a market-research study, sending questionnaires to the highest sellers. Hoping to use the questionnaires to get to the bottom of how these sellers were able to move so much product, Tupper's market research garnered an unexpected bonus—Brownie Wise.

○ ○ ○

"Get rid of your shower caps!" urged members of the Michigan area's West Side branch. "Turn your leftovers into makeovers!"[9] Those were two key catch-phrases from the stable of salespeople preaching the money-saving benefits of vacuum-seal Poly-T products to a growing base of enthusiastic homemakers. At demonstrations, Wise urged dealers to turn sealed Tupperware containers upside down or throw them across the room to prove they didn't leak.[10] It was August 1949, and Brownie Wise didn't let her disappointment with Stanley derail her ambitions in the least. She overhauled the dowdy line of brooms and brushes, substituting the bouncing pastel bowls and canisters with the seals that burped. Other than the change in what Brownie Wise and her sales force sold, the who, when, where, and how remained nearly identical to what they'd been doing with Stanley. She turned the lack of variety and scarcity of the new Tupperware product into a positive by putting would-be customers and dealers on a waiting list to have the privilege of buying and selling the new line.

"We started ordering the product fast because it was selling so well and recruiting was pretty easy," Gary McDonald remembered, "because this was something new and magic and different."[11] He and virtually all of the Stanley dealers in the West branch switched to Tupperware as soon as they saw how well customers reacted to their demonstrations. Wise ordered all the product she could, recruited new dealers and supplied them with Tupperware as fast as she could get it. If she ran short on cash, Wise put people on the waiting list, and that just added to the appeal.[12] Less than five years after World War II, people remembered what it was like to have to stand in line for the commodities everybody wanted like butter, stockings, and automobiles. The method proved so successful that Wise used it even after she had the money to stay stocked in Tupperware. "It was the strongest recruiting tool we had,"[13] McDonald said. Recruiting is the key to building any home-based selling business. As more dealers sign on at the bottom, the manager and distributor above sells to them at a discounted price. In the end, everyone profits. Once a territory is saturated with dealers, one of the peak performers is promoted and given a new territory to develop.

"Facts and Figures from the stack of orders and reports this week point to Nola and Jayne as super-duper on the 50-oz. canister," Wise reported in the August 18, 1949, newsletter. "Nola is making hey-hey this week on a fun-leave from Poly-T Parties . . . and here's news to warm the heart—Norma Kelly's husband has just gotten home from the South Pacific after a year's absence, which is by way of explaining the glow Norma gives off these days."[14] It wouldn't be long before Wise and her West Side branch dealers rechristened their gatherings "Tupperware parties." On October 17, 1949, with a stable of nineteen dealers and the Poly-T operation taking off, Wise moved distribution out of the Melborn Street house and into a warehouse space at 24912 Ford Road. In 1949, the Wonder Bowl and seal—the staple of the Tupperware line for decades to come—cost Detroit-area dealers $1.98 (before their discount). The line also included canister sets at $2.98 each, six nine-ounce tumblers for 99¢ cents, and cereal-bowl seals at 25¢ each.[15]

Wise and McDonald had much more in common than the "rubber dishes" they were selling at such an accelerated pace.[16] Both grew up in nontraditional households. As a child of divorced parents in rural Tifton, Georgia, Wise was often left behind with her aunt Pearl while her mother did long, risky stretches of road work for the hatmakers' union.[17] Young Brownie often played with black children and didn't have ingrained in her the racial divide so entrenched in the Deep South.[18] McDonald's mother died when he was sixteen, and his care was also entrusted to an aunt. Wise became a mother figure to her teenaged protégé, and he like a big brother to her only son. "Flashy as hell and not afraid of anything," Jerry Wise said of McDonald.[19] It was the end of a turbulent decade for the woman who liked to call herself Hibiscus. Things were looking up, and the future smelled as sweet as confederate jasmine.

"I remember filling a lot of orders in those days," Jerry Wise recalled. "Everything she touched seemed to turn to gold."[20]

◦ ◦ ◦

Earl Tupper was starting to get his first up-close-and-personal look at some of the highest-performing party-plan dealers who shared his enthusiasm for

Poly-T. He placed a call to the home of Ann and Tom Damigella. "It was a long-distance call," Tom remembered. "Boy did that cause some excitement! People just didn't get too many long-distance calls in the late 1940s."[21] Still in his market-research phase, Tupper wanted to know more about the Damigellas' early success in using the party plan to sell Tupperware. Since Boston is only forty-six miles east of Farnumsville, Tupper invited the Damigellas to drive out for a tour of his manufacturing operation. "I remember how proud he was to show us his plant where the molds as well as the Polyethylene products were made," Ann said. "He told Tom and me: 'I have the finest tool and die makers in the entire world.'"[22] Each color of Tupperware product had its own formula of dye and blending time to achieve Tupper's rigid standard of perfection. "Weigh all dyes *accurately*," he lectured employees; "do not allow dye canisters or dyes weighed on cellophane to be exposed to dust and dirt—keep covered. Never use the same spoon for more than one dye. Remember—care and caution in the Blending Room will reduce scrap in the Molding Room."[23]

On return trips after that first meeting, Tupper personally would help the Damigellas load boxes of product into their car, much like the old-fashioned Yankee peddler he purported to be. Ever the owner of surplus cars, trucks, air bases, office equipment, and assorted bric a brac, for $350 Tupper sold Ann and Tom their first pickup to better haul their Tupperware. Things were going so well that they had resigned their Stanley franchise and begun selling Tupperware full time, putting on parties, and recruiting new dealers. The Damigella family would go on to become a multigenerational legend in the annals of Tupperware. Unlike many other early distributors, the Damigellas never had to move their distributorship from their own backyard or from the Stanley framework of dealers and customers that facilitated their success with Tupperware.

"Paint this truck green," Tupper advised them, "because green is a lucky color."[24]

For the once-bankrupt tree doctor, the 1950s would bring a lot of lucky green cash Earl Tupper's way. He now had the infrastructure in place to begin Tupperizing America. All he needed were those willing to pull up stakes and preach the gospel of Tupperware in places with fertile fields to plow. From 1948 to 1953, more children were born in America than in the thirty years previous. There were myriad population-rich cities. Former soldiers were taking advantage of special low-interest loans to buy homes in developing suburbs. It was time to make the young war veteran Poly-T a bona fide, all-American, civilian superstar.

○ ○ ○

The golden touch of Brownie Wise showed up in her end-of-the-year Poly-T sales figures for 1949. From the local Poly Supply Company in Hazel Park, Wise ordered $65,741.98 worth of merchandise. Direct from the Tupper Corporation's factory in Farnumsville, Massachusetts, Wise rang up a whopping $86,407.15 in orders. Leading the way among her roster of star dealers, Jayne Boltz of Detroit brought in $7,398.52 in sales, outpacing Florence Zewicky of Wyandotte by less than ten dollars for the entire year. In the winter of 1950, the home office rang up Brownie Wise and dispatched a man named Victor Collamore to size up the go-getters in Detroit.

It was all very impressive for Wise and her still teenaged sidekick Gary McDonald. The Tupper Corporation's representative traveled halfway across country to take them to a get-acquainted dinner at a fancy downtown Detroit restaurant. It wasn't long after the water was poured that Collamore came right out with it. "You guys have gotta tell me," he implored, "just what in the hell are you guys doing to sell the amount of Tupperware you're doing? You're selling more Tupperware than the J. L. Hudson department store by far, and that's the biggest department store in the world!"[25] Wise and McDonald were glad to share their secrets, but by 1950, ambitious direct sellers all over the country had started their own Tupperware operations and Tupper's people knew it. Collamore was really sizing up Wise for a promotion. Less than two years after her Stanley ambitions had been crushed, Wise was poised to ascend to the highest level of Tupperware distribution.

Wise would be breathing rarified air. In 1950, 95 percent of American women were confined to low-paying jobs in one of four categories: light manufacturing, retail, clerical, and health and education. That left just 5 percent in professions and management.

Wise and Collamore sealed the deal at her home on Melborn Street. The entire state of Florida would be hers as distributor, to populate with Tupperware dealers and branches. With almost 3 million residents in 1950, Florida promised to be a lucrative territory as well as a dream place to call home. In the midst of a frigid Michigan winter, Wise broached with Jerry the idea of moving south. "Gosh yes, it's warm," the eleven-year-old gushed. "Let's go!"[26] Rose Humphrey moved down first to find a temporary place to live and space to store Tupperware stock. Brownie and Jerry would stay until the end of the school year, tie up all the details, hand over the reigns of the Michigan branch, then head to Florida themselves. Wise was pleased that some of her star dealers decided to stake a new claim in the Sunshine State.

After fourteen years in the Motor City, one turbulent marriage and divorce, the birth of her only child, and a couple of career changes, Brownie Wise was leaving forever. Florida would be home for the remaining forty-two years of her life. Like anyone starting out in a brand-new place and trying to build a new business, Wise would find the coming months exhilarating and terribly stressful. Not only was she uprooting her own family, Brownie Wise would need to stand on the shoulders of other dealers who'd been comfortably established in Michigan. They were pulling their kids out of school, selling their homes, leaving friends, and placing their faith in Wise. She, in turn, was placing her faith in a company and product without much of a track record. Success would not come easy.

Five

A Turbulent New Home

On Saturday morning, April 29, 1950, Brownie and Jerry Wise loaded into their car for the 1,425-mile drive from Dearborn to Fort Lauderdale. In March, Gary McDonald had joined the marines and headed off to Camp Pendleton, California. His aunt Dorothy Shannon, "the true Samaritan," made the trip with Brownie and Jerry, to help out with the twenty-one hours of driving.[1] Another couple, Ed and Millie O'Connell, along with their son, Pat, were driving a second car. Snow fell in "January-like flakes," making for a frosty, mid-spring send-off. Wise was sad and anxious—so much was on the line. "I could never tell you how hard it was to leave," she wrote.[2]

As the two-car convoy made its way out of Michigan, traversing the long miles of eastern Ohio, south through the heart of Kentucky, the elevation increased and the mood lightened. "We oohed and aahed at the sudden glimpses of beauty from the mountain curves," Wise reflected. "We ogled at the heights."[3] Hidden meadows burst with springtime fragrance and the color of dogwood and mountain laurel; oleander and buttercups lined the wooden, barbed-wire fencerows. "We gradually began, somewhere along between Tennessee and Georgia," she wrote, "to get the idea that life was a smooth, serenely flowing business, and that there isn't really any hurry about the thing at all."[4] Almost seven hundred miles into her new life with Jerry, Wise and her contingent stopped for the night along U.S. 27 in Cedartown, Georgia.

Breakfast got the next morning into gear with native smoked sausage, hot biscuits, waffles with strawberry jam, and farm-fresh eggs "that you KNOW the hens laid to order just for *you*."[5] By midafternoon, the group had hi-balled 450 more miles into north Florida, east to U.S. 1, intending to do some sightseeing in America's oldest city, Saint Augustine. By horse-drawn carriage, the group traveled narrow cobblestone streets dating back to the Revolutionary War, under live oaks "dripping with Spanish moss,"[6] and past the nation's oldest house, which was once a pub for British soldiers. The boys discovered and toured the Castillo de San Marcos. Situated behind earthen berms built from native coquina shell stone, the imposing fortress protected the sea route for seventeenth-century treasure ships returning to Spain. The women bathed in the glorious Florida sun, "and considered seriously the fact that life can be a b-e-a-t-i-f-u-l [*sic*] thing. . .!"[7] It's much like something fictional that Hibiscus would have written to her readers in Detroit five years before, except that this trip was the stuff of dreams and ambition coming true.

After a final stop at the Marineland oceanarium, the group raced madly down the coast, ending the 285-mile last leg of their journey to Fort Lauderdale at 10 p.m. At their temporary ocean-view apartment, Rose Humphrey had two surprises awaiting them: fried chicken she had prepared at five that afternoon, and a seven-week-old Boston terrier puppy, a replacement for their other dog, Pat. Like the Tin Can Tourists of the 1930s, Brownie Wise, along with her son, her mother, and their friends, marveled at the Atlantic Ocean's nighttime majesty, the sense of infinite possibilities in its salty breezes. It was Sunday, April 30, 1950. "Our place faced the ocean, with only a roadway between our front door and the surf," she wrote. "The white-caps lulled us to sleep."[8]

On Monday morning, Wise swirled in to motion, looking to set up her new Florida home and business. Her mother thought she'd found a good store space, but Wise decided it wasn't big enough. After much searching around Broward County, Wise settled on a storefront just a block away at the corner of Highway 7 and West McKinley Street. Since you could get more land at a better price farther inland, Wise shopped an area known as "Old Plantation" in hopes of finding a house for herself and Jerry. Five miles west of Fort Lauderdale, Wise settled on a three-bedroom block home situated on an acre of land. "There is a little stream at the back of the property," Wise noted, "where Jerry can park himself under a patch of shade, stick his toes in the water, and lean on a fish-pole to his heart's content."[9]

On May 4, Wise entered into a contract to buy the home and property for

The first Tupperware business Brownie Wise opened in Florida, at the corner of McKinley Street and U.S. 441 in Hollywood, 1950.

$15,000, more than twice the median price for a Florida home in 1950. As an indication of the prosperity that the switch to Tupperware sales had brought in the previous year, Wise was able to pay for the first two-thirds in cash. She'd pay off the remaining $5,000 in monthly installments of $94.30. Now, with a measure of contentment at having found a home and storefront in less than a week, Wise wrote to her friends back in Michigan. "I'm sure you'll be right if you catch a mind-eye glimpse of Wise setting out bougainvillea vines and hibiscus bushes and cabbage palms and putting elephant ears in the ground floor boxes," she mused. "Nothing could be so blue as this tropical sky . . . and the sun is like melted gold."[10] A salesman stopped by the new store and dropped off a fifty-pound bag of Valencia oranges as a welcome gift.

On Monday, May 15, Wise opened her first Tupperware business in Florida and called it Patio Parties. The same day, she was already heading south to Miami to meet with seven or eight prospective dealers. She drew up her own manual instructing recruits on Tupperware, the party plan, and the "urgent musts"[11] of her operation. For years to come, this system would become standard issue for all would-be Tupperware Ladies. "This plan has proved itself a tremendous and profitable success in other states, and with your cooperation, we will attain the same success here," Wise wrote in the foreword of her training manual. "While this policy may be flexible in some respects, any deviation from it, on your part, will result in the loss of your rights as a dealer."[12]

The Patio Party Plan

A patio party is the organized presentation of the values of your products.

It is the KEY that unlocks the door to sales, through good product demonstration and good product display. It is your means of creating a desire for the product through visual demonstration.

The congenial atmosphere of a Patio Party is relaxing. All the guests are imbued with the group spirit of the party. The social spirit of a party tends to lower sales resistance of those present, as well as increase a competitive buying spirit. The buying spirit is *contagious*; it is a proven fact that you will sell more to a group of 15 women AS A GROUP than you will sell to them individually.

This is the essence of the Patio Party Plan.

A good demonstration is a source of entertainment, information, and the purchase of useful products. It is to your interest to work toward the accomplishment of all *three* purposes.

In the course of a Patio Party, three people must gain—you, the dealer, through the sale of your products and the booking of future parties; the hostess, who in a sense is your sub-dealer, and upon whose hospitality and initiative, the success of the party plan depends; and finally the guest, who through the medium of the Patio Party plan, enjoy a sociable get-together. In addition, the guest is impressed because she is shown, to her personal benefit, definite uses for the products she purchases.

As a hostess incentive, the following plan has been patterned for Patio Parties:

1. The hostess receives _____ for having a patio party.
2. The hostess receives $1.50 for each party booked at her party. It is suggested that no more than 2 parties be booked from each hostess' party.
3. The hostess receives 5% of the total amount of merchandise sold at her party, including outside orders, which should definitely be encouraged. (See the points on verification, regarding "outside orders.") A list of the hostess gifts and their credit value will be supplied by your manager. A hostess may pay a balance of up to $1.50 on her hostess gifts, regardless of the amount accumulated in hostess credit.

A successful party always includes entertainment in the form of games, with prizes and favors. Please make good use of the game book, with which your manager will supply you. Game prizes will be supplied to you, on your order form, at a very nominal cost. Your manager can give you excellent advice on the variety of games you can use, suitable for various groups. When circumstances do not permit the playing of games, prizes should still be awarded, and they can be given for a lucky numbered card, the oldest or youngest person, the newly-wed, the mother of the most children, etc. You will receive party favors free of charge, at the rate of one favor for each wholesale dollar, with your orders. They may be used as gift souvenirs, as game prizes for relay games, etc. Suggestions along this line are included in the section of training devoted to games.[13]

It was soft sell—sophisticated, social, and fun. The Brownie Wise Patio Party Plan became to home selling what Earl Tupper's Poly-T was to plastics. Those two factors became the nucleus of Tupperware's widespread appeal.

Back at her new home, Wise sat down at the typewriter, producing a three-page, single-spaced "round-robin" letter, bringing everyone in her old Michigan all-star crew up to date. "I AM NOW A BONA FIDE RESIDENT OF THE SOVEREIGN STATE OF FLORIDA," she announced.[14] "My car has a native license plate, and I'm sporting a driver's license . . . which means, in the Florida vernacular, I have, 'sand in my shoes.'"[15] Her warmth and attention to the details of all her former dealers' lives foreshadowed the kind of one-on-one relationship Brownie Wise would foster when the number of people in her charge multiplied many times over:

NOLA: I hear from Betty that you are turning in your case soon . . . I hope you're going to enjoy every minute of your new-found freedom.

MARGE: Betty wrote me about Hank's good fortune, and I'm SO glad for you!

IRENE TYLER: Let me know how the den turned out, will you? Good luck!

EDNA: A kiss to the angel child . . . (still haven't seen one more beautiful than she is even in Florida!). . . . Boy, do I need a permanent!

In between lighthearted quips and witty asides, the true affection Wise shared for her Michigan team shone through. She had helped nurture, coach, and cajole them to success, and in turn their performance resulted in Wise taking a big step up the ladder:

As I unpack these beautiful things and make them part of my Florida home, please know that they are the essence of the home itself . . . they will give me cheer and encouragement every time I look at them, and I will love you and your kindness all over again.

With thank you and good-bye now properly expressed, it was time to get down to business. "I could go on for pages and pages," Wise wound up her long letter, "But in the meantime Patio Parties must be about the business of setting their little roots down here and there in Florida, and having their little roots watered and fertilized . . . and I can't do it sitting at this typewriter."[16] Brownie Wise zealously embarked on building a new cadre of Florida dealers, with the hope of surpassing the success she'd had in Michigan. On May 25, Wise celebrated her thirty-seventh birthday and Jerry his twelfth. To continue the family's musical tradition in their new Florida home, Grandma Rose presented a fancy electric organ to budding pianist Jerry.[17]

It wasn't long after the establishment of Patio Parties that the Florida storm clouds started to roll in. One of the Michigan dealers who followed Wise to Florida, Jayne Boltz, along with her husband, Bob, hoped to open a branch in Tampa. Their move was as hellish as the trip for Wise was joyous. The couple sold their home, moved their two young children, invested in a second station wagon so both could work their Tupperware Florida operation full time, and left behind an established dealership in Detroit. Upon their arrival, they learned that the Tampa region had already been claimed by a Tupperware dealer named James Evans in nearby St. Petersburg. He was throwing his weight around, offering better sales commissions, and, according to Wise, not properly training his dealers. Wise had known about Evans but had gotten assurances from Collamore that it would not be a conflict or problem for the new branch she wanted to establish across the bay in Tampa.

"The burning point is that Mr. Evans has set up in Tampa, and intends to stay there," Wise wrote to Collamore, "while I felt very secure in telling the Boltz's that the Tampa area would be theirs, and they have slanted all their plans and efforts in that direction. They have gone to a great deal of expense in running off their primary literature and distributing it."[18] Meanwhile, Evans was also advertising in Tampa, and offering a more attractive system of distribution than Jayne and Bob Boltz could offer. "Two of our other dealers from Michigan arrived in Tampa Saturday to work with the Boltz's," Wise reported, "and I'm sure you can imagine the turmoil all four of them are in at the present time. Their hands are tied."[19] Just a month after her own arrival, the Tampa situation had gotten so bad that Brownie Wise was desperate. "To be perfectly frank, Mr. Collamore," Wise confessed, "if I had only myself to consider, I think I would be discouraged enough about this, right at this time, to drop the entire enterprise; however, there is so much at stake for other people that I can't afford to."[20]

Brownie Wise and her son, Jerry, ca. 1954.

As May dragged into June, her former star dealers in Detroit focused their fury upon Wise. Jayne and Bob Boltz weren't getting quick answers to their concerns, and, making matters more difficult, the telephone service was bad and the couple felt Wise had left them twisting in the wind. "Brownie, this may well sound like a sob story, and well it may be," the couple wrote. "How would *you* like to sit on a fence waiting, waiting, waiting for just a few words that would put us straight as to your plans and policy? All during this waiting please keep in mind that our resources are NOT increasing, but rather the contrary, are DE- creasing." The tone of the letter turned personal and bitter, reflecting the couple's desperation. "Yes—we know that no one can tell you what to do," they criticized. "We are just trying to ascertain just what you intend to do here in Tampa."[21] In fairness, Wise had already written to Collamore, describing how dire the situation was. When the letter from Jayne and Bob Boltz arrived at her store, Wise fired back, but in a measured and empathetic tone.

"I have a genuine respect for both of you," Wise wrote. "YOUR resources, YOUR condition, YOUR possibilities are also mine in a business sense. As things go for you in Tampa, so they go for me."[22] Wise explained to the couple that she'd gotten assurances from Collamore before she left Detroit that Evans had agreed to limit his operation to Saint Petersburg. She had called Collamore and written a letter to get his clarification on the matter and was waiting out on the same limb with them. "'Yes—we know that no one can tell you what to do,' I'm sorry you wrote that Bob," Wise quoted. "I'll try to forget it as soon as possible . . . because I have never, sincerely, had the attitude that noone could tell me what to do."[23]

Despite the territorial battles, in the first two months of Patio Parties' existence, Brownie Wise had ordered $14,180.13 worth of Tupperware. Most of it went to customers in South Florida, where Wise, her mother, and local dealers could operate without sniping from competitors. Wise poured herself into holding weekly training sessions with dealers and two-hour weekly seminars with her unit managers, and she spent Fridays on the road visiting the West Palm branch. "In the long run," she wrote, "well-trained dealers will pay for the effort spent on them; the first three or four months doesn't always show this, but after that, the results are plain. I would go on the record for the statement that one well-trained demonstrator will outclass two, and sometimes even three dealers who are handed a line of samples, given a pat on the back, a price list and sent on their way."[24]

It would take time for new female recruits not used to public speaking, let alone selling an entirely foreign line of product, to start seeing success. Each received a cardboard box containing a big suitcase full of the Tupperware to be shown and demonstrated at home parties. In the early days, dealers could expect to shell out $35 on their sample case, putting them in a significant hole before they sold even one Wonder Bowl. On July 29, 1950, the first Orlando dealer, Gwen Lord, had her inaugural Tupperware party and reported back to Wise:

> I am enclosing the order form from my first party (hope it is done Right) which could not exactly be called a "howling success." Owing to some plague or virus or whatever about half those invited were sick.[25]

In July, Wise proposed splitting Florida in two, east and west, with the idea of settling the feud with Evans and getting on with business. "Whatever we can do will have my wholehearted effort in forgetting the things that are past, and working toward a good future," Wise wrote Collamore, "This thing must be good for all of us—Mr. Evans, Tupperware and Brownie Wise, or it will eventually be good for none of us."[26] As the hot summer of 1950 wore on, it was clear the fight over territory would not be settled so quickly. In a letter dated August 1, 1950, Wise reported to Collamore that Evans had ordered her dealers "out of town," and said that if they insisted on staying, "he would continue to fight them in *every* way, and *any* way he could."[27] Wise had her back to the wall, and it's clear from the tone of her letters that she might well have reclaimed her Michigan operation and said to hell with Florida. "It is true that I have, in a business sense, made steps that I cannot retrace," Wise told him. "I know I CAN build a good business here; I'm right now in the process of doing it; but I can't go on doing it with the present handicaps. I hope I can make you understand Mr. Collamore, that all I have is at stake here."[28]

◦ ◦ ◦

Earl Tupper was aware of the territorial problems going on in Florida and elsewhere. Very early on, Peter and Elsie Block accepted his invitation to move their powerhouse Poly T distributorship from Detroit to Los Angeles. Not long after establishing their headquarters in Pasadena, the Blocks received a phone call from a man who told them he'd been distributing Tupperware in the area for four years. "Why in the world did we come to California?" Elsie Block wrote. "We could have stayed in the east in our own back yard. This is a serious business and we staked our future on its success. Can we depend on any word coming out of Massachusetts?"[29] If Tupper hoped to continue to expand his burgeoning force of Tupperware missionaries, he would have to find a way to get them "singing off the same song sheet."[30]

By the summer of 1950, distributors across the country were starting to develop their own success stories selling Tupperware on the party plan. To mini-mize territorial disputes, Tupper needed to find a way to harness that selling power under one centralized umbrella, with a formalized approach to sales and distribution. He thought he had found it in the person of Norman Squires, who ran a Long Island–based company known as Hostess Home Accessories. Squires's family credits him with drawing up the first Hostess party plan for Stanley as early as 1938. Together, Squires and Tupper formalized rules of what would come to be known as Tupper's new Hostess Division, much of it looking like the system of distribution employed by Stanley, with some subtle differ-ences. Dealers like Wise who switched to Tupperware were starting to feminize home-party selling, with more emphasis on the social and emotional aspects and far less dependence on the hard sell. Dealers asked the Tupper Corporation about expanding the product line, setting up nationwide guidelines of demon-strations, pricing, discounts, and distributor territories.

Tupper hired Squires as general sales manager of the newly created Hostess Division. On September 5, 1950, the Tupper Corporation put higher prices into effect and started selling direct to all of its home dealer demonstrators. Old distributors like the Damigellas in the Northeast, Brownie Wise in the South, and the Blocks out West were asked to "terminate and liquidate" their own companies and invited to work for the Tupper Corporation as area manag-ers.[31] Tupperware would be sold exclusively through its new Hostess Division based in Long Island, New York, under the Tupper Hostess Party Plan. The area managers would take on the responsibility of appointing qualified branch managers, district managers, and unit managers. Each would receive a specific percentage discount on product on a sliding scale corresponding to their rank within each newly outlined area. This framework was much like the systems under which distributors were already operating, but it would end the territo-rial competition, create a rigid price and profit structure, and standardize all dealer training. Distributors who didn't want to sign on as a Hostess Division manager could not get a supply of product.

In California, Peter and Elsie Block received a telegram from the home of-fice in Farnumsville: "Tupperware no longer available on party plan, no fur-ther orders will be acknowledged."[32] The Blocks and their Poly-T business had been operating well without the help of Norman Squires and Hostess, and they weren't signed on. "The business was over," Elsie Block wrote. "Peter and I were crushed beyond words."[33] It was the Hostess way or the highway. The Blocks and a small group of their dealers, "Block's Believers," met and decided to carry on by selling items as similar as they could find. "It wasn't Tupperware," Elsie Bock said, "but the party didn't stop."[34]

In September 1950, U.N. soldiers fighting the two-month-old Korean War succeeded in driving North Korean troops out of the South Korean capital of Seoul. An obscure senator from Wisconsin named Joseph McCarthy had risen to prominence through a six-hour speech on the Senate floor in which he claimed to have a list of more than two hundred Communist subversives working within the federal government. For mediating the Arab-Israeli dispute, Dr. Ralph Johnson Bunche had become the first black American to win the Nobel Peace Prize. Diners Club was the first company to issue a credit card. The Tupper Corporation now had the infrastructure in place to handle the growth of its sales side, but the manufacturing would soon start falling behind the demand its new Hostess Division had created.

○ ○ ○

Squires immediately recognized Wise as a rising star and took quick action to address her concerns. Barely a week after his appointment as general sales manager, Squires had his secretary send her a letter. "He wants me to impress upon you that he is more than anxious to make your acquaintance," Squires's secretary wrote Wise. "He feels sure that you will be figured very prominently in the plans and policy which are now being drawn up for the future."[35] Two weeks later, Squires traveled to Florida to meet Wise and offer her praise for the "consistent progress" she had already made.[36] Like a good soldier, Wise dissolved her Patio Parties business and closed the warehouse along Route 7.

In the following weeks, Squires and the Hostess Division gave Brownie Wise and her dealers a way out of the first serious crisis of her Florida move. The "Florida East Coast Area"—encompassing Fort Myers, Miami, north through West Palm Beach, Orlando, Jacksonville, and ending at and including Savannah, Georgia—was now officially hers. The vast, 650-mile stretch included a half-dozen growing, sunny, southern metropolitan areas in which Wise was free to locate many of her old Detroit teammates and new recruits. They now had the assurance that there would be no renegade distributors to disrupt things once they arrived. It was win-win. The battle for Florida ended in a truce: Brownie Wise didn't get the entire state as promised, but—like the birthday gift of Savannah that Sherman gave to Lincoln during the Civil War—it was an attractive consolation prize.

With a renewed vigor and focus, on November 25, 1950, Wise published the first edition of her *Go-Getter* newsletter as part of Tupper's new Hostess Division. "A warm handclasp to all of you who join me in celebrating the birth of the Florida East Coast Area, Tupper Hostess Division," Wise began. "No other issue of our new "Go-Getter" newsletter will give Ye Editor quite the sense of elation and anticipation that laying out this one does!"[37] Each page had three holes already punched so dealers could put them in binders for future reference. It was the kind of manifesto Wise would use to tell people in the field exactly what was expected of them, to offer tips on presenting the best parties possible, to recognize peak performers, newbies, and those transitioning out of the program, and to deliver inspirational messages intended to focus eyes on the prize:

> The newness of the Tupper Hostess Division plan is fresh in our thinking our minds are alert to all these changes, because we must fit them into our way of working. We must take *advantage* of the newness—in hostess gifts, in products, in the plan . . . and while we are making way, ourselves, for the new mechanics of the business, let's expose our customers and hostesses to the enthusiasm we feel . . . selling is showmanship, and showmanship thrives on what's NEW![38]

The newness and enthusiasm was contagious. With Wise prodding them to do so, ambitious women were scouting for places to establish new Tupperware units in Florida towns like Kissimmee, Fort Pierce, and Plymouth. Over the Thanksgiving holiday, her mother, Rose Humphrey, got into the act, braving wind and rain to scout out possibilities in Sanford, a historic hamlet on Lake Monroe where gangster Al Capone once spent winter vacations. The noted Harlem Renaissance writer Zora Neale Hurston penned her first novel, *Jonah's Gourd Vine,* in Sanford. Humphrey liked what she saw there and made the 230-mile move north to open a new Tupperware business. In keeping with the family tradition, Humphrey would become a trailblazing and successful Tupperware powerhouse in the years to come, often ranking among the top sellers in the country.

With this hard-fought freedom and entrepreneurial spirit sweeping the East Coast Area, party sales started to roll in. As one example, a receipt during this time period from Tupper Plastics to Brownie Wise via ACME Fast Freight shows an order for forty dozen, fifty-ounce Tupperware canisters. If those shipments didn't make it to Wise on time, she couldn't get them to any of her dealers. At first, the factory couldn't keep up with the number of orders, and shipping delays became more and more frequent. Dealers lost money on Christmas orders for fear the orders wouldn't arrive on time. "I don't know, of course, what the trucking companies are promising you at that end," Wise complained to Squires, "but they're simply not coming through with deliveries as they should be down here."[39] One unit manager resigned because he hadn't received a commission check in months. "The company hasn't been fair enough to offer any explanations why they haven't answered my letters," he wrote in a letter of resignation.[40]

The continual frustrations and workload started to take a physical toll on Wise. For the last two years, she'd been experiencing chronic headaches. By the middle of December 1950, they had become so excruciating she had to be hospitalized for exploratory brain surgery. Doctors thought it possible they might find a blood clot or, worse, a tumor, and Wise was subjected to the long ordeal of doctors going into her brain to tie-off a series of blood vessels they suspected were causing the problem.[41] She was allowed a two-day home respite over Christmas, and then it was back to the hospital. In true Brownie Wise, stiff-upper-lip fashion, she never reported any of this to the home office; one of her managers related the medical issues to Squires. Brownie and Jerry Wise ended up celebrating the holidays belatedly, once she was finally well enough to go home from the hospital.

It was the end of a year where Brownie Wise cut loose from the unhappy remnants of a bad marriage in Michigan. She gambled on the promise of her new love, Tupperware, transporting her to the kind of successful life of which her alter-ego Hibiscus had dreamed. At times, making that happen took all the energy, diplomacy, and perseverance she could muster. Perhaps not quickly enough for a go-getter like Brownie Wise, Florida was starting to pay off. The year 1951 would be even more eventful than the year before. It would take her to the pinnacle of Tupperware's sales operation, to the kind of position Frank Stanley Beveridge told her a *woman* would never have on his watch. For the first time, she'd meet the Tupperware wizard himself and tell him just how things ought to be. Stanley's loss was Tupperware's gain. This time, the guru at the top would listen.

○   ○   ○

At the start of 1951, Earl Tupper had already seen his company expand to Cuero, Texas, and across the northern border into Canada. At Tupper Plastics and Chemicals Limited in L'Epiphanie, near Montreal, Quebec, the office personnel spoke French and English. The Canadian distributor in Montreal was on a pace to reach more than $1 million in sales by the end of the year. By the middle of 1951, there were 1,925 Tupperware dealers scattered across Canada. Tupper Texas encompassed a 500-acre tract containing remnants of an air base. The parcel had a fire station and eleven buildings housing production equipment, maintenance, and research labs. Tupper took his family there, living in an abandoned barracks, and relocated his personal laboratory on site. There were molds produced at Tupper Texas to supply Tupperware across the United States, and a beryllium casting shop with some of the "most expensive machinery in the south or southwest."[42] Tupper was eyeing this operation as the potential world headquarters for all his ambitious expansion plans.

Tupper had drawn up the deal for the Cuero property and had his lawyers state everything very clearly. The town council approved Tupper coming in and setting up shop, but not everyone else in the small town did. Soon a whispering campaign started: When would this *Yankee* start hiring people? Where are the advertisements? Could it be he's really here for some *other* reason? Could he be using the whole plastics angle as a front when his real intention is to prospect for oil? "People started pressuring the mayor saying he shouldn't have given away the airbase so cheap," Tupper's son Glenn remembered.[43]

Before the local leadership could go back on any of the things Tupper had already negotiated, he demanded they put it to a vote of the people. A majority of Cuero residents sided with Tupper, but that wasn't the end of it. Some of the good-old-boys didn't like it because they were convinced "a Yankee was getting a better cut than they were."[44] Even though there was no indication there really was oil under the base, the mayor's back was against the wall. There were too many people of influence convinced that "this damn Tupper has won in the courts and made us look like jackasses."[45] There were rumblings that Tupper might not even be safe if he continued to press the issue. "You could fight this and get a bodyguard," Cuero's mayor told Tupper, "but I've got to live here the rest of my life. I could keep helping you, but it's going to put me in a bad way too."

Ever the pragmatist, but not one to back down or walk away from a good business deal quickly, Tupper said, "I'm no pistolero, and I'm not going to get into this sort of thing." According to one of his sons, that's when Tupper "began to seriously think about pulling out."[46] Without the approval of people in town, how harmonious could their coexistence be? What prospects for long-term success could Tupper Texas expect to have?

Besides, Tupper's Yankee sensibilities and deeply rooted work ethic clashed with the locals' "do it mañana" attitude. Within a matter of months, Tupper pulled out of Cuero and shopped other locales around the country for a more favorable reception to his Texas-sized dreams. While Tupper was interested in preserving the mineral rights to his Cuero land, there's no evidence to suggest a big gusher was ever discovered. Instead of being the world headquarters for the empire Earl Tupper eventually built, today the Cuero land is home to a prison.

○ ○ ○

In January 1951, Brownie Wise was out of the hospital, and she noted in a letter that it was the "first time in two years I've been completely clear of headaches."[47] Squires had notified dealers that the division's name was changing to "Hostess Associates Inc." and dropping "Tupper" off the letterhead. Wise complained she'd been inundated with a "flood" of letters from her people concerned that Hostess might be on the verge of dropping Tupperware from its line of products. Squires assured them that the name change was just a technicality, but Wise pressed, "Will you please reassure me about this in a letter, mentioning that I have called it to your attention because of the dealers' questions to me?"[48]

By February, Squires had responded as Wise had requested, and that helped relieve some of the nagging insecurity Wise was still feeling about the Hostess Division. She told Squires that his letters "have driven away the sense of being 'lost' in the tropical hinterlands."[49] Still, the "needle that bit the deepest" for Wise was learning after the fact that an area managers' meeting had been held in Worcester, Massachusetts, and she had not been invited.[50] There were problems with end-of-the-year commissions that Wise was forced to cover out of her own pocket. "Frankly," she wrote, "I don't consider this fair at all Mr. Squires."[51] Confusion over shipments forced all of her dealers in Fort Lauderdale and Hollywood either to drive twenty-five miles to the Miami airport or to pay more freight to have them redirected. Worse still, the customers who paid to take a chance on this new product started questioning if it would ever come. For Brownie Wise, that was more than just bad business, it was an outrage.

As the weeks wore on, the situation worsened for Wise and the stable of twenty dealers who received their Tupperware directly from her. One of them, Abbie Brant, had moved from Miami to Fort Pierce hoping to establish a unit there, but with the shipping, supply, and ordering problems, she ended up back in Miami. Dealers in Miami were starting to drop off, too, discouraged by the lack of support and consistency. In a March 16, 1951, letter to Squires, Brownie Wise was all business: "I have little reason to do a good job of taking the company's side when my own affairs are as loosely attended to as they are, and I can't continue with my present stand if these conditions don't improve."[52]

Wise couldn't get display cases for her new dealers, and they had to use "make-up" cases far beneath her rigid professional standards. For a month, she'd been waiting for letterheads and stationery bearing the new Hostess name and had received nothing. When Wise tried to call Squires to convey the urgency of the matter, the operator told her Squires was not free to talk and then advised that he wasn't in at all. After such a promising start, it seemed as if Wise and her dealers were back in the dire straits they had experienced before Squires and Hostess came on board. For a woman so devoted that she carried a piece of Tupperware with her twenty-four hours a day, this would not do. "Most important of all—Will you see that I get some sample cases to work with?" Wise implored. "Or if I'm not going to get them, let me know, so I won't use up any more time, money, and effort on a futile cause."[53]

Exasperated, Wise decided on another phone call, only this time she decided to bypass Squires and Long Island and take her concerns straight to the top. It was a fateful conversation.

Six

THE CONFLUENCE OF GENIUS

If you know more than
the boss, tell him so.
He will appreciate your
ability and help.
—Earl Tupper

On March 27, 1951, the latest spring freeze on record hit eastern Massachusetts like an Arctic blast. The lingering winter in Farnumsville, however, was about to get some searing south Florida heat via the long-distance telephone line.

The unassuming operator at the Tupper Corporation was met with a woman's screaming voice on the other end: "I *demand* to speak to Mister Tupper!"[1]

The call was put through immediately; he picked up.

"This is Brownie Wise! In Miami!" she shouted.

"I know who you are," Tupper replied.

Wise was fed up with the fouled-up orders, and she was going to let Earl Tupper have it. "I wonder if you know how serious a problem this is?" Wise lectured. "It's a very serious problem!"

That kind of insolent talk from an employee could very well get that person fired on the spot. Respect for the boss was of paramount importance to Tupper. Then again, Brownie Wise, for all intents and purposes, was not an employee per se. She was more of an independent contractor building a business from which she and Tupper were benefiting. Despite the problems, Wise was moving more Tupperware per week than "anyone, any where."[2] That would explain why Tupper himself moved quickly to make sure her orders were straightened out and then called her back that very day to let her know he was handling it.

Tupper had bigger problems on his hands. Barely eight months into its existence, the Hostess Division was going down in flames, and he suspected Norman Squires of stealing money. Scholar Alison Clarke reported that Tupper later sued Squires for absconding with "$200,000 in invested monies."[3] Squires strongly disagreed, contending that Tupper had appropriated the knowledge he had brought to the corporation and then "unlawfully dismissed him."[4] The messy divorce between Tupper and his Hostess Division left him looking once more to redirect the sales end of his business. Brownie Wise's screaming voice was actually the Siren's song he needed.

When Tupper called back, he asked Wise how she was managing to move so much Tupperware, and would she come to meet with him? "I'm busy," Wise fumed. If Tupper wanted to meet, she told him, "You'll have to come to me."[5] It was the first interaction between two titanic personalities who, in the next seven years, would guide Tupperware to spectacular sales success. "Their relationship was set right there,"[6] the writer Charles Fishman observed. The back and forth continued. If Tupper wanted to meet, Wise told him, he would have to invite everyone else who had experience building their party-plan businesses before Hostess got involved. Tupper agreed, inviting the likes of Brownie Wise, Ann and Tom Damigella, Russ Bassett from Connecticut, and a few of the other most successful home-party people.

On Monday, April 2, 1951, Brownie Wise met Earl Tupper for the first time, during a two-day sales conference at the Garden City Hotel on Long Island.[7] His Hostess area managers sat at the meeting table with Earl Tupper and filled him in on how they were making American housewives coast to coast fall in love with Poly-T. The party plan, they told him, was the future of his product—not retail, not showroom. To ensure they could mine the profits of their hard work—setting up networks of dealers and training them to put on the best parties and offer the best service to their customers—they needed exclusivity. On the surface, it seemed what they were asking Earl Tupper to do was take a monumental risk—to put Tupperware, the pinnacle of his life's work, solely in the hands of a sales network comprised almost entirely of female business novices like Brownie Wise. In truth, many of them had already earned their stripes through Stanley and had shown the smarts to see the potential of Tupperware and the guts to stake their own futures on the product. They stood committed to doing this despite the seven months of hell they had endured riding the Hostess Division roller coaster. They had earned the right to try to make it fly their way. "I learned long ago," Wise said, "that a kite rises against, not with, the wind."[8]

Overnight, as Tupper thought about what the group was proposing, he was taken by its persuasiveness, especially that of Brownie Wise, and on April 3, he called Wise in her hotel room. "You talk a lot and everybody listens,"[9] he told her. It was a calculated gamble, and Earl Tupper was signing on. On Tuesday, April 3, 1951, Tupper formed Tupperware Home Parties Division (THP) and offered Wise the position of general sales manager. Within a few months, the Hostess Division remnants would be absorbed into THP, and the association with Squires largely ignored in the annals of Tupperware history. Tupper was giving Brownie Wise the opportunity to correct the infuriating stumbling blocks she had faced under Squires, and the upper-management brass ring that Beveridge said she would never attain at Stanley.

In 1951, there were few women in upper business management Wise could count as contemporaries: During World War II, when her husband became seriously ill, Olive Ann Beech stepped in to provide a steady hand for Beech Aircraft; Dorothy Shaver was setting new trends at Lord and Taylor; and the industrial designer Freda Diamond blazed the trail for women at Libbey Glass.

From a pragmatic standpoint, the offer was not immediately attractive to Wise. Tupper wanted to establish the new home-party operation a stone's throw down Main Street from Farnumsville, in Fisherville. For Wise it would mean not only having to give up her home in warm, sunny Florida after only eleven months, but she would also have to give up the lucrative distribution end and draw a regular management paycheck of $400 a week. At that rate, she'd equal her entire income for 1948 in less than a month. As a compromise, Tupper allowed her to split time between Massachusetts and South Florida, and she agreed to run the home-party operation at least until it was well established enough that someone else could take over.

During the time Tupper was waiting for the newly franchised territorial distributors on the home-party end to take hold, inventory started to back up. Using it as collateral, he took out a $300,000 loan from a Worcester bank to keep the business going. On May 3, Tupper sat down and drew up a plain-talk letter intended to woo dealers back into the fold and reassure those who'd been holding fast through the Hostess debacle:

Dear Tupperware Dealer:
    We have plenty of Tupperware right in stock ready to ship—And that includes the entire line. You can also look forward to new items soon unless materials become more difficult to get. Rest assured that Tupper will have

materials as long as they can be had legitimately. If anyone tells you that you cannot get Tupperware, please let us know.

You are in a lusty business; and like in all the old gold rush days, you will make a lot of money if you stake your claim wisely. As in the gold rush days, there seems to be every sort of scheming afoot and everyone seems to be trying to grab off of someone else's claim.

Those of you who are selling Tupperware, know that it is pay dirt because it was the first of its kind to be made and still is first by far in volume sold and in quality. People remember and ask for it. It is the backbone of plastics parties. No imitation will ever be as good. There is just exactly as much difference between the Tupperware original and imitation, as between an original painting and a copy—or an original in anything and the copy that comes later. Those who copy do not build to do that job; they copy to ride on the good will that another had built.

We want Tupperware dealers who recognize that fact; and who will not offer other products of similar appearance at Tupperware Home Parties and lead people to think they are getting all Tupperware. If any person suggests you do that, please let me have the details. You and the buying public are going to be hearing a lot about Tupperware and other Tupper Products. Here is a glimpse:

1. The complete line of Tupperware available now!
2. A national line of top quality, flat, soft plastics now!
3. Also a competitive line of fill-in soft plastics that will stand your competitors on their ears. These items will be adapted to your particular area now!
4. An improved line of chemicals and so forth, for those who want to sell them—if shipping is not too much of a problem. They will not be crammed down your throat. We are working on the chemicals.
5. Sales aids; Will develop line.
6. Gifts: We have the cooperation of the best national companies in the business who will supply these to you.

But here is the best of all, Tupper plans to turn over to his franchised territorial distributors, at cost, all items other than our own proprietary items. That will be the Tupper service to you. Can anyone else do that?

The distributors will take reasonable profit and sell to you as a dealer. You are going to make money. As you know, we are closing out some old items now from Hostess Division stock below cost or slightly above (as the case may be) direct to the dealers. You can make money on that deal and get set for the real future.

If you do not know the distributor for that territory, please write us for the name. If there is no distributor in your territory, we will arrange to have the nearest distributor serve you, or we will serve you, until a person is found to qualify for your territory. We are going to give you real service thru franchised exclusive territorial distributors. To do that, we are going to rewrite the rule book to simplify your dealings with us and give you quick, accurate service.

We are going to weed out the dealers who are the chislers so that we can spend our time serving the dealers who mean business. If you happen to be one of the few dealers, or if you know any such dealers, who have been lured from us by misleading statements, I here[by] extend the hand of welcome. Come back—if you will play honest ball.[10]

On May 7, 1951, Tupperware announced to the world the appointment of Brownie Wise as general sales manager for the Tupperware Home Parties Division. To round out THP's two-person executive staff, Wise turned to an old friend from her days in Michigan.

While Gary McDonald was still a new marine recruit in California, he and other soldiers had been enlisted to help fight range fires in the southern part of the state. After three days and nights of breathing in noxious smoke, McDonald "was hit with asthma big time, could not breathe."[11] In a field hospital, as McDonald was receiving pure oxygen, an absent-minded doctor strolled in with a lit cigarette. The attending corpsmen dove out of the room at the sight of it, but fortunately the blunder didn't ignite anything. After McDonald was moved to Pendleton's base hospital, another doctor prescribed an ether enema. "I called that doctor every word I ever learned in the Marine Corps," McDonald laughed.[12] As many of his contemporaries marched off to the Korean War, the end result of twenty-year-old Gary McDonald's asthma and tribulations was a medical discharge.

The military's loss was Tupperware's gain. Upon his return to Michigan, a wire was waiting for him: "Unpack your sea bag and pack your suitcase, we need ya, Brownie Wise and Earl Tupper."[13] After just a few days back home, McDonald was given the title of sales promotion manager and joined Wise at a Fisherville mill Tupper had purchased to house THP. It started humbly with a couple of offices, four clerk secretaries, and one "green eyeshade," a bookkeeper named Louis Seabury.[14]

Tupper also approached two stalwarts from the early days, Pete and Elsie Block in California, to see if they would put the power of their Poly-T business back behind Tupperware where it belonged. "Earl Tupper assured us that we would have a continual flow of Tupperware again," Elsie Block said. "We trusted his word as final. We agreed to cover all the counties north of San Diego County to Madera and Modesto counties. That was roughly half of the Golden state and we were ready to start mining."[15]

The plastic gold rush in California was on. The Blocks and their dealers booked a hectic schedule of parties, "actually more than we could handle."[16] Despite their reticence with the Tupperware Corporation, the Blocks and their dealers never lost faith in the product. Before long, they promoted three dealers to unit managers, and then divided all of the remaining dealers between them. With that accomplished, they could start their weekly sales bulletin, promotions, and contests, letting the three units battle it out for sales supremacy. That same kind of business-building started to sprout all over the United States.

Once Wise was installed as general manager, Tom and Ann Damigella lost the one-on-one contact they had enjoyed with Tupper, now having to deal with Wise as go-between. "I give the man credit," Tom Damigella said of Tupper. "He aligned himself with Brownie Wise immediately. She was brilliant. She had the real gift of gab."[17] It would be up to Wise to be a conduit between manufacturing and the distributors, and McDonald would handle scouting and recruiting new distributors in non-Tupperized territories. In the spring of 1951, Tupper pulled Tupperware from store shelves and rolled the dice that his network of motivated distributors would deliver.

During the first weeks of Wise's tenure, in a show of trust Tupper didn't like to bestow on outsiders, he took her on a tour of the Farnumsville plant, through his development laboratory, pointing out all the equipment he used to design and develop Tupperware. "Walking down the line of work tables," Wise wrote, "I saw this block sitting on a shelf and I guess I asked about it just because of feminine curiosity being as violent as it is."[18]

"Oh that?" Tupper said. "That's the first piece of material they gave me one day at DuPont and asked me if I could do anything with it."[19] It was the ugly piece of slag the DuPont people saw as worthless.

"It just stopped me in my tracks," Wise remembered. "I think it is the most potent lesson any one of us can have about the power of man's imagination."[20] At that instant, in Tupper's laboratory, the persistence and vision of her boss dawned on Brownie Wise—all she had known previously was his finished products. "From this," Wise wrote, "came the magic of Tupperware in all its beauty of design, all of its lovely coloring, all the artistry, and think of the imagination it took, the tremendous imagination it took. But always remember that the imagination had to be followed by a great deal of persistence through the years, to turn *this* in to *that* . . . the best sales story I have ever heard in all my life."[21]

Brownie Wise and Earl Tupper at the Tupperware factory in Farnumsville, Massachusetts, 1951.

Tupper gave "Poly" to Wise, who made it her most prized possession. She gave speeches about it as if it were a person, had dealers and distributors touch it for good luck and be photographed with it, and had Lloyds of London insure it as a valuable artifact. One person was assigned to make sure Poly was where Poly was supposed to be, and God help them if it wasn't. "Just get your fingers on it, wish for what you want," Wise would implore her dealers, "know it's going to come true, and then get out and work like everything . . . and it will!"[22]

Wise toured the length and breadth of the Tupperware empire, including the L'Epiphanie operation in Canada, the Fifth Avenue showroom in New York, and Tupper Texas, which could have been the long-term home of Tupperware Home Parties had things not gone so badly for Tupper with the locals. Wise compared her journey to a magic-carpet ride that offered her the awe-inspiring big picture; now it was time to get the sales side off the ground and keep all those factories humming with orders. "Sometime I hope to set up a museum of the first hand-made pieces of Tupperware produced," Wise wrote, "when it was a dream to Mr. Tupper and an impossibility to the rest of the plastics industry."[23]

After her orientation road trip across North America, in Detroit Wise gave what is believed to be her first speech as general manager of Tupperware Home Parties. With an abiding sense of pride and overflowing optimism, Wise addressed a crowd of friendly faces, hoping to bring more of them back into the Tupperware family. "It's a new day for Tupperware Home Parties . . . for Tupperware," she told them, "for our distributors, for you and you and you and YOU. It's a new day for our customers in the field, who will be introduced to more and more new, useful, unique pieces, original pieces of Tupperware, designed for modern living."[24]

The speech was vintage Brownie Wise, coaching dealers to be the best "service representatives" they could be, not mere salespersons:[25] "Are you yourself as fresh as you should be—is your hair well arranged and shining and your hands well-groomed (remember they frame every piece of Tupperware they handle!) Are your white shoes WHITE and your dark shoes gleaming?" she asked the audience.[26] "When you make your delivery, is your appearance as inviting as it was when you put on the party? Have you time to be pleasantly cordial with your hostess, and relaxed, and friendly—or are you in a mad rush, because you got off to a late start?"[27] She urged the audience to keep their minds refreshed and learn all they could from customers, fellow dealers, and managers. "We are not building for tomorrow only," Wise told them, "or next week or next month; all of us are building for the future. To build is to USE all you have."[28]

The new THP Division was about to embark on an "old, old dream" of their new general manager's, to make a movie featuring a demonstrator and audience. Wise hoped it would be a filmed version of the perfect party demonstration. "Well, 99% perfect anyway . . . we have to save the 1% to grow on," she mused. Wise thought it could be the best possible training tool for old and new dealers, "the most potent ammunition," she wrote, "anyone could have with which to fire the guns of ambition." On August 18, filming began in Norwalk Connecticut, of a forty-five-minute, full-color feature complete with sound track, at a cost of almost $1,000 a minute. The star demonstrator was Marge Rogers, one of the alumni from Wise's former Michigan branch.

With the flow of Tupperware restored, Elsie Block reported hefty sales among her Golden State dealers. In one week, the Block's Poly-T company ordered 1,140 sets of Wonder Bowls and 6,360 cereal-bowl sets. By the end of 1951, Block said her operation reached $365,000 in sales for the six months they'd been back in Tupperware business. At their year-end celebration at the Pasadena Elks Lodge, their dealer numbers had grown from 30 to 130. Because of all the money the Tupper Corporation laid out to get the new division rolling, as of September 30, 1951, Ed Creiger reported that Tupperware Home Parties was operating on a $32,171.46 deficit. Tupper's expansion plans were undeterred; clearly the early sales reports from operations like the Blocks' were an indication of good times ahead.

In September, Wise presided over the first sales conference of eastern, southern, and Canadian Tupperware distributors held in Worcester, Massachusetts. To complete her ascent within the new company, the Tupper Corporation's board elected Wise vice president, also bestowing on her the title of general sales manager. At that conference, Wise announced to the twenty-two distributors operating in the United States, a contest to award a Cadillac to each of the seven who had the highest sales for the coming year. Wise also announced in Worcester a policy to "appoint distributors only from within the company."[29]

In November 1951, an ad in *Salesman's Opportunity* magazine featured a smiling woman holding fistfuls of cash and the promise that Tupperware "must make $10 to $50 for you in one evening—or pay nothing."[30] Those interested could mail off a coupon to the Tupper Corporation and receive a "free approval sampler." All people had to do to earn the "quick money" was attend parties, have good times, and expect a shower of "crisp bills and jingling silver."

The same month, acting as "editor, writer, artist and copy girl,"[31] Brownie Wise churned out the first edition of *Tupperware Sparks*—the companywide newsletter intended to boost employee morale and motivation:

> First came Earl Tupper's vision . . . beauty of design for kitchenware, plus the unique utility of "material of the future.
> Then came his invention in distinction . . . Tupperware!
> Now, the third great development is well on its way—Tupperware Home Parties Inc. the modern American plan to distribution.
> YOU are the most important single factor in the far flung Tupperware PLAN.[32]

The inaugural issue, complete with photographs, took "Tupperware Folks" on an eye-opening tour similar to the one Wise herself had taken just months before. Across America, distributors and dealers had to be every bit as impressed at the size and scope of Tupperware North America. Immediately, *Tupperware Sparks* was a public relations bonanza for Tupper. The woman who paid homage so dutifully would in time use the newsletter for her own purposes.

More importantly, *Sparks* became a crucial motivational tool, with dealers vying to get their name in print, their accomplishments recognized, their picture next to Tupperware big shots like Wise.

With the ultimate demise of Cuero inevitable, Tupper started to shop the southern United States for one thousand acres to house Tupperware Home Parties. Still dead-set on the warm weather of southern states, where unions were not prevalent and land could still be had cheaply, Tupper scoured the Carolinas, Tennessee, and Alabama. "We were urging him to pick Florida," McDonald remembered, "because we could have all of our salespeople come down there on family vacations and we could have them there for seminars and big meetings and not have to worry about paying expenses."[33] Wise remembered the morale boosting, team building, and educational aspects of the Stanley pilgrimage and thought Florida could add to the draw a hint of tropical sunshine and glamour. With Tupper it was all about the deal, the most land at the cheapest price, which would explain why one of the first Florida locales he seriously considered was in Starke, Florida—home of the state penitentiary and death row, where condemned inmates met their fate in a native oak electric chair, "Old Sparky."

Thirteen-year-old Jerry Wise, with his thick, jet black hair and bushy matching eyebrows, now stood eye-to-eye with his mother. On slower weeks, Brownie would load her son and mother in the car and go land shopping around South Florida. The trio spent a lot of time up and down U.S. 1 eyeing land for $35 per acre in Miami; investment property could still be had during those days for $10 per acre. Farther north in Jupiter, Wise found the stretch she fancied most: "It's in what is known as the 'Indian Hills' section—rolling land, and closer to the ocean than most," she reported to Tupper.[34] In a hurriedly typed letter, she took time to write in her own hand about this property, "very nice!"[35] A three-hundred-acre parcel near Boca Raton was also under consideration, right along U.S. 1.

The pragmatic and cost-conscious Tupper told Wise she should shop around Florida for an abandoned airport—not exactly the kind of tropical glamour she had in mind. He once made the 1,500-mile trip to Miami just to take her to one such airstrip in the town of Stuart. Wise yawned the whole way and made it clear she had better ideas in mind: "If you want an old airport, buy one," she told him, "but my headquarters won't be at any airport."[36] An old hanger could provide plenty of cheap space to operate, but it would also be hot in the summer, cold in the winter, and noisy almost all the time.

At the end of 1951, Tupper took an interest in the Orlando municipal airport and initiated talks with the Orlando Industrial Board. From 1941 through 1946, the airport had operated as the Orlando Army Air Field, and perhaps Tupper could sense the piles of military surplus as well as cheap space available. In the five years since control had reverted to the city, it had built a new passenger terminal and put the word out that the so-called city beautiful was friendly to new business. For Tupper, that in and of itself was a welcome change from the hostile treatment he'd gotten in east Texas.

The Orlando airport was steeped in history: In 1935, Amelia Earhardt was among barnstormers who took part in the annual Florida Air Party; three years later, Eddie Rickenbacker celebrated the grand opening of Eastern Airlines's passenger service to exotic places like Key West and Havana. During the war, German POWs housed there worked the citrus groves and nearby packing plants. Some received such humane treatment that they made central Florida their home after their incarceration.

During her own barnstorming days with the Patio Parties business, Brownie Wise had made a number of trips to Orlando. The small city was far more landlocked and less glamorous than the places she'd been eyeing as the future home of THP. She tried to discourage Tupper from putting the company there: "PLEASE don't make a deal on the Orlando land right away," Wise implored. "If you want to go up there, just go in on a temporary basis in the airport building, and wait a few months before you commit yourself to a building site. PLEASE . . . because I honestly think you could be terribly disappointed."[37] Of course, Wise was trying to convince the autocrat who nearly put the home-party operation near Florida's state penitentiary. For his part, Tupper became aware of a cattle baron offering some well-located land near the town of Kissimmee at a very good price.

Tupper mulled his decision—Tupperware Home Parties could relocate from Fisherville, Massachusetts, to a temporary home at the Orlando municipal airport, with the idea of building a new headquarters somewhere in central Florida. Orlando wasn't the oceanside glamour spot Wise was looking for, but perhaps she could make it work. Area tourist attractions like the Bok Tower, Cypress Gardens, and Gatorland; the warm climate; and lakes and palm trees provided a suitable enough image with which Wise could draw dealers. And the beaches were still close enough to suit Jerry. Besides, she had her hands full with an important distributor conference in Miami. Details of the Orlando idea would have to wait until after she was done with that summit.

At the end of 1951, this still-sleepy, agrarian part of the Sunshine State was just beginning to awaken to the tourism and technological boom the rest of the decade had in store. Despite the promise of the economic and civic transformation that forward-thinking companies like Tupperware Home Parties could bring, Orlando was still entrenched in the ways of the Deep South—schools, pools, and restaurants were segregated.

On Christmas night of 1951, forty-two miles to the east in a little, forgotten outpost town by the name of Mims, Harry T. Moore and his wife, Harriette, were also celebrating their twenty-fifth wedding anniversary. Harry Moore was an educator, head of the Progressive Voters' League, and Florida representative for the NAACP. To Ku Klux Klansmen, he may have been the most hated man in the state at the time. That night, after Moore turned out the lights in his wood-frame home and fog had settled in around the area, someone detonated a bomb planted directly beneath the Moores' bedroom. Harry was injured fatally; Harriette died a week later.

"The state is swarming right now with FBI agents," a newspaperman commented, "and we want the perpetrators caught and punished. Ninety-five percent of our folks are fine, decent-minded people. The other five percent are trash. And it is that trash that causes that kind of trouble. I suppose they do what they do because they feel they have to have somebody to look down on."[38]

The Moore bombing remains the most notorious Florida murder case for which no one was ever prosecuted.

Brownie Wise would bring a progressive attitude toward race relations to Florida. In Michigan, some of her early dealers were black and made good sales in their neighborhoods—working-class people more than anyone needed ways to stretch their limited budgets. But it went deeper than that for Wise: As a young girl, some of the playmates she counted on for company while her mother was on the road for such long stretches were black children. Jerry Wise said his mother always opposed segregation despite it being the tradition where she had been brought up.

Despite the violence, a new day was dawning across central Florida. Pulitzer Prize–winning Associated Press war correspondent Hal Boyle noted that many of the "new pioneers" were young veterans who had fallen in love with the climate while stationed in the Orlando region who had returned to launch their civilian careers.[39]

"Florida is a land of reward for almost any fresh talent," Boyle wrote. "Anyone who likes to turn his hand to new jobs might find a real opportunity in a recent newspaper ad offering $75 a week for an alligator wrestler. When I remarked the pay didn't seem too attractive an oldtimer remarked: 'Well, the hours are short and it's more than the alligators get.'"[40]

In 1951, Earl Tupper finally found the sales formula he needed to make his dreams of being a millionaire possible. Poly-T provided the foundation from which people like Brownie Wise, Gary McDonald, Ann and Tom Damigella,

Peter and Elsie Block, Rose Humphrey, Dorothy Shannon, and some names that would later become legendary would shape more prosperous lives. And 1952 was another watershed year—Tupper would bring THP to its permanent home, central Florida. Distributors emboldened by Tupper's confidence to do things their way started to hit big numbers and bring in new dealers from many walks of life. Wise would make two more moves in 1952, the latter of which would bring her to a waterfront mansion fit for a movie star—a Hibiscus dream come true.

Seven

PERMANENT
ROOTS

Have you ever stopped
to think what a decision
Mr. Tupper had to make
in turning this entire
sales distribution over to
a seemingly frail handful
of people . . . [when] none
of us were able to assure
ourselves or Mr. Tupper
100% that it would work?
—Brownie Wise

On New Year's Day of 1952, Brownie Wise
wrote Earl Tupper from the distributors' conference she had called in Miami Beach. The
fifteen who assembled held the fate of Tupper's
dream product in their hands; it would be
their responsibility to grow their regions
under the franchised distribution agreement
he had put into place. "These distributors have
gone nuts over Florida," Wise gushed. "They're
like kids at their first circus . . . never saw anything like it."[1] Wise was obviously campaign-
ing to solidify Tupper's thinking about putting
his new sales headquarters on her Florida
home turf. She'd been busy running around
looking at property all along Florida's eastern
seaboard and held out hope that Tupper might
change his mind and move the headquarters
to South Florida, not Orlando. "If it's possible
to find land for the building site no further
north than Stuart," she wrote, "I believe you'd
be able to operate from the temporary quarters at Boca Raton if you couldn't find anything closer."[2]

Some of the distributors were not thrilled
about kowtowing to Brownie Wise. They had
built their own businesses, recruited their own
dealers, and gotten things off the ground without her help. But they also had to deal with the
supply and shipping problems, inconsistent
training methods, and general uncertainty.

Tupper was asking them to put their faith in Wise as he had. Some felt she had not had as much experience as a distributor. Her old nemesis in St. Pete, J. B. Evans, expressed his own ideas at the summit about how things should be run. Wise was insisting that no other sales meetings be held until she called one in June or July. "We're in for a bad session of it, I'm afraid," Wise reported to Tupper. "One sour apple y'know. . . . Not that I think any serious upheaval will result—it's just too bad to waste distributors' time, when they need so much help as they do, with bull sessions on J.B.'s brainstorm."[3] Wise gave all of her distributors the first edition of *Tupperware Know-How,* her primer on how to give better demonstrations and ring up more sales. She called it "the most complete and effective manual of its kind in the direct selling industry."[4]

Despite that milestone, Elsie Block not impressed. When she and Peter reported to the other distributors that the line they were selling was already 90 percent Tupperware, their peers wanted to know more. Some were just coming into the new party-plan system and carried a wide variety of other "saleable merchandise." Elsie remembered that, "We were riddled with questions about warehousing, licensing, recruiting, training, premiums, and so much more."[5] Apparently Wise also took notice and wasn't pleased. In their hotel room later that evening, the Blocks got a visit from a Canadian distributor.

"I think I should warn you of something that I don't think you're aware of," he said. "I have been watching Brownie's reaction while you are answering questions coming from the folks at the meeting."[6]

Peter asked what he meant.

"It's not sitting very well with her. You folks are getting too much attention."[7]

"We were so cautious from then on," Elsie Block wrote. "I could understand her feelings, if it were true about her. After all, she was the newly appointed leader of the pack and coveted their recognition."[8]

If Wise indeed felt a rivalry with the Blocks, she didn't mention it in her New Year's Day letter to Tupper. He needed to know how much demand he might expect from his manufacturing end, and he wanted Wise to put the question to her distributors. What kind of sales figures could they project for the coming year? It was of great importance to them, too: If they wanted the new plan to work, an uninterrupted flow of Tupperware to their customers was vital. The Blocks projected $1 million in sales for 1952. With that kind of performance promised, even if Wise did feel a rivalry with Elsie Block, this early, team-building stage in the company's existence was no time to press the issue.

The tone of her letter to Tupper was upbeat; Wise knew he was on his way to Orlando to prospect for THP's new home. "Have a pleasant trip," she wrote. "Be careful . . . these tourists are crazy drivers."[9]

Tupper was further along in his negotiations than he may have let on. Just one day after she wrote that letter, the Orlando City Council unanimously approved a seven-month permit for Tupper Corporation's use of a massive hanger, T-129, at the city's municipal airport. Tupper promised to bring new jobs to the area; even at the temporary location, he expected the airport operation to employ close to one hundred locally recruited tool and die makers, machine operators, and clerical staff. Tupper also left the impression that Orlando would be the permanent home for his permanent manufacturing and distribution center.

On Thursday January 17, 1952, the manager of the Orlando Industrial Board appeared with Tupper in Orlando to make the historic announcement to an assemblage of photographers and newspapermen. The next day, the *Orlando Sentinel-Star* newspaper ran the front-page story under the headline, "Million Dollar Plastic Firm to Come Here."

"The combined distribution center and plant will give Orlando a new annual payroll of close to $250,000 to begin with," the article stated, "while future developments will increase this to one million dollars."[10] The writer described the Tupperware line as "air and liquid-tight flexible covers made with a groove into which the rim of the container fits snugly." As an added bonus, the Industrial Board's manager pointed out, the manufacturing process "is clean, odorless and noiseless."[11]

The group of volunteer Orlando businessmen who made up the Industrial Board had a reason to puff out their chests with pride. Tupperware Home Parties was just the kind of year-round diversity the area's evolving, citrus-based economy needed. "We are indeed happy to welcome an industry of this type to Orlando," one official beamed. "It will do a great deal for the city with its plans for a big future and we think Orlando is an ideal place for it."[12]

The *Orlando Sentinel-Star* lauded Tupperware's arrival in an editorial titled "Another Central Florida Triumph." In a statement that had to thrill Tupper, the paper's editors promised, "The organization and its officials will receive every possible assistance from the city and its citizens."[13] There would come a time when Tupper's people would need to call in a few favors, from the newspaper especially.

For Wise, the announcement had to be bittersweet. She had only been in her South Florida home for a year and a half, and she had had to fight like hell to get her business established. But there was little time for looking back, and Wise was always one to concentrate on what was around the bend, not what was behind. She had two moves to make: her home from Miami to Orlando, and her home office from Fisherville to Florida. Tupper announced to the newspapers that his people would arrive to begin setting up offices at Orlando's municipal airport on Saturday, January 20. To make that timetable, a lot of grunt work was required: clerical staff packed up the office, and the Farnumsville workers packed the Tupperware into a red truck for the Florida trip, with heavy items shipped by railcar. McDonald supervised the operation and got a firsthand look at Tupper's stern attention to detail.

It was nightfall, and workers were well into the job of filling up the freight car for the Florida move. "I was supervising the thing and went back to the office where Brownie and Tupper were," McDonald remembered. "The first thing when I walked in, I told them they were about half full, and the first thing he said to me was, 'Did you line the thing with plastic film?' I said no. He said: 'Good grief man, those cartons *breathe*; they *breathe* in and out as it bounces along and will pull all the dirt in from that box car into the containers and it could ruin everything that's in there. Now get your ass over there and fix it!'"[14]

McDonald double-timed it back to the loading platform and had the men pull everything out of the freight car and start all over. "I told the factory guy that was over there about what Tupper said, and he said, 'He didn't fire ya?' And I said, 'No, not yet anyway.' That's the kind of guy he was—harsh."[15] McDonald was a Wise guy, and Tupper wasn't about to fire someone so crucial to her confidence vis-à-vis the new company's success.

When it was all loaded, the staff of Tupperware Home Parties incorporated piled into two vehicles: the now-famous red truck driven by McDonald, and a four-door sedan with the women and the bookkeeper. With the railcar already bouncing its way down to Florida with its precious stock fully protected with plastic film, this puny little two-car procession comprised the entirety of Tupper Corporation's executive sales branch. The shocks and front steering on the truck were so bad McDonald kept crossing the center line. In the Carolinas, a police officer took notice and pulled him over on suspicion of driving while intoxicated. The procession of Tupperware pioneers ground to a halt as McDonald pleaded his case before the justice of the peace. "The judge heard the story and said, 'Get out of here, drive the best you can,'" McDonald chuckled.[16]

As promised, on Saturday, January 20, the group finished the 1,260-mile trek down most of the eastern United States. When Gary McDonald made that historic turn off Colonial Drive and pulled directly into Orlando municipal's hanger T-129, his red truck full of Tupperware, the sense of relief overtook any notion of what a historic moment it was. "We were so relieved to be here, you know, Florida," McDonald remarked. "It had the magic that all northerners used to have in their minds about Florida. So just being in Florida was wonderful."[17]

The hanger was a sprawling, cavernous space in which the team set up shop. Downstairs, they unloaded all the Tupperware they had into a small area blocked off with chicken wire. A lot of people in those early days remained direct Tupperware dealers, and it was up to the fledgling THP to supply them as if they had their own distributorship. Upstairs were the desks, phones, and supplies necessary to start spreading the new gospel of Tupperware cross country. It was decided that McDonald would continue to do the road work, developing distributorships, and Wise would do the dealer/distributor liaison work on the phones from the office and home.

Wise sold the Plantation property for a tidy $5,500 profit and picked out a house on Orlando's northwest side at 303 Dubsdread Circle. With its pleasing aesthetic lines and art deco influence, the single-story house rented for $100 per month. Rose Humphrey stayed behind in Miami to take over the South Florida network, the roots of which dated back to Wise's Stanley days in Michigan. The Orlando place was situated just off the second hole's green at Dubsdread Country Club's golf course, Orlando's oldest. The buzz the week Wise moved in was that West Virginian "Slamming" Sammy Snead had agreed to play in the upcoming International Mixed Two-Ball Tournament with one of the greatest female athletes of that era, Babe Zaharias. Seven years earlier, Ben Hogan had bested Snead at Dubsdread to win Orlando's Victory Bond Open. Golf historians credit that inaugural event with providing a springboard for central Florida's emergence as one of professional golf's epicenters.

Rich folk and golf pros could drink freely in the Dubsdread lounge and gamble openly on its fairways. "Full orchestras played on the club's patio which featured a barbeque pit, colorful gardens and a swimming pool," writer Steve Elling noted, "where kids skinny-dipped at night."[18]

The socializing would have to go on without Brownie Wise—she didn't have the time. Within a few days of her arrival in Orlando, she adroitly began courting the press. She continued to use her married name, but no mention was made of something as personal as her true married status. She took out ads in *Opportunity* and *Specialty Salesman* magazines looking to cultivate entrepreneurs interested in becoming distributors. An article in the January 24 *Orlando Evening Star* featured a photograph of a regal-looking Wise to the left of a headline that read: "Plastic Firm Official Spreads City's Fame." "National publicity in connection with the moving here of distribution headquarters for Tupper Corp., manufacturers of plastic consumer products, has begun to spread far and wide," the article began. It made note of the fact that Wise had sent notices throughout North America informing the Tupperware faithful of the move:[19] "Like Tupperware Home Parties," Wise wrote, "Florida is progressive and ambitious, it is the third fastest growing state! We sought a location that would lend itself best to national publicity and we felt that many of our people would like to visit us, especially with the wonderland of Florida to add warmth to the invitation."[20]

In late January, aside from the cheerleading PR of Brownie Wise, there wasn't a lot of wonderland or warmth in hangar T-129, the less-than-auspicious environs for Tupperware's new queen bee. Each morning McDonald had to coax an old boiler into warming the place. There was no timer on how long you pushed the starter button to let the oil run in before you lit it. The old machine began each day's work with such an explosion that the early employees of THP were assured of starting the day with a bang. "I never knew if it was going to be the beginning of the day," McDonald remembered, "or the end of my life."[21] Wearing coats and sweaters, people in the upstairs office waited for the big space to heat up.

The remains of the old air base provided a never-ending source of wonder and amusement for thirteen-year-old Jerry Wise. "I had the run of the west side," he remembered. "I used to drive my mother's '51 Hudson or Rose's Ford around the abandoned runways." There were remains of old World War II trainer planes he could explore and a "mountain of supplies just sitting there."[22] It was as if the soldiers and the airmen just packed up their own personal belongings and left all the government's toys behind. "There was no guard," Wise said. "You just drove in and drove out."[23]

His mother busied herself with churning out her first Florida-based edition of the *Tupperware Sparks* newsletter. In a one-inch-high headline, Wise announced the company's relocation and establishment: "Tupperware—Orlando!"[24]

"So, we started in the sunny state of Florida," Wise wrote. "The welcome we received in Orlando made us want to take the time to stop and look around. And what we saw we liked! Orlando, as you know, is in the heart of Florida and is known by many pleasing names such as 'City Beautiful' and 'The City of Camellias.' Within the city limits are 43 lovely lakes. We are not the Junior Chamber of Commerce of Orlando, but we do love it here."[25] Brownie Wise was the living, breathing personification of all the Orlando Industrial Board hoped for when they rolled out the welcome mat to her boss; she was already promoting Orlando as if she were on the chamber's payroll.

But Brownie Wise was about far more than promotion and public relations: She had a shrewd, almost uncanny sense of what to look for in a perspective "Tupperware Lady," whether she would be successful, and how to keep her motivated. In addition, this woman of limited formal education had a genius for effectively putting it on paper. These were the "eight basic qualifications" she instructed managers to look for in scouting new dealers and growing Tupperware's business:[26]

> *Health* Her health must be excellent, so that she can work steadily and so that she can work on her feet, as must be done in conducting a party.
>
> *Need of Money* She must have a real need to earn at least $50.00 a week, and it is still better if she must earn a good deal more than that.
>
> *Full Time* She must be willing to devote her full working time to this business. Of course, this does not mean that she will have to work forty or forty-five hours a week—as she would have to do in ordinary employment. What it means is that she should have no other employment, to distract her attention from this business.
>
> *Evening Work* She must be able and willing to devote several evenings a week to this work.
>
> *Family's Agreement* Her family must approve of her work. For example, if she is married, her husband must be willing to see her give several evenings a week to our work. We must *know* that this requirement has been met. We cannot safely accept her statement that "my husband won't object." We must see him ourselves, explain our work to him and sell him on it, so that we can be sure of his full cooperation. This same principal [*sic*] applies to any other members of her family who are likely to influence her.
>
> *Field Dating* She must be able and willing to do field dating, if and when it is necessary. This is especially important during her earliest weeks, when she may not have developed enough skill in dating Parties at Parties.
>
> *Residence* She must live within easy reach of you, so that you can visit her personally and so that you can phone her readily—and so that she can attend your training classes and your meetings.
>
> *Training* She must be willing to spend at least four or five afternoons (or an equivalent amount of time) and at least two or three evenings, in our regular course of training. AND, it must be more than mere "willingness." She must *want* to be well trained. If she isn't eager to devote enough time to her first training, you should not appoint her. Beware of the applicant who thinks she doesn't need thorough training. The odds against her are huge.[27]

"Field dating," was the equivalent of making cold calls to friends, relatives, even strangers with the hope of getting someone to put on a party until the dealer network was such that one party just led to another. Wise also advised her managers to pick a woman who was at least twenty-five or who had "outstanding ability that makes you feel sure she will succeed despite her youth."[28] If the woman had children, she would need someone who lives in the house to care for them, not just a sitter: "The expense of paying the 'sitter' generally leads the Dealer, in time, to drop out of the work."[29] The prospect needed to know how to drive and have regular access to a car and a telephone. Wise also offered a thorough analysis of fourteen personal characteristics, the intangibles that play a part in a prospect's odds for success or failure. An example: "Appearance . . . on this point, you need little guidance. Is her appearance attractive? She need not be beautiful, but she should look attractive and interesting, so that people will naturally tend to like her when they first see her. And she should dress neatly and conservatively."

At the end of her dealer-recruiting drill, Wise cautioned: "You aren't looking for perfection. *You'll never find it!* All you are trying to do, in selecting new Dealers is to put the odds in your favor—by picking the women who rank highest on those characteristics."[30]

Tupperware Sparks would inform the growing family of dealers and provide a key place to recognize their accomplishments and stoke their competitive fires. Distributors held their own sales conferences in their subfamilies across North America. Earl Tupper's gamble was starting to pay dividends: Tupperware Home Parties was gelling, distributors were starting to get product on a timely basis, and dealers were selling it to a new generation of customers.

On February 27, 1952, Wise sent out a newsletter to the new distributor network. "Pull out that bottom desk drawer," Wise wrote in a folksy tone, "put your feet in, lean back, and let's visit for awhile." She paid homage to Ann and Tom Damigella just for calling long-distance from Boston to say "hello." Wise lauded Pete Block—no mention of Elsie—for "his" January Tupperware orders totaling $25,353.18 "Number one for the States!" Then came the motivational push: "I'm sure you'll agree with me that sales like these do not just happen! It takes a lot of dealers putting on a lot of parties, demonstrating to a lot of consumers."[31]

Earl Tupper was taking notice of those sales figures and sent a handwritten motivational note of his own to Brownie Wise:

Brownie,
    Just this little line to be sure you know I appreciate what a whale of a job you are doing in spite of all the many problems. It's the first time I've ever had anyone so good on my team. Believe me it's a *good* feeling. We are going to do a real job.
Earl Tupper."[32]

Wise could use the reassurance. In addition to all of her responsibilities with distributors and dealers, she was in charge of the Orlando office, and she sometimes butted heads with male employees not used to taking orders from

A glimpse of the good times. Tupper and Wise suited up for a masquerade party in Orlando, 1952.

a woman. When the machine-shop man came in and asked to use the keys to the company car, Wise asked why. "I want to use it, that's why," the man replied, looking surprised. Wise rebuked him but later fretted to Tupper: "I'm on the spot with him about it. Do you want him to have it? I don't want trouble with him."[33] The company car problem continued in to March; it was as if the machine-shop man who was derisively nicknamed "the big wheel downstairs" was making his own rules just to get under the boss's skin.[34] "Believe me, I hate these fourth-grade arguments for authority," Wise fumed to Tupper. "I'm fed right up to my teeth with this deal. But until I receive further instructions from you, the station wagon is to be used as you originally outlined."[35]

Orlando's stormy spring weather brought with it a more serious problem—a blowing rainstorm flooded the hangar and damaged some of the inventory. The machine shop downstairs had standing water, and for Tupper this provided impetus to keep moving forward the long-term plans for finding land to build on. Despite those issues, some photos from that time period show Tupper and Wise decked out for a costume party, he in a top hat and handlebar mustache, she smiling beneath a flowery hat. Both have on formal retro attire with a modern twist; and, like loving parents, both hold Tupper's Poly-T bowls, pitchers, and canisters close to their hearts.

By April, THP had added Herbert Young to its ranks as head of accounting—they needed the extra bookkeeping help to keep up with the orders streaming into headquarters. By the company's first birthday on April 5, 1952, the number of U.S. dealers had swollen fivefold to 1,400. Tupperware had been chosen for the Housewares Award in the Modern Plastics competition, given recognition at the Industry and Handiwork show in Germany, and at the Modern Living exhibit at the Detroit Institute of Arts. *Charm* magazine called Tupperware "the miracle on the pantry shelf" and featured three accompanying photographs. Most importantly, the rise in dealers meant Tupperware was gaining critical word-of-mouth, neighbor-to-neighbor, party-to-party popularity.

On April 2, 1952, Brownie Wise and the Orlando staff celebrated the first birthday of Tupperware Home Parties with a formal dinner. Secretary Ann Fortier smiled on one side, and Gary McDonald, dressed sprightly in a bow tie and dinner jacket, did the same on the other. Wearing a bright flower corsage, Brownie Wise cut a three-layer company birthday cake complete with a single candle on top. "Now the swaddling clothes have been shed," Wise said. "Our infant has by-passed years and has grown to effervescent adolescence. Adulthood is just ahead."[36] Missing from the party was the evening's honored invitee, Earl Tupper. As a first birthday present, Wise sent him as candy, nuts, and a mustache cup with a matching saucer. She also included a couple of photographs from the birthday party.

In a handwritten letter dated April 7, 1952, Tupper sent back a letter of uncharacteristic warmth, even giddiness:

Brownie,

I've just opened your package tonite. The one with the two party pictures! You sure look Super! Anyone that cute has no right to be so smart. I'm eating the nuts and candy right now—the picture of the cake didn't bother me until I started eating . . . but now yum! yum! I'm sorry I missed the party—pounds or no pounds. Where did you pick up the mustache cup? The saucer has a beautiful ring. Many thanks to you, Brownie, on our first birthday . . . for the happiest hours this business has known . . . and for doing the greatest job ever done for me.

Sincerely,

Earl S. Tupper[37]

In May, the Tupperware Home Parties juggernaut surged forward with completion of *A Tupperware Home Party*. The fifty- two-minute feature, filmed in vivid Technicolor, starred Tupperware dealer Marge Rogers as demonstrator and costarred fourteen Tupperware distributors. This was the ultimate training tool Wise envisioned, to be shown by distributors at their sales assemblies across North America. Dealers would learn the best way to arrange a table to keep items easily accessible during their own demonstrations. "You will be shown how to say the right words at the right time: how to handle your product with grace and poise," Wise wrote, "how to deal with your audience and how to get their participation. You will be shown how to do a concise but complete demonstration of every item in the Tupperware line in a 45-minute session."[38]

Given all the effort Wise had expended on developing a thorough and uniform training and motivational program, she found it hard to sympathize with distributors who weren't keeping pace with the leaders. That unfortunate distinction fell upon distributor Russell Bassett of Hamden, Connecticut—one of those who had convinced Tupper to use the exclusive party plan in the first place. Brownie Wise's letter of May 3, 1952, showed that, along with being an expert cheerleader and motivator, she could be the taskmaster ready to use her ruler on a student not getting the job done. It also foreshadowed the kind of autocratic style she would develop. Former underlings say Wise would never admit failure.

"First, I hope you can appreciate fully, Russ, that the only sense of failure we can ever get here at the home office must necessarily come from some failure on the part of one of our distributors. We have in all cases given an equal share of sales aid and encouragement to all distributors," Wise wrote. "I have re-read every piece of correspondence in your folders, and I cannot help coming to the conclusion that you simply have not followed through, Russ. If you had used all the suggestions that have been given you, I truly believe you would have succeeded even without the past experience you have had on the party plan."[39]

Wise warned Bassett that his distributorship could be at stake: "We have not received appreciable cooperation from you in reporting on the leads we have forwarded to you for your territory," She complained. "My serious advice to you (and it is also friendly advice) is to put everything you have into this operation for the next 60 days and prove what you are really capable of doing. I wonder if you fully realize how much money a number of other distributors are making Russ. Let me hear from you."[40] It turns out Russ Bassett was not the only distributor Wise thought was underperforming.

A letter later that month showed that contrary to popular belief, in 1951 Tupper had not pulled Tupperware entirely from store shelves. He was considering putting a new line of Frosted Crystal Tupperware in department stores. This was where Wise had to draw the line; she felt retail outlets were hurting her distributors' progress and undermining the training program she worked so hard to install. Wise was not afraid to take issue with her boss and state her case in a forceful and analytical way. "The average home demonstrator does not realize how little is sold in stores where the product is displayed," Wise wrote Tupper. "He simply is conscious that our products are for sale in a store, and that this fact knocks out his punch line in the presentation of Tupperware to the effect that it is sold exclusively on the Home Party Plan. It further knocks out the reason we give for this type of merchandising. . . . Tupperware must be demonstrated."[41]

Wise went on to disagree with Tupper that it was prestigious to have Tupperware in stores, or at least certain pieces of it, even if it did not produce much sales volume. "I cannot agree with you on that," Wise told him. "If you had visited as many stores as I have had to do to buy out what was left of a stock of Tupperware which had gotten dusty, and been reduced to cost, and stacked up any old way, you would realize that unless Tupperware is displayed properly, it is better not to have seen it at all. I believe you do realize this, because I think I have heard you mention some incidents along that line."[42]

Tupper worried that Tupperware's potential for future publicity in magazines dependent on retail advertising could be compromised if the products were not available in stores. Wise was concerned about unrest among the foot soldiers charged with doing the real work of selling the product.

In California, Pete Block was the first to make an issue of the chain Van Kepple Green still selling Tupperware retail. In Detroit, J. L. Hudson still had a supply. Many top distributors blamed the retail stores for undermining the product's exclusivity. "I feel we're just on the threshold of receiving the kind of recognition that all our efforts have been slanted toward," Wise complained to Tupper. "I hope you realize that I am giving this careful consideration; I am not pulling a mother-hen act with our distributors, most of whom I could cheerfully kick in the teeth at least every other day. I have truly given this very serious thought for three days before answering you, and these are my firm convictions."[43]

Wise had a good point: across America new dealers were buying into the home-party plan. In letters to Wise, Tupper was clearly pleased with the way his new division was performing. Wise finally had the plan in place to make sure all the new dealers would read from the same sheet of music while training. Why compromise distributor morale by sticking to the old, failed, retail distribution methods? In this sense, Wise was firmly telling Tupper to let her handle the sales end, and he was demonstrating once more why he needed someone like her at the helm.

Tupper sent off a sketch to Wise of an invention he had in mind—a funnel to be used for "feeding or watering an invalid in bed."[44] Like a master guiding his apprentice, he sent her inspirational messages: "The Madness of Genius . . . is only the difference which makes the Genius tackle new things . . . believe they can be done . . . and do them! Quite naturally the plodders consider such a person unusual . . . even mad. E.S.T."[45]

More importantly, at the end of May Tupper flew back to Orlando for another historic announcement: he had reached a deal with State Senator Irlo Bronson on a thousand-acre tract of land just north of the city limits of Kissimmee. Bronson, the Speaker of the Florida House of Representatives, was also the largest landholder in all of Osceola County. If Orlando-area leaders were looking to find some property on which to establish a substantial new industry, it was natural to look to Bronson. The Kissimmee newspaper noted that Bronson "counts his holdings in number of townships not thousands of acres."[46] In just two real estate sales, one to Earl Tupper, the other to Walt Disney, Bronson forever changed the central Florida landscape.

Gary McDonald remembered how Tupper wanted to check out the swampy property for himself before making the deal final: "Tupper true to his own style walked the property carrying an iron stake with rubber gloves and rubber boots and a hammer and he would push the rod down in the ground and hit it with a hammer to chase the snakes away."[47]

On May 30, 1952, Bronson and William Bennett from Orlando's Industrial Board joined Earl Tupper and Brownie Wise in making a formal announcement of the land deal. Situated along the main artery bringing tourists in to central Florida, the Orange Blossom Trail, the property encompassed a mile of highway frontage. For Tupper, the land's easy access to transportation routes was a big plus. For Wise, the proximity to tourist attractions up and down the Trail could be exploited in promoting the new headquarters to her stable of dealers. Wise told reporters that Bronson himself had purchased, at his own cost, the remaining acreage necessary to bring the parcel to the size Tupper required.

Tupper hired John A. Templin of Lakeland-based Templin Incorporated as the contractor; Lakeland architect Donavan Dean is credited with designing THP's inaugural building. On Wednesday, June 16, 1952, workers started grading the site of Tupperware World Headquarters. In the *Kissimmee Gazette,* the announcement of work starting on the new THP headquarters was front-page news.

Despite their widely disparate personalities, Tupper and Wise can be seen in photographs from this period enjoying one of the warmest periods of their

Earl Tupper handing Wise the keys to a new Cadillac in front of her Orlando home, 1952.

professional relationship. They belie the notion that Tupper was humorless and didn't know how to have fun. One classic photograph taken in front of the Orlando Dubsdread golf course home shows a smiling Earl Tupper handing Wise the keys to a brand-new Cadillac. Tupper rarely posed for any public relations photographs of this kind.

The land announcements had to be jammed into the breakneck schedule of cross-country travel Wise was keeping. In June, she flew to San Diego, Pasadena, and Miami to award "oxblood leather" Diplomat cases to the highest performing dealers.[48] Each carried an inscription, "To a Star Distributor—Compliments of Earl S. Tupper, President of Tupperware Home Parties Inc."[49] In Miami, Wise awarded the case to none other than Rose Humphrey—nowhere in the June-July issue of *Tupperware Sparks* did Wise mention that Humphrey was her own mother, but Tupper didn't seem to see it as a possible conflict of interest. In San Diego, dealers jammed into the assembly hall to see Wise present another prized leather case to top performers Eli Schofield and "his charming wife."[50] The biggest gun of the three winners was the Pasadena-based Poly Sales Company, which had done $165,899.02 in sales over the seven-month contest period.

Elsie Block wrote that at that award presentation she asked her dealers: "We've got millions of people in our area. Are we going to get out there and get the sales personally or do we all have to recruit new people to do the job?"

All over the banquet hall at the famous Biltmore Hotel dealers chanted back, "We'll get all the sales!"[51] "When I sat down," Block wrote, "Brownie turned to me and said, 'So that's how you do it!'[52] I thought, 'She doesn't know?' It was on that night that Brownie got a glimpse into some of the reasons for our rapid growth."[53]

Clearly in this instance Elsie Block is self-aggrandizing in an attempt to minimize Brownie Wise's knowledge and stature. By this point in time, Wise had literally written the book on sales know-how and dealer motivation. It is interesting to note, however, that Wise does some minimizing of her own in the June–July issue of *Tupperware Sparks*. A photograph shows Wise addressing contest winner Peter Block, with no mention or recognition in the caption of Elsie, despite the fact that she is smiling and very evident in the picture. Given Wise's penchant for diplomacy and attention to detail, this was more than an oversight on her part. She did, however, give both some written recognition: "The Poly Sales family turned out in full force for a giant rally and sales assembly. In honor of the occasion they had run a "Brownie Wise Week" and their total sales for that week set a new record. Both Pete and Elsie Block paid glowing compliments to the cooperation of their dealers, managers and sub-distributors."[54] The Blocks' distributorship would go on to produce some of the most important and successful alumni in Tupperware history.

Keeping with the new company's habit of holding conferences on holidays, Tupperware Home Parties held its semiannual distributor conference over the Fourth of July weekend at the Alpine Inn in Ste. Marguerite Station, Quebec. Highlights included the introduction of seven new Tupperware products, bringing the product line to thirty-two. Wise had a chance to preview to the audience of almost seventy distributors, the company's demonstration film featuring the ideal Tupperware party. Cooperation, not competition, she told them, was the key to their young company's continuing success. "It is a source of sincere pleasure to me to know that I don't have to stand here and sell any of you people on the truth of this," Wise told distributors, "that all of you have accepted in this program a wonderful community spirit."[55] It's also interesting to note that her relations had come so far with J. B. Evans—the St. Petersburg distributor with whom she'd practically gone to war two years before—that Wise presented him an award "for general cooperation with the Orlando office."[56] In the face of prosperous sales figures, it seemed almost anything could be forgiven.

"Brownie has kept me well-informed on your progress," Tupper wrote Evans, "and we are happy to renew your franchise as you request."[57] The August

4 letter was also Tupper's chance to let Wise's old rival know just exactly who is in charge of the Home Party operation. "I'm happy because this just tells me again, as I've been told in so many other ways, that at last we have someone (in the person of Brownie Wise) who has the knowledge, ability and character to handle the difficult job of liaison between the factory, upon which you depend, and you folks, upon whom the factory depends, for a sound, successful operation."[58] Tupper also gave a glimpse into his paranoia, which enveloped his paternal feelings about his proprietary products: "Believe me, we are here, with malicious glee, very busy stewing some vile broths for those who step foot into our domain with products designed to annoy us."[59]

In return for his confidence and praise, Wise had promised Tupper that her THP distributors would double their business in the second half of the year. With that deadline bearing down, Wise penned a memo on August 15 to "All-of-You," where her motivational techniques seem to be bordering on neurosis:[60]

> The vacant stare in my eyes is due to the serious contemplation that there are still five months to go before the deadline for my nibbling away at this tasty testimony. Now gather round, chillin, my voice is growing weaker. Self-preservation, they say, is the first law of nature, and I find myself strangely concerned about my own digestive welfare.
>
> I can appreciate that this *personal* matter is of more concern to me than to any of you, but when a person is backed up to the wall with only a narrow avenue of escape, you can expect him to make the most of that avenue. I can assure you I will do just that. My only avenue of escape is obviously a 100% increase in sales volume from you and You and YOU . . . and from here on, you can expect me to resort to almost any means to achieve it. I may call you at three o'clock some morning to find out how many parties your dealers have coming up the next week.[61]

Perhaps the stifling work environment had something to do with the memo's neurotic tone. "It is, shall we say, quite warm in our office quarters there," Wise said of the home office hangar, "which is another reason for all of us looking forward to September and the move to our own building."[62] As Wise hopscotched around North America projecting a professional image and speaking of Orlando's glamorous locale, working back home in the central Florida summer with no air-conditioning was pure hell. The upstairs office in the metal hangar was cooled by huge, noisy box fans; to keep papers and files from blowing away, the staff weighed them down with two-by-fours. During the summer of 1952, Wise had a full-on campaign of courting local civic groups in Orlando, speaking to the Junior Chamber, the Orlando JayCees, the Central Florida Advertising Club, the Orlando Civitan Club, and the Orlando Exchange.

The final four months of 1952 were every bit as historic and tumultuous as the first eight. In September, Wise was encouraged on two fronts: The shell of the modern, spacious, and air-conditioned new headquarters was nearing completion, and sales during the month of September hit an all-time high. In San Diego, Esther La Venture recorded a "sensational" $1,303.67 sales week.[63] She had a hunch that it was not too early in the year to include a small Christmas tree in her presentation: "I had the smallest pieces of Tupperware tied with ribbons and placed beneath the tree. This must have been good idea as the guests did buy, plan and talk Christmas shopping with their friends. My party sales climbed, I mean leaped."[64] *Tupperware Sparks* featured a picture of a California dealer smiling proudly, a tiara on her head after being named "queen of the week."[65] Wise seized upon the accomplishments of star dealers to urge on others. "Hitch your wagon to a Tupperware star," Wise wrote, "and begin breaking some sales records yourself."[66]

On October 15, Tupperware made headlines by awarding a new Cadillac to each of the seven highest-performing distributors over the last twelve months: Peter Block of Pasadena; Tom Damigella of Everett, Massachusetts; J. B. Evans of St. Petersburg; Rose Humphrey of Miami; Eli Schofield of San Diego; Mildred Thompson of Lindenhurst, New York; and Ronald Tremblay of Montreal. The scope of the prizes awarded gave an indication of how far the company had come from just one year previous, when they had an operating deficit of $32,000. Reaction was quite different among some of the winners: "When we saw the Cadillac we could not help but gawk at what we saw. There had been mounted on each of the front fenders long bugle horns," Elsie Block wrote. "We even kidded about entering it in the Rose Parade. That would have been a great way to advertise Tupperware."[67] Rose Humphrey never even drove hers, preferring to trade in the Cadillac for a more modest Ford; her vehicle of choice dated back to the family's Detroit days. Tom and Ann Damigella wrote Earl Tupper a letter of thanks: "In spite of your absence, we could not help but feel your presence there in Orlando, especially since most of us present there had had the pleasure of your personal acquaintance and also the happy experience of growing with Tupperware."[68]

These were some of the best times Wise would ever experience in Tupperware. In 1952, Tupper paid her a salary of $20,933.33, far more than she had ever made since being on her own. He also agreed to provide her a home near the new company headquarters. That concession might have helped Wise get over her initial impression of Kissimmee, with a population hovering around four thousand, as something of a "hick town."[69] She was very attracted to a 19,000-acre lake just south of the city's small downtown, Lake Tohopekaliga—known to locals as Lake Toho.

Jerry Wise remembered his mother driving him around the northeastern edge of Lake Toho to their new home, and off in the distance on a peninsula, "it was all you could see; it looked like a castle."[70] It was a home of which Hibiscus would be proud, only this time there was nothing fictional about it. It would provide a kind of regal southern lifestyle Brownie Wise could have only dreamed about that cold spring day in 1950 when she left Michigan for an uncertain future in Florida. It was Tupper's payoff for all Wise had done to bring Tupperware Home Parties to fruition. It was another setting upon which Brownie Wise would capitalize to attract homebound housewives to Tupperware. She called her Hibiscus mansion Water's Edge.

Eight

GROUNDWORK FOR A REVOLUTION

This is a cooperative
organization the success of
which has confounded many
of the best thinkers in direct
selling today who, a year and-
a-half ago, said what we have
done could not be done.
—Brownie Wise

In 1952, Ernest Hemingway culled his classic *Old Man and the Sea* from his long days of deep-sea fishing off the coasts of Florida and Cuba. His central character, Santiago, is a broken man said to be cursed with bad luck; held together only by strength of will, he lands a giant marlin and proves his detractors wrong. In November 1952, the pride of Abilene, Kansas, Dwight David Eisenhower, was elected president, and less than a month later he made good on his promise to visit the war zone in Korea. In America, Dave Garroway hosted the first-ever edition of the *Today* show on NBC, the first open-heart surgery was performed, and Siamese twins were successfully separated for the first time.

In 1952, the first full year of Tupperware Home Parties' existence, distributors sent in wholesale orders totaling $2,170,617.62. And there was every indication that those numbers, like the ranks of Tupperware dealers and subdistributors, would continue to grow. On the Orange Blossom Trail north of Kissimmee, workers had dug a reflecting pond to provide fill material on which to build THP's new 40,000-square-foot headquarters. In late November, as soon as the shell of the building had a roof, Brownie Wise and her team moved in. In many ways, the huge space was reminiscent of the airplane hangar they had left behind in Orlando—there were no walls or dividers nor proper office space. But mercifully, it did have air-conditioning. Workers installing the metal roofing overhead made such a clamor that each strike of the hammer sounded "like a rifle going off."[1] For Wise, the move finally felt like the company had arrived:

> We now have our roots firmly down in Florida's tropical soil, our new building has attracted wide attention and is a modern, efficient and comfortable home for our operation. In that home, large enough for us to spread our wings, we will be able to do a great deal more in the way of promotional work for our national program. Now that it is over, we can look back with even a smile at the handicap under which we operated during the first year of Tupperware Home Parties Inc.[2]

Her choice of residence ensured that Brownie Wise would live a regal existence compared to most of the Florida Crackers and their kinfolk around Kissimmee and Osceola County. On November 14, 1952, the *Kissimmee Gazette* ran a front-page story reporting that the Tupper Corporation had bought, for a hefty $35,000, the sprawling home Brownie Wise had spied along east Lake Toho. The house featured "eight spacious rooms" and 1,900 feet of lake frontage, "the most of any other property in this area."[3] The architecture showed Spanish influence with red tile shingles surrounded by tropical palm trees. The home featured one of the few indoor swimming pools in the area, filled by a spring that flowed into the pool, out of the house, and back into Toho. There were sweeping staircases, broken-tile floors, and plenty of room to entertain. According to local legend, the home had been built in the 1930s for a film star whose name no one could recall. As it turned out, the star had a change of heart and never moved in anyway.

For fourteen-year-old Jerry Wise, the home was nothing less than awe-inspiring. "Yeah, what a castle, wowee!" he exclaimed. He found the indoor pool inviting but the water "colder than hell, oh gee."[4]

His mother almost changed her mind about moving in when she spied some squatters who'd already taken up residence outside the estate. "Gators," Jerry said, "big ones."[5] No matter how big, alligators have a natural fear of humans, Brownie and Jerry soon learned. And as a last resort they could always, "shoot 'em if they got too close."

Wise swept into action, hiring a maid, surveying what renovations and repairs were needed, and installing a dining room table fit for a queen. "Good lord," Jerry exclaimed, "that thing must have been fifteen feet long with matching chairs."[6] Brownie Wise painted her bedroom pink and quickly assumed

Water's Edge, on the shores of Lake Toho in Kissimmee.

an aristocratic mantle in a very small, out-of-the-way cow town. At the time, Kissimmee had just over four thousand residents. It wasn't the glamorous oceanside home Wise had envisioned for THC the year before.

Common newspaper stories featured people like Frank Darden, proprietor of the Gulf service station halfway between Kissimmee and Saint Cloud on Highway 441. For sport, he'd take his five hounds out and go hunting for big cats around Canoe Creek. His prowess bagging the critters was becoming legendary; when his count reached five hundred, Darden proudly accepted the nickname "Cat Killer."[7] A front-page photograph in the December 12, 1952, *Kissimmee Gazette* shows Darden proudly posing in front of his pickup next to three of the dead varmints. In recent years, populations of big cats like the Florida panther or the more common bobcat have dwindled to the point that the rare occasion of seeing one is treated like beholding an apparition. Livestock auctions, the Boat-a-Cade, bass-fishing tournaments, and the Silver Spurs Rodeo were always front-page news around town. Many articles noted the moonshining and gambling misdeeds of area "negroes." In 1952, there wasn't a single integrated school in all of central Florida.

During this period, another key player in the early days of Tupperware

Home Parties came on board—Jack Marshall. Dark-haired and broad-shouldered, Marshall had a salesman's smile almost as big as his personality. He'd worked in the trenches with dealers, managers, and distributors dating back to his days as a brash Stanley man. Marshall's wife, Irene, had been a Stanley branch manager in the Detroit suburb of Royal Oak. Notice who Brownie Wise makes the real center of attention when describing Marshall:

> He studied Brownie's vision, her product and her plan. What other company had ever built a dealer strength of 3,000 in so short a time? How had they done it? As Brownie talked, he realized that she had made sound plans in the beginning . . . and followed them. It indicated solid foundations. So Jack Marshall decided to become a part of Tupperware's growth. He was appointed general sales manager.[8]

By the time Wise wrote this, in 1956, Tupperware was "her" product, and that conceit in the coming years would grow more and more prominent, many would say malignant. As Tupperware sales soared, so did the ego of Mrs. Brownie Humphrey Wise—or at least of her alter ego, Hibiscus.

Another key personality in the worldwide spread of Tupperware, Elsie Mortland, was a humble, diminutive, and soft-spoken Deland, Florida, housewife. It was by chance that some friends from a nearby self-service laundry recommended Mortland the day a woman came around asking if anyone might be interested in becoming a dealer. "They did it mostly to get rid of her," Mortland laughed.[9] In those days, Mortland, like many housewives, thought plastic products coarse and inferior; when you poured hot water in them, "they would almost melt."[10] Tupperware was different; "that's when women started using it and telling each other how wonderful it was."[11] Before long, Mortland became a star dealer in Rose Humphrey's distributorship. Through hard work and practice, Mortland perfected demonstrating the Tupperware seal, or burp. "People could just see, it was virtually a vacuum seal," Mortland remembered;[12] "I remember one of the early parties in Deland, a woman came in and the first thing she said was, "I want a set of those salt and pepper shakers with the toilet seal tops."[13]

As Tupperware found its way into the hands of more and more ordinary women like Elsie Mortland, something happened. "No women got praised for scrubbing floors, mopping floors," Mortland reflected. "But when they got praised for selling Tupperware, they had something to be proud of."[14] That simple yet profound concept was making its way onto the national scene. It's almost funny to read a very important piece of publicity Tupperware received during this time period from *Salesman's Opportunity* magazine. In an article entitled "How a Typical Homemaker Learned the Secret That Can DOUBLE Your Family's Income," the article delves with a sense of wonder into the very notion that a sales*man's* opportunity could come to an average, yet enterprising housewife–Tupperware dealer, Eleanor Sterhan.

First things first, though. The article reinforced very plainly where a woman's place remained: "The orderly five-room Sterhan bungalow in a quiet residential section of Detroit, her well-mannered youngsters, and her proud husband are ample proof of her success in every woman's most important job . . . that of wife and mother."[15] Yet, here's what the article concludes makes her exceptional: "But her top-flight success in the dual role of homemaker and career woman is what draws special attention to her. For although she is not a career-woman type, Mrs. Sterhan has been operating her own business for more than three years."[16] Whatever the "career-woman type" was up to that point, articles like this one offer a sense of how revolutionary the notion of the female-based Tupperware home-party sales system was. Imagine, housewives could go out and earn their own money and yet not shirk their "most important job" or, worse yet, have to be the dreaded "career-woman type."

The article described how Sterhan got over her first party jitters, despite the fact that the experienced demonstrator assigned to her was too busy with her own parties to show up. To enhance the upbeat, soft-sell Tupperware philosophy: "She began by dividing the group into two teams. Then she placed an orange under the chin of each captain, instructing them to pass it chin to chin, to the members of their teams without touching it with their hands. The team that returned the orange to the captain first was the winner."[17] Only after several games were played and prizes awarded did Sterhan start her demonstration of Tupperware samples set up on a card table.

Mrs. Sterhan was no salesperson and didn't know how to give a so-called "sales talk."[18] These were friends to whom she described the polyethylene products, their uses appropriate for every room in the house, and their pastel colors: lemon, lime, peach, raspberry, plum, and frosted crystal. She demonstrated the patented Tupper seal, passed the samples around, and then "chatted with her prospects while they drank their coffee and placed their orders."[19] That first party, which Sterhan had held with no outside help, netted her a respectable $80 in sales, of which she kept $25. From that point on, the Sterhans went into the Tupperware business as a family team. The two teenaged daughters pitched in with the housework, and Mr. Sterhan "packed and unpacked merchandise, made deliveries," and even "prepared many a dinner for the family."[20]

Before long, Eleanor was putting on five parties a week, pulling down around $100 in weekly profits, and "practically" doubling her husband's postal

Brownie Wise having her portrait painted at Water's Edge, ca. 1956.

service income. Now for the part that really appealed to post–World War II baby boom families: "The Sterhans quickly replaced their 1937 Packard car with a new automobile, practically refurbished their home, bought a TV set, took a motor trip to California, and made financial problems a thing of the past." More than the money, Sterhan said her main sense of satisfaction was the very feminist feeling of "security and independence" she had achieved. "There's as much money to be made as anyone needs," Sterhan reflected. "All you have to do is put a little effort back of your desires. There is no profit in hoping . . . but there is profit in selling."[21] It was a quote that could well have been written by Brownie Wise herself.

With these kinds of typical, yet extraordinary, women coming into the Tupperware family daily and with the kind of publicity this phenomenon was generating, the 1953 catchphrase of Tupperware Home Parties was "There's gold for me in '53." For Tupper and his manufacturing division, it was like a call to arms; orders flooding in did not always translate into product expeditiously rolling out. In a memo early that year, Tupper deftly addressed his "Fellow Workers" about the need to keep up with ever-increasing demand.[22] "From what you have seen lately, you know we have a real live-wire sales division. We have a hard job ahead of us to keep up with them," Tupper wrote. "That means you and I all have that job—but it offers a dandy reward in the way of greater success and promotion and better pay—if we come through. I need your help!"[23]

It was Tupper's plan to use the Farnumsville plant to "hatch out and develop supervisory help in all classes."[24] Designs were already on the drawing board for a 100,000-square-foot manufacturing operation as phase two to the Home Parties building nearing completion in Florida. "If you should not want to go and you have a man or woman under you who would like to go—and is fully capable, then we want to send that person," Tupper wrote his employees, "and that person could go if he or she has trained someone lower down the line to do his or her job here. You can see how it goes—there is opportunity all down the line here. We are not holding people back; we are trying to urge them upwards to success."[25] Tupper was correctly anticipating the polyethylene gold rush about to overtake America. "This company can grow and provide jobs just as fast as you folks can grow up to handle the jobs. Don't be afraid to believe that you can do the better job."[26] Perhaps Earl Tupper was reading some of Brownie Wise's memos to her distributors for inspiration. "If you folks will all take hold and heave together," he proposed, "this can be a lot of fun as well as being profitable, how about it?"[27] Tupper would soon embark on plans to expand the factory operation at Farnumsville.

On the sales end, Brownie Wise closed out 1952 with another cross-country trip to California to award THP's first-ever National Merit Award. Wise designed the award with the notion of recognizing Tupperware's top dealer in the nation out of a very crowded field of top-performing candidates. "The qualifications of so many were so high," Wise wrote, "we pitied the three outside individual judges who had the problem of choosing the winner."[28] The judges decided on Corliss Levitt of San Francisco, the mother of three young children who had to borrow the down payment for her Tupperware sample case. Wise called her on New Year's Day to pass along the good news. "I was in heaven!" Levitt wrote. "What I did, others can do and will do . . . just as soon as they have the want to!"[29] The December–January issue of *Tupperware Sparks* shows a photograph of the smiling winner, with flowers on her arm, accepting the specially engraved silver-vase trophy. As was the case with many super dealers, Levitt would go on to be awarded her own distributorship.

At the Pasadena distributor conference held at the posh Huntington Hotel, Wise made the "thundering announcement" that sales for the last half of 1952 were triple those of the first.[30] Part of the credit has to be given to Wise for standing up to Tupper when it came to keeping his product exclusive to dealers and out of the big department stores. In 1952, it was obvious that notion still went contrary to his inclinations, regardless of what he might have been saying publicly. Appropriately festooned with flowers, Wise awarded Hawaii trips to the two distributors who had done the highest percentage of volume over her goal of "double-in-the-last-half of '52" quota.[31]

In typical Brownie Wise fashion, she found a way to congratulate her distributors' success yet ensure that no contented stagnation would set in:

There are outstanding examples, of course, of distributor growth during the last six months. Amazing examples of dealer sales records broken, of high weeks, of high parties . . . new sales territories have blossomed over night . . . older territories have taken on new life . . . new Tupperware items have sold three times the volume ever anticipated for them . . . dealers have averaged more parties and higher parties and more sub-distributors have been added to service territories. In spite of all this, and it is all good, we still have a long, long way to go. We still have territories unfranchised, we still have territories new in development, and with a lot of growing to do; for all of our growth and development and achievement—and for all of it we must be happy—we still have not scratched the surface.[32]

Wise compared Tupperware dealers and distributors to miners from the nineteenth-century gold rush days and concluded with a quote from Earl Tupper on how to prepare for success: "The first step is learning to realize how little time you have in the world . . . the second step is pushing yourself to hurry and make the most of that time."[33] Judging from her own schedule and workaholic tendencies, Brownie Wise had taken that message as gospel.

Back at the company's new home near Kissimmee, work was going "full blast" to complete the building in time for a big July conference.[34] Workers bored into the walls with air drills to carve out air-conditioning ducts, and carpenters buzzed away pieces of lumber to complete detail work in the lobby. The "ear splitting blasts"[35] that Gary McDonald compared to rifle rounds were actually .45 caliber shells used in what Wise described as "specially-designed guns to attach metal to cement block."[36] On the grounds, steam shovels and cranes positioned tons of sand, gravel, cement, and landscaping. Outside, the placing of "giant *cocos plumosus* palms" added a windblown, tropical look.[37] Photographs show accountant Herb Young trying to concentrate on processing orders despite all the construction commotion. The largest photograph on the front page of *Tupperware Sparks* features Brownie Wise smiling peacefully, and she is quoted as calling the noise "music to our ears."[38] The headline of the March issue, written by Wise as always, read: "Brownie Wise Creates Startling New Look for World-Famous Orange Blossom Trail." As Earl Tupper took to including just his initials, E.S.T., at the bottom of some correspondence, Wise was starting to use her own, B.W., to reflect her growing status.

Some distributors felt Brownie Wise was taking on too much, and their orders were getting muddled in the process. In California, the Blocks received the following message: "Upon receipt of this notice, all further orders are to be sent to Tupperware Home Parties, Inc. in Florida."[39] For long-timers already smarting over the loss of one-to-one contact with Earl Tupper and the manufacturing operation in Farnumsville, this posed a more practical problem: sending orders to Massachusetts by way of Florida increased the chances of delays or mistakes. "Our concern was soon justified," Elsie Block wrote.[40] A first order to Kissimmee went in with no acknowledgment nor ensuing shipment of product, then another. For Poly Sales, time was money, and Peter and Elsie Block were running out of patience.

Peter called the factory in Farnumsville. "I'm sorry," the voice on the other end of the line said, "you'll have to call Florida."[41] When he did that, there was still no satisfaction from the operator. "Nobody can help you with that information except Mrs. Wise."[42] Problem was, Mrs. Wise was out attending to something on the grounds and wasn't reachable. Exasperated, Elsie finally gave the Florida operation an ultimatum, "Tell her that if I don't get a call from her in twenty-four hours we are going to send a message to all our dealers to stop putting on parties."[43] In less than an hour, Block says Wise called her back: "Don't do that please," Wise begged, offering that the ordering delays were due to a mold that had broken down at the factory.[44] "One mold?" Elsie asked. "Is it true our whole order was held up because of one item? Dear Brownie, why wasn't everything else sent? Why weren't we notified?" Later Elsie Block said, "I learned from employees at the Florida office that Brownie Wise hadn't delegated authority to anyone other than herself."[45] It was only after Peter Block's persistent phone calls to Farnumsville that their company had a constant flow of product restored; in the meantime, they supplied dealers with what they had in stock.

There were more problems with the new headquarters. Tupper felt the phone service and drainage were too poor to proceed with plans for the second phase of construction on the Orange Blossom Trail site. Tupper had already sent down a freight car full of equipment to set up a tool shop in hopes of the problems being cleared up and construction proceeding on the new addition. He also broke ground on the addition to the factory in Farnumsville.

Despite those issues, Wise continued getting the headquarters ready for the July conference. In May, she hosted a tour of the new building for Stan Tasker and Caryl Bailey, husband and wife art professors at Rollins College. It was

Bailey who Wise commissioned to paint a forty-two-foot, ten-panel mural inside the headquarters building. "The mural will portray in a modern rendition the evolution of dishes," the *Kissimmee Gazette* reported, "from their earliest beginnings and continue through the centuries to a typical Tupperware mold. The hands of Earl S. Tupper, president of the firm, will be used as a model for the final panel."[46]

Wise cultivated the notion of business supporting art in public places, a move that in 1953 was far ahead of her time. She would go on to establish Tupperware art fellowships and hire a director for the Tupperware Art Fund. Recipients were chosen on the basis of their work, regardless of race, creed, or color. They could use the money for study, travel, or supplies. When asked why Tupperware got interested in promoting art and painting, she replied: "It's just one of the ways we've chosen to help pay for our room on earth. We believe that a company should exist for more than just to supply useful products."[47] The notion of "paying for our room on earth" came from a phrase Wise remembered and often quoted from her own grandmother.

April brought THP's second birthday, which Brownie and her staff celebrated at headquarters and Water's Edge. Although Wise's own birthday wasn't for another month, *Tupperware Sparks* included the musical serenade "Happy Birthday Dear Brownie, Happy Birthday to You." Brownie sits at her desk smiling at the congratulatory telegrams and flowers; Brownie is seated as staff stand around her also admiring the flowers and telegrams; Brownie, in her party dress, beams as she prepares to cut into the five-layer birthday cake with the "2" on top; in a wider shot, a group of Tupperware "party dolls" assist Brownie in cutting the cake; Brownie "cuts a rug" with Gary McDonald at the after-hours party at Water's Edge; Brownie poses with the cake again at Water's Edge, this time surrounded by the Tupperware men; Brownie mocks surprise at receiving a congratulatory phone call. It's unclear if Tupperware's "star" photographer, Jack McCollum, insisted on Brownie being the absolute focal point, or if Wise herself felt she deserved such ultrarecognition for all THP had accomplished.

In another attempt to establish a sense of the company's growing national momentum, in the spring of 1953, Wise and her THP team barnstormed into Boston's Somerset Hotel for a sales rally. Leading the cheers was sales-promotion manager and boy wonder Gary McDonald with trademark bow tie; the now-famous National Merit Award winner Corliss Levitt smiled at his side. Brownie Wise took the opportunity to pay homage to the East Coast's longest-running distributors, Ann and Tom Damigella. Her new right-hand man, Jack Marshall, gave an award to Artie Watts—an African American unit manager. In 1953, it would be hard to imagine a black woman holding even a low-level managerial job in many other companies, especially if it were located in Birmingham rather than Boston.

The April issue of *Tupperware Sparks* was proof enough that despite supply problems, the slogan "Gold for me in '53" was coming true. Each dealer who had registered at least one so-called "Victory" week—where sales totaled at least $300—would have their name listed on an honor roll. The list of names, flanked by gold columns, numbered three hundred. Some had had more than six Victory weeks; others had rung up weekly sales of more than $1,000. Sixteen of those on the honor roll ended up getting their own distributorships.

When Wise returned home from many miles on the road, it was time for her and Jerry to share a milestone birthday. On May 25, 1953, she turned forty and her son fifteen. To mark the occasion, and in an obvious show of the esteem in which he held Wise, Earl Tupper sent her a Palomino horse on which to ride the grounds of Water's Edge. On her birthday card, he included this:

A Verse for Brownie Wise

I have a Palomino
Named Golden just for me

Because the way the tale goes
There's Golden '53.

Introducing Golden, the 5-year-old Palomino
Gelding

from Earl Tupper
to Brownie Wise on
her May 25th Birthday[48]

Earl Tupper shopped around Kissimmee before settling on the "golden" Palomino. It wasn't until later that Jerry Wise discovered Mr. Tupper hadn't gotten all he'd paid for. During a rainstorm, the horse's color started to run. Unbeknownst to Tupper, the previous owner had taken the liberty of filling in discolored spots—"Golden" was part gelding and part painted pony.[49]

Young and precocious, Jerry Wise found this all very amusing. While his mother kept up her breakneck schedule, he had the run of a curious teenager's paradise. His main hobbies during the carefree days at Water's Edge included "riding horses and chasing girls, what else?"[50] He'd play a practical joke on his mother or spout off a dirty word just to get her reaction—always the same disgusted look, a pointed finger, and sharp rebuke, "I don't like that word!" Despite the move to Kissimmee, he still attended Seese private school on the shores of Orlando's Lake Eola. For forty-six cents to Orlando and back, twenty miles each way, the Greyhound bus picked him up and dropped him off at Tupperware headquarters. "That was the only place Brownie would be," her son remembered.[51]

Jerry Wise had a ringside seat to the spirited brainstorming sessions his mother and her staff held to try to come up with the next great whiz-bang marketing idea, dealer incentive, or training technique. In those days, it was a democratic process, even a family dynamic, with little attention paid to the long hours. After the workday was over, Wise and her small team of managers would head back to Water's Edge for more hours of strategizing; some of it could get intense. "Oh, it was interesting; I liked those," Jerry remembered, "because they were arguing with each other and really fighting and I was afraid they were gonna kick each other's ass."[52] But Wise channeled the energy by requiring those around her to write down what they said. "She wanted everyone to sit down with a piece of paper," Jerry said, "and at the end of that meeting she wanted that paper full.[53] And don't throw it away—it's going in the file with your ID number on it."[54]

That summer, some of the suggestions that emerged from those brainstorming sessions bore fruit: THP produced a new game booklet to give dealers ideas for anniversaries and parties; a new product brochure kept them up to date on the Tupper Corporation's ever-expanding line; new color recipe cards brought "ideas for dishes from across the land, and additional uses for Tupperware."[55] The team decided on what would become Tupperware's new symbol—the Tupperware Beauty Rose. To make it official, the July-August cover of *Tupperware Sparks* featured the rose surrounded by an antique frame and this caption: "Both symbolic of enduring perfection—the exquisite artistry of Tupperware . . . and the matchless and delicate beauty of the regal rose." Standing larger-than-life to the left was the ubiquitous Brownie Wise, dolled up in a shimmering gown and pearls, looking like Hibiscus personified.

On Tuesday, June 30, 1953, to kick off the distributors' conference, Brownie Wise hosted a buffet supper and cocktail party at Water's Edge. It was a chance to give dealers and distributors a first look at her "palatial home."[56] Subliminally, it was yet another motivating tool; work hard, sell Tupperware, and a life like this is within your reach, too. At the same time, just to buy into a piece of this fantasy, the Tupperware faithful were expected to make these trips on their own dime. Hence the importance of being in a location that people regarded as a travel destination, where their children could enjoy the sunshine while they attended long days of speeches, training, and workshops. Often it was left to Jerry Wise to be tour guide for younger members of the Tupperware family.

Wise in front of Tupperware's first permanent building along U.S. 441 near Kissimmee, 1953.

In the headquarters' Pacific Hall, Wise delivered a speech entitled "Our Place in the National Selling Picture."[57] While she would gladly play the part of aging debutante for the cover of the company's in-house publication, Brownie Wise was also a shrewd, astute businesswoman keeping in close touch with regional employment trends, giving long-range sales projections, analyzing the effects of explosive growth on the company's relations with dealers and distributors, and a host of other less glamorous minutiae that came along with the job. When the legions weren't coming to her, Brownie Wise was going to them, logging an exhausting amount of travel in 1953.

Soon after the conference wrapped up on Sunday, July 5, Wise and Jack Marshall embarked on the most grueling travel schedule of their days at Tupperware Home Parties. Starting in Hawaii, the vice president and her general sales manager intended to put in 100,000 miles to personally tour Tupperware distributorships across North America and meet thousands of new Tupperware dealers.[58] Wise wrote in 1953: "Our ties are particularly strong with our people because we have planned it so. The close personal contact of rallies, assemblies, seminars etc. have kept us very close to the dealers."[59] It also sent out the message to dealers that while distributors ruled the region, Brownie Wise and her Kissimmee office ruled the entire sales end of the Tupperware roost.

During the first three days in Hawaii, Brownie Wise hosted what has become, in company circles, a famous Tupperware party right on the Pacific Ocean. In a photograph later run on the cover of *Tide* magazine, Wise stands next to a well-appointed table of Tupperware products; the tablecloth has "Tupperware Home Parties" in plain view. While the nine others in attendance are dressed in casual clothes and bathing suits, Wise is all the while a resplendent Tupperware Lady with coiffed hair, pearls, earrings, and not-too-casual summer dress. This was just the beginning of an all-out publicity blitz and coming-out party for the woman soon to be America's executive "it" girl, Brownie Humphrey Wise.

"I have the feeling," Brownie Wise wrote in a memo to Earl Tupper, "that you don't realize how close you are to rocking this whole direct-selling picture right back on its heels."[60] Sales for 1953 were on a course to far surpass the year previous; in 1954, Wise forecast to Tupper that the number of Tupperware dealers would surpass ten thousand. Tupper himself had already made a shrewd move of his own that would help his baby, Poly-T, reach the coveted "next level" in the consciousness of consumption-hungry 1953 America. He hired a Madison Avenue public relations firm in New York by the name of Ruder and Finn to

Wise giving a Tupperware party in Hawaii, 1953.

help guide his company's corporate strategy. They, in turn, locked arms with the formidable and enthusiastic public relations machine from THP, Brownie Wise and Gary McDonald.

In September, THP held its first unit managers' seminar. From 8:30 each morning until 9:00 each night, 108 students studied the new Tupperware training way. "They have learned to lean more and more on us in the way we want," Wise wrote, "and they have, at the same time, learned that in certain phases of their work we hold them responsible for certain performance. This is what we slanted everything toward two years ago and the fruit is just beginning to ripen now."[61] Each of the department heads lectured the eager students about sales technique, public relations, and order processing. The seminar culminated in a dramatic, formal, candlelit graduation ceremony where each student actually received a diploma. For some women who didn't even graduate high school, this was a proud moment and another form of that rarest currency, recognition.

Wise and McDonald were about to embark on a difficult test of their own—impressing editors from some of the most important and influential national magazines. With the backing of Ruder and Finn, Tupperware Home Parties was planning to host its first-ever New York press party. Bigwigs had been invited from many major magazines, newspapers, and wire services: *Business Week, American Journal of Commerce, Newsweek, Tide, American, Ladies' Home Journal, House Beautiful, House and Gardens, Mademoiselle, Cosmopolitan, Coronet, Retailing Daily, Opportunity, Glamour,* King Syndicate, the United Press International, the *Philadelphia Inquirer,* and many others. To present Tupperware in the best light, they chose one of the most glamorous and ornate hotels in the entire city, the St. Regis on Fifth Avenue, which was within walking distance of Tiffany's, Rockefeller Center, and Saint Patrick's Cathedral. Just five years earlier, Wise and McDonald had been selling mops and floor wax in working-class Detroit neighborhoods. Now the former secretary and her red-haired sidekick were about to take on the Big Apple and a bunch of big-city editors. "My knees were shakiest of all," Wise remembered.[62]

Nine

SUCCESS AND JUBILATION

Tupperware isn't his business, it's his *baby. It's his child.* Brownie is causing his child to be loved and adored.
—Gary McDonald

The press party was scheduled for Wednesday, October 21, at 12:30 p.m. Invitations featured a whimsical cartoon of a dozen women smiling and chatting while holding their stackable Tupperware. "I believe you will notice that the layout man for Ruder and Finn developed very quickly a real feeling for Tupperware," Wise wrote Tupper. "Notice its apparent light weight by the way in which the feminine figures hold it in the sketch!"[1] The invitations also included this:

> We're having a party and we hope you'll come to meet the newest members of the famous TUPPERWARE family of Polyethylene table and refrigerator ware and hear about the plan that is revolutionizing the buying habits of American women.[2]

Far from the Pacific Ocean shores and swimsuit-clad guests, Brownie Wise would host this Tupperware Party at the famous St. Regis Maisonette, a posh dining room one floor off the hotel's main lobby. Built in the French Beaux Arts style, the St. Regis itself had been a landmark in New York City since 1904. From an architectural standpoint, it looked like it could just as easily be situated along the Boulevard St. Germaine in Paris. Singer Mel Torme once recorded a live album at the Maisonette. In the 1940s and 1950s,

Dorothy Shay, the pride of Jacksonville, Florida, became a fixture there; she would wow the audience with her smoldering charm, then break into a surprise version of "Uncle Fud."[3] The song so delighted her audience that they often asked for more like it, and Shay soon came to be known to the sophisticated New York crowd as "the Park Avenue Hillbilly."[4]

As Brownie Wise moved from the board room to an assembly hall packed with dealers, to an ornate dining room like the Maisonette, perhaps her own southern roots were what gave her such versatility. Her years of public speaking—beginning with the days as a teen orator for her mother's union work—prepared Wise for the big moment, and she did not disappoint. She wrote, "The setting for the Party was the most beautiful, undoubtedly, that I have ever seen."[5] The Maisonette's small round tables were set on blue gray linen, and making striking centerpieces were vases filled with Tupperware's new Beauty Rose. A "rosarian" who had patents on such flowers as the first thornless rose had been brought in to make the arrangements himself. In all, 130 press people, many of them men, packed the room for cocktails, lunch, and the Tupperware "pitch."

About her fifteen-minute presentation, Wise wrote:

> It was necessary for me to slant certain information to the business magazines who were primarily interested in our method of distribution; toward the versatility, stability, and the utility of Tupperware itself for the women's editors; and then I had to shed a little personal glamour for the benefit of the editors of such magazines as *Vogue* and *Glamour* who were primarily engrossed in determining just how any appreciable amount of honest-to-goodness business was conducted by "a mere woman."[6]

Her presentation also addressed why Tupperware was available only on the home-party plan, the establishment of the new "Orlando" headquarters, and the introduction of the new Beauty Rose. Also in attendance, Gary McDonald demonstrated to the audience how to apply Tupperware's patented seal.

According to Wise, Ruder and Finn's people said the affair was "undoubtedly the most successful press party they had ever had." Wise obviously agreed in her letter to Tupper: "I am sure that you would have been proud of every separate detail of it."[7]

Ruder and Finn saw considerable potential in this "mere woman" as a revolutionary marketing tool. What Wise had started doing herself months before, they wanted to amplify on a national level. In-house, consciously or subconsciously, Wise had presented to Tupperware dealers an image of herself as the ideal Tupperware Lady. She also did this in the Orlando and Kissimmee newspapers, having herself photographed explaining Tupperware to State Senator Bronson, getting noticed for giving speeches to myriad area civic groups. When Ruder and Finn looked at Brownie Wise, they saw something new and different to present to America's rapidly developing, suburban-based, consumer culture.

At a meeting with THP executives Brownie Wise, Gary McDonald, and Jack Marshall, the Ruder and Finn people talked about the "three *P*s" to consider in a campaign: the Product, the Plan, and the Personality. "They made a major case that we had all three things that made a product unique," McDonald remembered.[8] Two of them would be a tough sell, though: people still had a negative opinion of styrene, or breakable plastics, and people saw parties as potentially high-pressure and an imposition on their friends. "It's the third one," McDonald recalled, "the *woman* who's the leader of this company, and we could position her as such and build her up totally. Get great press on the fact that she's the leader of a company and that it's a company of women all across the country."[9] It didn't take a lot of convincing to sell those at the meeting. "We agreed," McDonald said, "and then Brownie talked to Tupper on her own and sold him on it."[10] Earl Tupper himself signed off on the idea of making Brownie Wise the national pitchwoman for his baby, Poly-T.[11] And why not? With a few supply hitches Tupper planned to address with the factory expansion, the party plan was working: more dealers were signing up, dollars were rolling in, and more and more people were seeing the need to have Tupperware a part of their home lives. As evidenced by all the traveling and promoting she'd done that year, Brownie Wise was making Earl Tupper's invention a household name and bringing him closer to his goal of being a millionaire—albeit several years later than he originally planned.

As an executive, Brownie Wise was hitting on all cylinders and wasn't afraid to take to task others who were not, even if they happened to have the last name *Tupper*. During this time period, relations between Tupper and Wise were at the point where they discussed many matters of business one-on-one via phone calls. He'd given her a $10,000 raise, and in 1953 Wise was making $30,800. By all indications, Tupper had to feel that investment was paying off. On November 21, 1953, Wise typed an eight-page, single-spaced interoffice memo to Tupper, outlining "how your potential sales picture stacks up with the national economic outlook."[12] But it was much more than that; it was an opportunity to challenge him on what she perceived as some of his shortcomings.

"If this company had a President, who was active at all in the sales picture or would even permit his name to be used," Wise complained, "we could have a President's Club like Avon, Fuller and Real Silk have. . . . This is a club for star salespeople who qualify by meeting a certain required volume, but since we don't have that kind of President we make do with other gimmicks."[13]

She stressed how important it would be to take care of supply problems if he wanted more expansion in 1954. "If you intend to carry on this selling program," Wise lectured her boss, "I certainly hope that you have already laid a good groundwork for a greatly increased production output for the next year."[14] She told Tupper that all the positive sales projections could be out the window if he didn't: "This is so serious an affair and the outcome can be so explosive that I would be a fool to try to forecast now what will happen next year without knowing whether it will be necessary tomorrow or the next day or the first of next week to call our distributors off from further sales until after Dec. 15th."[15]

Wise did much more than complain and criticize. The tone of the memo is upbeat. In the coming year, Wise expected the number of Tupperware dealers to surpass ten thousand (which it did); she said sales could more than double. And despite all that she wrote about the organization's expansion, she admitted, "We have at this time less than half the country franchised."[16] There was a lot more gold to mine, many more claims to stake. Dealers were rising through the ranks, and Wise expected to grant as many as fifteen new distributorships within the first sixty days of 1954. The uniform training program Wise developed was motivating the sales force and bringing in big dividends; the distributors were running their own contests and programs regionally. For a man who couldn't get much of any sales program going on his own watch, Earl Tupper had to be very impressed, even awestruck, at the phenomenon he saw unfolding across the country. In as many words, Wise told him he should be.

"I think it is time for you to decide whether you want Tupperware to step into the big time," Wise declared. "You have the possibility of an amazing amount of orders for pre-sold merchandise pouring in a steady stream and increasing on a regular basis if you can outline a program without delay that will give you the assurance you can handle it."[17] Brownie Wise was taking a page from Earl Tupper's playbook, as visionary and coach to her own boss. For the direct, take-charge Tupper, it had to feel strange for anyone to question his abilities.

"And then," Wise concluded, "for the benefit of everyone concerned, I think it is time we received a forecast from you. What can you do next year? That's all. B. W."[18]

By the end of 1953, two more key early staff members came on board: Don Fuhr, director of premium purchasing, and "Texas" Jack McCall. From "the Pecos to Peoria," the colorful Texan had learned Tupperware from the ground up, ascending to distributor before joining the staff. Not so much one for the creative or sales sides, Fuhr had great contacts with companies from whom Tupperware was buying items to give away as hostess gifts. "At one point I was going to eleven countries in a month," Fuhr recalled. "We could put our finger on anything in the way of consumer products."[19] A hostess gift accomplished several things: It rewarded the person who granted use of their home for the Tupperware party and provided subliminal encouragement for someone in attendance to have the next. THP executives could also try out a product in development as a hostess gift. If reaction to it was enthusiastic, they could move it right into the permanent Tupperware line. With the addition of Fuhr and the central premium purchasing system, THP could buy hostess gift items in bulk at a deeply discounted rate.

Finding someone to hold a Tupperware party—or "dating," as it was called—sometimes required dealers to make cold calls or phone up women who had hosted one in the past. "I stopped at the same gasoline station several times, with my station wagon loaded with Tupperware," Wise remembered of her South Florida days. "The station man got curious, asked me about it. It wound up with his wife putting on a party."[20] To close out 1953, Wise initiated a program called "Operation Doorbell." The idea was to knock on doors or phone willing friends with the goal of dating as many parties as possible. Elsie Block reported that some recruits told her: "Not on your life! I thought I was going into a business that would never subject me to such demeaning things to do."[21] Despite the reticence of the faint of heart, like everything else Brownie Wise initiated in 1953, she once again struck gold. "Telegrams from nearly every distributor at the end of the all out dating drive," Wise gushed, "told the story of all-time dating records being broken."[22] It was a fitting end to a record-breaking gold rush year. In 1953, distributors had increased their sales output by a whopping 102.5 percent over 1952.[23]

If 1953 was the coming-out party for Tupperware, 1954 would herald its arrival on many fronts: the new national headquarters would be dedicated through an inaugural jubilee—now a Tupperware tradition—Earl Tupper would embark on an enormous expansion of his New England manufacturing operation; Brownie Wise would make history in the business world; and the number of Tupperware dealers would skyrocket.

The onward and upward drive to Tupperize America was embodied in THP's slogan, "10,000 more in '54."[24] In her November memo, Wise told Tupper she thought it entirely possible to bring the number of Tupperware dealers to twenty thousand by the end of 1954 and to double sales. She initiated a "Full Steam Ahead" contest in which five "lucky" dealers and one "outstanding" manager would win a six-day transatlantic cruise to Paris on board the

Queen Mary, "one of the most comfortable and luxurious liners in the world." *Tupperware Sparks* described the prize to dealers as a lifelong dream trip come true—an example of how Brownie Wise could speak to the dreams of her growing legions. "Winners will find that Paris is fascinating . . . fun . . . and French!" said the author of the *Sparks* article. "While in Paris, the dealers and managers will sit in the sidewalk cafes along the Rue de la Paix and watch the Kaleidoscope of Parisian life flow past."[25]

With that kind of contest gold at the end of the rainbow, some dealers booked frenetic party schedules. In the Blocks' Poly Sales Company, dealers held what was called a "six-party fete" that started at 9 a.m. with parties held at two-hour intervals until the last one was held at 8 p.m.[26] "During those marathons the dealer engaged a helper," wrote Elsie Block. "There had to be two sets of displays. The helper set up a display for the dealer at the first party destination before she got there and then proceeded to the next party address to set up a display for the dealer while she was putting on the first party."[27] The hopscotch continued with the helper then going back after the first party was over, to take the display to the third house, while the dealer put on a second party. Then, after the all-day home-party blitzkrieg, participating dealers would meet that night for coffee to see who had tallied up the most sales. Elsie Block reflected, "It was an excellent way to learn how to cut down on time spent at a party and not sacrifice good results."[28] So much for the Brownie Wise axioms about a Tupperware Lady showing up early and never being rushed.

In January, Wise welcomed a crowd of two hundred students to the second managers' training seminar. In order to become an officially "Accredited Tupperware Manager," they were obligated to attain the "know-how and training that could be obtained nowhere else."[29] The newspapers described the feel of a graduation ceremony: "Organ music and a candle lighting ceremony lent an atmosphere of dignity and emotion to the ceremony more like a college graduation rather than the commercial feeling one might expect in a sales conference. Tupperware officials said this serious tone of the graduation reflected the earnest purpose with which the managers had come here."[30] As a writer once observed, "Emotion is the high-octane fuel of direct-sales success."[31] Another building block in that success is free advertising—*Printer's Ink,* a magazine of sales and advertising management, carried an article about the unique training seminars in its April 1954 issue.

On January 11, 1954, THP's National Promotion Day, 345 dealers were promoted to manager. Four managers would make distributor. Six days later, Wise wrote a congratulatory note to a long-time member of the Tupperware faithful who had relocated her franchise to Orlando: her own mother, Rose Humphrey.

The distributorship known as Hibiscus Sales operated out of a storefront at 823 Virginia Drive in Orlando. Humphrey had taken the roots of her daughter's Patio Parties business and overseen tremendous growth throughout Florida and into Puerto Rico. It's interesting how the note from daughter to mother is all business. "Dear Rose," Wise writes, "We would like to take this opportunity to point out to you the responsibilities and duties of a Tupperware distributor go far beyond the usual meaning of the term, 'distributor.'" It wasn't enough for a distributor to go about the business of cultivating their region by holding their own contests, recruiting new people, and ringing up higher sales. "It is the responsibility of distributors," Wise wrote to her mother, "to help in Tupperware Home Parties Inc. as a national concern as well as to build their own local distributorships."[32]

In 1954, everywhere you looked within the Tupperware empire, the main theme was expansion. Charles McBurney joined THP'S new Public Relations Department with a singular mission: "To make Tupperware a household word."[33] Responding to the need for increased manufacturing and to his vice president's November challenge, Earl Tupper unveiled a new 25,000-square-foot expansion to the Farnumsville plant. Wise, McDonald, and other members of the THP staff "dug their overcoats from the mothballs" and flew up for a tour.[34] In just over two years since the small staff had left THP's first offices in nearby Fisherville, the sales side had grown to more than seven thousand dealers. Its local distributorships had done almost $7 million in gross sales.

It was not easy for Earl Tupper to open up his factories to anyone he didn't trust completely. "That's manufacturing, and I've got all kinds of secrets," Tupper would protest.[35] He took extreme measures to protect the operation; when product started disappearing inside the factories, Tupper ordered the workers strip-searched. For women, McDonald said, "it was very easy to put bowls in their bras and walk out with them."[36] But it wasn't some sinister plot to try to steal the designs and patents Tupper had worked so tirelessly to earn; the employees just wanted the Tupperware for their own use. Tupper used to worry about the vulnerability of New England to attack from unknown forces overseas. In response to the possibility that his own workers or union rabble-rousers could start any kind of trouble, Tupper had small living quarters added to his office where he could hunker down if need be. Compared to the sunshine, palm trees, and exuberant atmosphere in Florida, the Massachusetts operation was very staid, Old World, and low-key. That's how Earl Tupper wanted it.

The Farnumsville addition was only the beginning. Along the Massachusetts–Rhode Island state line, Earl Tupper purchased a stately old plant at Blackstone, Rhode Island. Located on two hundred acres, with the Blackstone River wind-

Earl Tupper gives members of the THP team a tour of his Farnumsville operation.

ing through its rolling terrain of towering elms and maples, the new acquisition increased Tupper's production facilities to 600,000 feet. Together, those moves doubled his production muscle, put the ball back on sales' side of the court, and eliminated the need to worry about expediting plans for a manufacturing operation in Florida.

THP executives kept the pressure on themselves to come up with the next great contest, incentive, or publicity initiative. Brainstorming sessions would continue late into the night, often out at Water's Edge. That could be a problem because the lakeside home was so isolated, and many of her staff who participated lived a good distance away. "We'd be out there late into the evening [and] then have to go home to wherever home was—Orlando or Kissimmee," McDonald recalled, "and we'd have to be in at eight the next morning."[37] The team discussed at length how to make THP's annual birthday party something much bigger than it had been the two years previous.

"We talked about the pilgrimage, which was Stanley. Brownie came up with the name 'jubilee,'" remembered McDonald of another important historical milepost in Tupperware lore. "Then we started working on how we could add a lot of pizzazz to it. We had very exciting things."[38] The event they hatched, the first annual Tupperware Homecoming Jubilee, would have a western theme, and like miners at a gold rush, dealers would have the chance to prospect for

$75,000 worth of prizes in a uniquely Florida way. That wasn't all. In concert with the long hours of training, speeches, and graduation ceremonies, dealers could win one of a fleet of automobiles, mink stoles, or "freezer units."[39] THP'S public relations department sent invitations to the national press and media, hoping they might be interested in an event so unusual and visual. That hunch paid off beyond their best expectations.

Before any of that could happen, plans had to accelerate on several new facilities at headquarters: workers welded together steel beams on the roof of the new Garden Pavilion, a venue they designed to seat one thousand people; they poured concrete into a quadrangle and planted shrubs and trees for the Garden of the Palms; and carpenters accelerated work inside to finish the Exhibit Home. With its Magic Kitchen, visitors could take in the glory of Tupperware products and all their many uses. With the ten-panel mural complete, the Museum of Art focused on a first- of-its-kind exhibit featuring the evolution of dishes. Tupperware headquarters was set to become a world-class tourist attraction just as Brownie Wise had hoped. As a finishing touch, floodlights bathed the headquarters building in dramatic light for those who drove by on the Orange Blossom Trail.

In 1954, the unbridled optimism and Tupperware team building, the all-for-one-and-one-for-all spirit, contrasted with some of the other events happening at the time in the United States. On March 9, 1954, legendary newsman Edward R. Murrow dedicated his entire *See it Now* program to skewering the Communist fearmongering of Senator Joseph McCarthy. Regarded as one of the great early milestones of television news, the program rocked McCarthy's credibility and hastened his downfall. In the U.S. Supreme Court, Chief Justice Earl Warren soon would compose the historic majority opinion on the case *Brown vs. the Topeka Board of Education,* declaring as unconstitutional the so-called separate but equal racially segregated schools. In 1954, the United States was still a year away from Jonas Salk's breakthrough polio vaccine.

With so much fear and uncertainty pervading the American landscape, people were ready for a dose of wholesome distraction. On April 2, 1954, the *Kissimmee Gazette* ran a front-page story, with an accompanying photograph of Tupperware headquarters, heralding the "Cinderella" company's plans for its first jubilee: "Mrs. Wise has led the company in its rapid growth to second place among all sales corporations merchandising on the home party plan. The multi-million dollar corporation has doubled its business during each of the past two years and is expected to triple this year." Interestingly, the article mentions that Tupperware Home Parties Inc. had been founded three years before by "the Tupper Corporation of Massachusetts."[40] Nowhere mentioned in the article is founding father Earl Tupper, still the president of Tupperware Home Parties, nor did he accept a role in any of the jubilee activities.

On Monday, April 5, 1954, the Edgewater High School band played, and Brownie Wise cut the ribbon on what amounted to a new era of prosperity and recognition for Tupperware dealers, distributors, Brownie Wise herself, and her boss, Earl Tupper. The state comptroller officiated at the dedication of the flagstaff, and the dean of St. Luke's Cathedral in Orlando gave the dedication. False-front, frontier-style buildings were constructed, and Brahman bulls and horses were carted in to give the grounds a real western feel. If there was ever such a thing as the golden age of Tupperware, it began on this date, without question.

Service to others was the theme of Wise's welcome speech in the new Garden Pavilion to the assembled throng of 633 dealers, managers, and distributors. It was an apt notion. Up and down the line, without people nearer the top bringing along eager but inexperienced people nearer the bottom, Tupperware's success could not have happened. "It is a time for gratification and it is a time for Thanksgiving," Wise told them. "We would not be human if we were not gratified at the success the last three years has brought us. We would not be very worthwhile human beings if we were not thankful for it. Thankful not for luck, in which I have very little confidence, but thankful for the strength which has been given to our hands and the ingenuity that has been given to our minds, and the willingness with which our spirits have been enriched."[41]

Tuesday brought the fun and excitement that many of the Tupperware faithful had traveled hundreds of miles at their own expense to experience. On an unseasonably warm, 90 degree, sun-drenched day, dressed in cowboy hats, boots, and other western wear, hundreds of Tupperware people, "90% of them women," were led to an area referred to as a "Forest of Spades."[42] Shovels that McDonald and his team borrowed from the Kissimmee street department stuck out of the ground waiting to be chosen and used. Each person in the assemblage would get a chance to dig until they unearthed a hidden treasure. The better-performing dealers would dig in roped-off areas with higher-end loot.

For five-and-a-half hours, with Brownie Wise barking encouragement through a loudspeaker, women hopped on shovels as if they were pogo sticks, prodding and pulling hidden treasure from the sandy Florida soil, while their curious, bewildered family members looked on, screamed, shouted, and exalted in one of the most unique and truly joyous experiences of their lives. Four women who fainted in the heat were carried off on stretchers and later revived with smelling salts.

Betty Long of West Rushville, Ohio, preened proudly after unearthing a carefully wrapped mink stole; Collette Maniaci of Dearborn, Michigan, beamed with pride at the $60 gold watch she prospected; Edith Berkenbile of Oklahoma City needed a titanic effort to pull a $70 radio from the ground; and Fay Maccalupo of Buffalo, New York, sat exhausted atop a toy Ford she had finally exhumed. When the Tupperware team showed her the real-life car it represented, Maccalupo pressed her face against the hood and, sobbing uncontrollably, kept repeating, "I love everybody."[43]

Originally, McDonald and his team had buried the prizes eighteen inches deep. Some of the soil was so swampy that items like diamond rings and pen-and-pencil sets that had been buried in small containers weren't recovered until Vanguard Lake was dug years later. "They dug the lake, ran the dragline," McDonald chuckled, "and came up with the Tupperware with the gift items still in them."[44]

The treasure dig had been a sensation; the press and media loved it, too. The leading television news network at the time, CBS, carried film footage on its evening news, and the British Broadcasting Company aired the story in England. *Life* magazine documented all the zany goings on in a multi-page photo spread entitled: "Life Goes on a Big Dig." The magazine reported tongue- in-cheek that the women, along with digging up thousands of dollars in prizes, "raised a crop of bonus blisters as big as doubloons."[45] Wise spun that golden piece of national publicity into more acclaim within the local community. "Brownie Wise, brilliant chief of Tupperware Home Parties Inc. called us Wednesday morning and she was so jubilant it was immediately apparent," the *Kissimmee Gazette* gushed in an editorial after Wise called them with news of the upcoming publicity. "And it all can be attributed to Mrs. Brownie Wise, who is fighting for Kissimmee heart and soul, day and night."[46]

As exciting as the *Life* spread and resulting local acclaim was, Brownie Wise received an even more significant honor as a result of the first annual Tupperware Homecoming Jubilee. In its April 17, 1954, issue, *Business Week* devoted a seven-page article so complimentary to Tupperware and its system of home selling that it could have been written by Wise herself. In a move that might as well have been a coronation of Wise as the queen of home-party sales, the magazine featured her smiling face on the cover—the first woman *Business Week* ever picked to receive that recognition. In the photograph, Wise is holding a polyethylene block like the one Earl Tupper was given all those years ago and from which he invented Tupperware. Beneath the photograph, the cover carried a phrase that through the years came to be known as the Brownie Wise sales mantra: "If we build the people, they'll build the business."[47]

The magazine described Tupperware's jubilee as being a three-part combination of "sales training session, circus, and a revival meeting."[48] At the center of it all was the woman *Business Week* called a "Prophet in Plastic," the charming forty-year-old "widow" who the magazine identified as "the heart and soul" of the three-part package.[49] With *Business Week* comparing her to Aimee Semple McPherson—an eccentric evangelist who garnered a huge following in the 1920s and 1930s—certainly some would grumble behind the scenes about Wise becoming the sole focus of so much attention. But the Tupperware believers, including her own staff and dealers spread across the land, would support the magazine's conclusion: "she's the greatest person in the world."[50]

Business Week showed Wise throwing a container of polyethylene into the small lake dug out in front of headquarters to provide fill dirt. From that point on, it was called "Poly Pond," and all dealers had to do was dip their hand in the water for good luck. "There's an alligator in the pond," Jack McCall joked, "for the dealers who don't work."[51] The article described the long, thirteen-hour training sessions: "Everything from a Dale Carnegie course on public speaking to brass tacks discussions of how to display premiums to lure the hostess."[52] The magazine remarked on the newly unveiled Tupperware rose silver pattern, unavailable for retail sale but very useful as a lure for hostesses who put on a Tupperware party. "The entire $1 million plant at Kissimmee, dedicated so lovingly last week," the article declares, "aims at creating dealer pride in belonging to such an organization."[53]

The article offered Tupperware's impressive sales performance: nine thousand dealers, fifty-four distributors, and an estimated $25 million in retail sales (equivalent to roughly $175 million today) as proof enough that their system was working. Jack Marshall reminded writers that, through it all, the one "safety valve against competition" was the Tupperware patented seal.[54] To keep dealers inspired, the article pointed out, THP's home office worked "indefatigably" on new contests and promotions culminating at the end of the year in "an orgy of prize giving."[55] The writers also noted a conspicuous aspect of the female-driven company's management ladder—once a woman was ready to be promoted to distributor, that's when her husband would usually "horn in" on the business.[56] Some of her critics say Wise helped perpetuate that glass ceiling by having only men around her in THP management; five years before, she had left Stanley because of the lack of managerial opportunities for women.

With the choruses of "I've got that Tupper feeling down in my heart" sung,[57] the treasure dug, and the lessons learned, it was time for the climax of the historic five-day affair—graduation. On a stage adorned with a row of ornate candelabrums, her male executive staff dressed in dark formal attire seated behind her, Brownie Wise cut a striking figure as she stepped to the lectern

BUSINESS
WEEK

INDEX ON PAGE 22

WHY BUSINESS
KEEPS SPENDING FOR
Capital Goods
PAGE 104

Brownie Wise of Tupperware: "If we build the people, they'll build the business" (page 54)

A McGRAW-HILL PUBLICATION

APR. 17, 1954

Brownie Wise was the cover
story of *Business Week*'s April 17,
1954, issue.

positioned between two large flower arrangements and delivered what was arguably her most memorable speech as the head of Tupperware Home Parties;
it was entitled "Ad Astra":

> I am glad that a graduation ceremony is termed Commencement. I believe
> that people sometimes make the mistake of considering a graduation a climax,
> an ending, a fulfillment. Actually, it is none of those things. This graduation is
> not an ending of anything. It is truly a beginning, a commencement; the com-
> mencement of a new course of study for you; the commencement of a new
> way of thinking, of new plans . . . definite plans; a commencement of goals, of
> new confidence and new growth.[58]

Wise told the audience that she chose the Latin title "Ad Astra" because "I
am primarily concerned with reaching to the stars."[59] In doing so, Brownie
Wise was rapidly becoming a national star sales sensation herself. "Since the
earliest days of our recorded history," she told the rapt attendees, "the stars have
always been an inspiration to man; partly, perhaps, because they constitute an
unknown quality that appeals to the imagination, to the adventure spirit, to the
curious mind; partly, also, because in their distant far-off splendor, they are a

source of steadfast wonder. Through the ages they have been in their appointed places, far beyond the reach of men, but not beyond their dreams."[60]

She spoke of challenges, accomplishments, positive thinking, and the tendency to look back:

All of us have to believe to live; and the more we are able to believe in with *firmness* and *conviction*; the more abundantly, the more prosperously, the more happily we live. What is it that prevents some people from realizing this amazing force in their own lives? Only one thing . . . the terrible tendency of the human being to look back. Like the biblical wife, some people keep turning to the past, and give it the power to destroy the present and the future.

"*Live* this day. Make it work for you; for in the magic of *this* day walks *tomorrow,*" she implored them. "Being completely satisfied would be a little like death. What *we* want is growth, progress, the consciousness that we are getting somewhere, and helping other people get somewhere. Our need is to understand that not a lack of problems is necessary to make us happy, but the *knowledge,* the *ability,* and the *desire* to *handle* the problems will give us what we need for happiness."[61]

Business Week observed, "When Brownie Wise made a farewell, inspirational address called "Ad Astra," there wasn't a dry eye in the house."[62] As a comfortable, matronly, highly successful distributor put it, "I don't know how it is, but Tupperware has become a religion with me."[63] It was simple: Brownie Wise had devised a way to build a better life for women and their families, as long as they were willing to make Earl Tupper's baby a focus and follow her training methods. As in any sales program, success is limited only by how hard you want to work, how much you are willing to let it consume you. In the case of Brownie Wise, it had become her raison d'être, her religion, her life, and she was shepherding the flock as its numbers grew and grew. "When she was on the lectern, on the platform," Gary McDonald reflected, "she would mesmerize them."[64] Innovation was Tupper's thing. Communication in many forms was the genius of Brownie Wise.

Top distributors Peter Block, and Harold Feinberg of Buffalo, New York, were awarded Cadillacs, and Rose Humphrey of the new Orlando distributorship was one of four others who happily took home a less showy Ford. To cap off the gift giving, "the company" awarded Brownie Wise herself a much-deserved Hibiscus pink Lincoln convertible. In typical style, she didn't take many rag-top days off to tool around Lake Toho. Nor did all the press and media accolades get the creative juices flowing adequately as the THP staff tried to brainstorm plans for the rest of 1954.

As Wise liked to do when the team wasn't coming up with what she wanted, she ordered all of them, herself included, to get a week-long change of scenery. On Friday, April 30, 1954, the THP staff boarded a plane for Havana, Cuba. Once ensconced at Havana's five-star, twin-spired, art deco masterpiece, the Hotel Nationale, Wise and her entourage mapped out sales, promotions, and public relations for the rest of the year. For fun they could take in the hotel's Parisian-style cabarets and the ambiance that had charmed famous guests like Winston Churchill and Frank Sinatra. They also toured the new Tupperware operation in pre-Castro, U.S. commerce–friendly Cuba.

The 1954 Homecoming Jubilee, *Life* spread, and *Business Week* cover story were the high points heralding the arrival of Tupperware on the American scene. That recognition would continue to pay huge dividends throughout the rest of Tupperware's golden year.

Ten

EXPLOSIVE GROWTH

The *Business Week* article didn't focus much on Earl Tupper's role in the Tupperware revolution. "Nominally," it read, "he is president of the sales company, actually Brownie Wise has just about carte blanche to run the organization."[1] In a memo he wrote to Wise, it seemed Tupper didn't mind her getting the credit as long as the publicity meant more people "hugging his baby."[2] But while the two mostly hashed out business during this time period on the telephone, he made a point, in writing, to remind her where the true focus should be.

"Thanks for the pictures with the interesting quotes on the back," Tupper wrote Wise. "The ones with your elbows on the ledgers, fingers interlaced with chin resting on fingers and smile on your face, looks like a very good executive in a very good frame of mind. Apparently the books balanced. However, good executive as you are, I still like best the pictures as a woman, of course with TUPPERWARE!"[3]

Upon the THP executive team's return to central Florida, they flung open the doors of their swank headquarters for public tours. On Kissimmee Day, an estimated five thousand area residents took in the new gardens outside and exhibits inside. Next in line were Spanish-American War veterans inspecting the Museum of Art, Magic Kitchen, auditoriums, and offices. "We were very pleased to welcome so many of our neighbors to the Tupperware national home," Wise beamed.[4] The team used tours as yet another advertising and recruiting tool. Long before Walt Disney put down roots nearby, THP headquarters became a regular stop for tour busses heading south for Cypress Gardens in Winter Haven. From 8:30 in the morning to 4:30 in the afternoon, and 8:30 to noon on Saturdays, one thousand visitors a week came through. Each got the Tupperware pitch; their names and hometowns were duly noted and sent to area distributors who would follow up for party dating.

On June 7, 1954, came what Wise called "the most outstanding event of the summer." At the National Association of Direct Selling Companies convention in New York, Wise and her staff received a plaque in recognition of the "most outstanding public relations program in the country."[5] And who could argue with THP's success in that realm? Tupperware was everywhere, and Brownie Wise was quickly becoming a media darling. "I thought it was sensational, sensational," remembered Gary McDonald. "The more I saw the better I liked it."[6] And there was plenty of press to see with articles in: *Specialty Salesman, Premium Practice, Printer's Ink, American Business, Fortune, Life, Business Week,* and *Woman's Home Companion.* In the August issue of *Woman's Home Companion,* the article entitled "Help Yourself to Happiness" brought a flood of calls and letters to headquarters. "The article attracted more dealers than any previous publicity piece," Wise noted.[7]

Wise and THP had every intention of keeping that juggernaut going. Tupperware dealer numbers across North America were taking off like some of the early rockets on Florida's burgeoning Space Coast, with their numbers soaring past ten thousand in the summer of '54. To help Charlie McBurney churn out more stories, the public relations department added a young Tampa newspaperman, Glen Bump. As the maintenance manager for the ever-expanding grounds, Wise brought in George Reynolds, who also had a say in executive brainstorming sessions. A former sales executive from Safeway, American Airlines, and Stanley, Hamer Wilson was brought in as sales counselor, to help manage the growing dealer ranks. "Genial" Elsie Mortland, the soft-spoken housewife from Deland, had become so proficient at giving Tupperware demonstrations that Wise hired her as "Hostess Demonstrator" to run the new Magic Kitchen at headquarters.

Mortland became a friend and confidante to Wise. While waiting for their Kissimmee home to be built, Mortland and her family moved into a guest house on the grounds of Water's Edge. "She was quite the fairy godmother," Mortland recalled. "She just loved the recognition, and I remember one time her mother told me she was in a high school play. She wanted the role of princess and if she couldn't have that part she wouldn't be in it."[8] Wise was also a very caring and maternal boss to some of the young women hired right out of high school for entry-level positions at headquarters. "After my mother died," one former secretary remembered, "Brownie came to me and said, 'I'll have food made—take some time off and come back as soon as you can.'"[9] The former employee never forgot the level of genuine kindness Wise extended.

To capitalize on the success of the *Woman's Home Companion* article, the THP team launched its "Top of the World" drive. With more people than ever showing an interest in Tupperware, THP challenged team members to recruit others and date parties with a goal of doubling dealer ranks by the end of the drive. Recruiting cards were issued for dealers to keep on the visor of their cars, "where it will remind you at all times of the people you are about to see becoming Tupperware dealers in the Top of the World Drive."[10] Successful dealers could win link pins and tie tacks commemorating their achievements; their names would represent a link in a shining chain being added to the new "Garden That Loyalty Built" at headquarters. The THP team kept up the relentless push for success: "Will you have had a part in it?"[11] was the question they posed to the growing legions. At the end of the contest, Wise and her executive staff planned to fly out and personally congratulate the highest-performing distributors at rallies throughout the country.

At the beginning of September, Brownie Wise and the rest of her well-traveled THP royalty joined her son and the six winners of the Bon Voyage to Europe contest. The September 10 edition of the *Kissimmee Gazette* showed the party of beaming executives and dealers preparing to board the *Queen Mary* in New York. "Would any of these Paris-Rome travelers have believed when they put on their first Tupperware Party," Wise reflected, "that within a year or so they would be putting on original Paris gowns in the fashion capitol [*sic*] of the world . . . or seeing their names in one of America's leading magazines?"[12] Now, ever-mindful of free advertising, THP invited along Ludwig Bemelmens of *Coronet* magazine to cover the journey.

Beyond the public relations, everything's-great veneer, Jerry Wise said his mother found the trip exasperating: "That was a mess," he remembered.[13] It was one thing to take dealers to New York or Hawaii, but Europe proved to be much more culture shock. Dealers didn't speak the language or understand the cuisine. That opened the door to some classic "ugly American" moments. At a restaurant in Paris, one unnamed dealer stood up and demanded, "I want the *real* Franco-American," not realizing they were in the very spot it originated. "From now on we'll pick the winners," Brownie groused to her sixteen-year-old son. "These people are so stupid it's pitiful."[14]

Wise in front of Tupperware's *Evolution of Dishes* mural, ca. 1956.

When Brownie Wise wasn't having fits of pique over the dealers' lack of so-phistication, she knew very well it was those same people driving Tupperware's enormous home-selling engine. On Saturday, October 16, hundreds of dealers from all over Florida gathered in Tupperware's Pacific Hall to celebrate the culmination of the Top of the World drive. Thirty-five phones were brought in so dealers nationwide having their own regional "auction" parties could call in with the number of new people they recruited.

As the phones rang, the flashbulbs popped, and the executive team tallied up the numbers pouring in from everywhere, THP celebrated a new milestone. As Brownie Wise mugged for the camera in mock amazement with a phone in each hand, like everything else in the golden year of 1954, the recruiting drive was a success. "We're 20,000 strong!" they announced.[15] After starting the year with a force of seven thousand Tupperware dealers, the avalanche of national publicity helped THP nearly triple that number in nine months. Like New Year's Eve in October, dealers from Rose Humphrey's Hibiscus Sales wore hats and sang, "We're sittin' on top of the world." Wise broke into an impromptu vic-tory dance with McDonald, McBurney, and Marshall. A photo from that night shows the early THP all-star executive team clowning around on telephones, another big goal realized: McBurney, McDonald, Bump, Hamer Wilson, Herb Young, Jack Marshall, Don Fuhr, George Reynolds, and, of course, Brownie Wise.

In Chattanooga, Mattie McNutt rejoiced with her team from Green Valley Sales; in Spokane, new distributor Corliss Levitt celebrated by promoting a new group of managers in her company, Live Oak Sales. In New York City, all-star distributors Edith and Jack O'Reilly posed for photographs with a team of five male branch managers; Wal-Dor Sales of Kansas City hit the top, as did J. G. Gould Plastics of McKeesport, Pennsylvania. October 16, 1954, brought victory dances from all over the world of Tupperware dealers, now twenty thousand strong. Not bad for a company that just three years earlier had risen from the ashes of the failed Hostess Division. Wise boasted that the Tupperware dealer force had grown from ten thousand to twenty thousand in just thirty days.[16] Even if that was a bit overstated, it was still powerful testimony to the effectiveness of the company's public relations campaign and to the strong chord it struck with prospective dealers.

To handle that enormous growth, Hamer Wilson brought in a "tabulating systems specialist" Dave Seraphine, to help organize THP's new IBM department.[17] "These magic machines could do in a minute," Wise marveled, "what clerks could not do in months!"[18] New offices were built to accommodate the cutting-edge equipment. That expansion included THP's printing and sales production department.

In November, another group of 135 were among those who attended the first "Postgraduate Managers Training Seminar, the first Prospective Distributors School and a Distributors conference." They ate steaks cooked in THP's newly dug three-grill barbecue pit and "feasted on rich food-for-thought" from Napoleon Hill and Charles B. Roth. Within a few weeks, six of the attendees became distributors and were given new territories to conquer.

Hill paid homage to Wise and Tupperware with a spread in his pocket-sized national publication, *Success Unlimited*. Happy to keep at arm's length and busy with his own ambitious expansion program in New England, Tupper took time to send Wise a confidential memo. "As a result of publicity in 1954, many people are going to be seeking a statement again on our sales," Tupper advised."

I believe we should stick to just one statement and not enlarge upon it. Our schedule remains the same. We plan to produce an annual retail sales volume well in excess of $100,000,000.00 by 1958. We are well on schedule."[19]

When Tupper and his handful of distributors met on that historic day in April 1951, such a figure would have seemed impossible. Thanks to THP's "live-wire" sales division and the enormous progress they made in 1954, everything seemed within Tupperware's ever-expanding reach. They had more than doubled their sales force, the sales volume had more than doubled, and Tupper had done his part, doubling his manufacturing capacity.

In Miami, special presses spit out a new, full-color Tupperware display folder. At Christmas, THP produced a new food preservation and storage booklet entitled *How to Guard Food Values in Your Refrigerator or Freezer.*[20] These were two smaller ways to get the Tupperware name and message out to the American consumer. Brownie Wise and Earl Tupper could look back on the ambitious expansion goals of 1954 and think, *mission accomplished.*

"The year 1954 drew to a close with the distinction of being the biggest year in the history of Tupperware Home Parties," Wise wrote. But that didn't mean she'd let the sales force sit back and enjoy it for long. "If you have met your last year's goal, set a higher one for next year," she urged.[21] "Great things are behind us in Tupperware. But because we are young and we have so much to offer, the greatest things are ahead—many of them to come this year."[22]

Not exactly. While Wise did get to enjoy the fruits of much success and recognition in 1955, the seeds of resentment and downright revolt had also been planted. Where everything seemed to come up Beauty Roses in 1954, the next year would bring the biggest trials. To quell some of the unrest, THP's executive team at times would have to get "down and dirty."[23] Brownie Wise would have to deal with some of the skeletons in her own closet.

Eleven

A Revolt from Within

Brownie basically had a kind of standing restraining order on my father.
—Jerry Wise

At infrequent intervals, a most commanding and well-dressed gentleman whom the great majority of employees didn't know showed up at Tupperware Home Parties' headquarters. Sometimes he would even have his cab drive him right up the sidewalk, and then he would still get through the front door very quickly. It was never during jubilees, and rarely during seminars or large-scale public events—he hated crowds. Even worse, the idea of having to speak publicly in front of a large gathering could make him sick to his stomach. Sometimes he announced himself as "Mister Esty."[1] Other times, he'd just show a business card with the initials "E.S.T." on it. Such was the low-profile, cloak-and-dagger way Earl Silas Tupper made his presence known to the sales division.

Sometimes he came just to take care of a business matter or to see how the Florida operation was shaping up. Or he would bring with him a new idea for the product line. That was where he entered the arena of an equally commanding personality, that of his vice president and general manager of sales, Mrs. Brownie Humphrey Wise. Coming to Florida with his mysterious air, conservative seersucker suits, and take-charge attitude, Tupper was known as "The Boss." Holding court seated in a regal peacock wicker chair, reading letters from adoring dealers, and still basking in the constant flow of positive press, Wise was "The Queen." If he thought one way about a product, and she thought another, the battle royal was on. Jerry Wise witnessed once such face-off after the bus had dropped him at headquarters.

"In the big front room, at that big kidney-shaped table," Jerry chuckled, "the rest of the staff sitting there afraid to say anything."[2]

Like two heavyweights in a prize fight, this wasn't just a battle over some product idea; it was two parents battling it out in front of their children. Such was Tupper's personality that when challenged, he could often blow his stack. But where other employees would have been intimidated, that only gave Wise more fuel. "She wasn't afraid of him at all," her son declared.[3]

"It's time to calm yourself down and sit down and listen to me for a minute," she lectured. "It's going to be too expensive to manufacture."

"Now listen to me, woman, I do the manufacturing and you do the selling!" Tupper shot back.

"Woman?" Wise dressed down her company president. "Is that the way you address your wife?"[4]

Tupper left the meeting red-faced, but with the numbers his sales department was posting and the dollars they were raking in, he wouldn't stay mad for long.

During visits to Florida, Tupper took Jerry with him to look at foreign sports cars at used-car lots. "He loved Jaguars," Jerry recalled. "I remember taking rides in thirty different Jaguars." When Tupper opened up his billfold, Jerry said, he had "nothing but hundreds." With that kind of money, Jerry asked, why don't you just get a new car? "That just tells everybody I have too much money," he replied. Tupper also had an employee incentive program at Farnumsville, where top performers could take one of his high-performance cars for a weekend.[5]

In his mid-forties, Tupper was completely bald except for a few wisps of hair. That often tempted Jerry's precocious sense of humor. "I always wanted to call him 'chrome dome,' and Brownie said, "Don't you *ever* call him 'chrome dome.'" In truth, Tupper's extensive holdings across North America and his inventive mind awed young Jerry. "He brought me the plans for a three-wheel car with a V-8 engine in it," Jerry marveled. "It was designed to be a police car . . . would take a corner at ninety miles an hour because the front-end was cantilevered." Instead of turning one way or the other, the vehicle's wheels would lay down. "I'm thinking, this guy's brain never stopped," said Jerry Wise of Tupper. "His mind was just like Brownie's, working all the time."[6]

Just as many people at the Kissimmee headquarters had no idea who Earl

Tupper was when they saw him, Tupper had never met some of his most talented new executives. One of them, Tony Ponticelli, was hired to take over as Tupperware Home Parties' special events director. "He met me in the hallway and said 'who are you?'" Ponticelli remembered.[7] That led to a meeting in Tupper's office where he quizzed the young executive about his background. When he found out Ponticelli had had real-world experience as the vice president of sales promotion and public relations at a Madison Avenue firm, Tupper often asked for his input on new product ideas.[8] Ponticelli believed Tupper liked his honest, straight-shooting style.

Barely in his thirties at the time he was hired, Ponticelli brought with him from New York a flair for showmanship and creativity. He designed a new wing at the Kissimmee headquarters, "offices and everything." Ponticelli was point man in planning some of the most spectacular shows in Tupperware's early jubilees. He had seen the New York office politics and analyzed what he saw going on at Tupperware Home Parties. "This was a step down," Ponticelli said of his career switch to the slower pace of central Florida. "The lifestyle was what I wanted from the rat race in New York. This was paradise. I didn't mind taking a back seat."[9]

For a worldly, streetwise New Yorker, his first impressions of the company and its people were indelible. "These are a bunch of flaky people, way-out nuts," he recalled. "Where do they get off singing, 'I got that Tupper feeling?'" Memories of his first jubilee are ingrained in his mind: "I'm watching these people singing; they got all these flaky people singing." By the second day, "I'm listening to it, not criticizing in my mind . . . watching the people." And that's when his attitude started to change. "In New York, you think you know it all," Ponticelli offered. "You're away from the people. Only with executives. So you're not down to earth with them. The third day I was singing the song with them."[10]

Why the change of attitude? Without a note of cynicism or sarcasm, Ponticelli replied: "I was converted. It wasn't a phony, staged kind of thing. This was spontaneous. People would get up and sing and people would join in. This was not canned. And before you know it, you got a new religion of helping other people." For the first time, he was overtaken with the feeling of wanting to climb the ladder but with a sense of altruism, a genuine desire to bring other people with him. "That was the idea that permeated the sales force," Ponticelli said. That was all it took to convince him to try for a new career direction with Tupperware Home Parties and a new life in Florida.[11]

He was invited in for an interview luncheon. Brownie Wise sat in her customary wicker chair, surrounded by her team of male executives. "There was a

Wise in her office, ca. 1956. Notice her trademark wicker chair.

Tupperware cup for coffee, and the handle had a hole in it," Ponticelli remembered. "You had to twist your hand a little to get it in your mouth. In those days everyone wore a suit. I was very careful on the first sip, but as I relaxed, I picked up the cup and it was all over me." His blunder was the perfect ice-breaker; everyone laughed, and Ponticelli was now part of the THP team. "Brownie used to kid me about it all the time," he laughed. Ponticelli was also struck by his first impression of Brownie Wise. "In viewing her, sizing up her body motion," he recalled, "I said, well, she really thinks she's a prima donna. But I had a look back and watched how the individuals are responding to her, and I said, 'Hey, I have to give this woman some credit. She's got something on the ball here.'"[12]

To keep that sense of respect in the male-dominated business world of the mid-1950s, Wise was "all business." There was never much talk about personal matters or private concerns. "She struck me as an individual who was over men," Ponticelli said, "and she never wanted to let her guard down as some individual male might try to take advantage of her weakness."[13] Beneath the image she liked to project of a vibrant, on-the-go, rising star executive, Brownie Wise had numerous personal challenges to overcome.

Wise continued to use the last name of the ex-husband who'd long been out of her life. *Business Week* had even miscast her as a widow. What most in the Tupperware family didn't know—and Wise worked hard to keep secret from the press—was that her alcoholic ex-husband eventually moved to central Florida and was a frequent cause of concern. "You just never knew when he was going to pop up," Jerry Wise remembered.[14] He once had to wear a disguise when there was word his father might try to kidnap him. On another occasion, Jerry found out from the local sheriff that Bobby Wise was back in town—and in the drunk tank.

"Your Dad's in jail here. You want to see him? His car's right out there in the lot," the sheriff said.[15]

Jerry declined. "I went through his car, and it looked and smelled like he'd been living in it for six months."[16]

Wise would call headquarters trying to reach his ex-wife. On one occasion, she came out of her office and told her new PR man, Don Hinton, that "Bob Wise" was calling from the Angebilt Hotel in Orlando, wanting to come down and see her. "I don't think he belongs down here at this time," she said dispassionately. With that, Hinton and a couple other staff members drove up to see him.[17]

"We assumed it would be embarrassing as hell for her," Hinton remembered. So he and his men assured Bob Wise that his now-famous ex-wife was far too busy to see him. They were prepared to restrain him physically if need be, but that wasn't necessary. Wise looked in no shape to go anywhere. He didn't have a car, and at the time he wasn't even quite sure where the THP headquarters was.[18]

Jerry Wise said his father was an intelligent man who had many successes in business. Again and again his business ventures would all go by the wayside, sacrificed—like his family life—to a river of destructive alcoholic binges. "My Dad just couldn't get it together, and he couldn't stand it that his ex-wife did," Jerry reflected. "Brownie basically had a kind of standing restraining order on him."[19] Because of the goodwill she and Tupperware had built up with law enforcement, Brownie could count on the authorities to pick up her ex if he crossed the county line drunk, to keep him in jail, and then to quietly transfer him to another lockup farther away from the area. During big events like the jubilees, Hinton always had to keep a wary eye out to make sure Bobby Wise didn't show up to embarrass his ex-wife.

That wasn't the only personal problem Wise had to mask from the throngs of adoring dealers, coworkers, and members of the press. After giving a speech at headquarters, Wise backed away from a new lectern different from the kind to which she was accustomed and fell directly onto the concrete several feet below. Her son says she injured her back so severely it required traction. After treatment she still needed a back brace, and the injury became a long-time source of chronic pain. From time to time, sinusitis and perhaps the stress related to job demands brought back the migraine headaches that had plagued her enough to seek surgery while she was living in South Florida. Beyond all that, Brownie Wise was still a single parent bringing up a red-blooded teen-aged son with a predilection for practical jokes and sarcasm.

It was a new year, and the pressure was on Wise to keep the 1954 momentum rolling. By 1955, Tupper raised her salary to $31,800. Wise lived like a movie star, rent-free in a glamorous lakeside estate, traveling to exotic places all over the world. Her name was being mentioned in the same breath with the few other top executive businesswomen in America. As her stature rose on the national scene, Brownie Wise was becoming a central Florida icon. Like other celebrities so well-known they needed no last names, "Brownie" was big news in the local papers. On January 9, 1955, the *Orlando Sentinel's Sunday Magazine* ran an article entitled "What a Woman!"

"A trim, brown-eyed ex-secretary who efficiently and swiftly moved into Orlando's back yard and established a multi-million dollar corporation in less than three years," the article begins, "that's Brownie Wise, vice-president and general manager of Tupperware Home Parties Inc."[20] The piece goes on to describe the career and personal life of this star business executive, a veritable superwoman working to balance what it called a twelve- to twenty-hour workday, and logging 150,000 miles a year traveling to seminars, rallies, and contest ceremonies. Considering her travels from 1954, that likely was not a huge exaggeration. Yet, the writer marveled, Wise still found time to "do a bit of fishing, boating or horseback riding" with her sixteen-year-old son. The article described their "rambling" home as a virtual paradise with two dogs, three horses, and a twenty-acre estate. "She's not famous," Jerry was quoted as observing. "Famous people are movie stars and people like that. She's just my mom."[21] But to the typical homebound woman of the 1950s, years before Mary Kay, Martha Stewart, and Oprah, this must have been the stuff of fairy tales.

Beyond the focus on Wise, the article delved into how she managed to take the business "by the heart instead of the purse strings." A generous helping of photographs taken by Jack McCollum showed one of the roundtable brainstorming sessions in her "spacious 30 x 75-foot office." Readers saw Wise in front of the Eiffel Tower on the recent Europe trip, Wise in front of headquarters, Wise reading to her son, chatting on the phone, and talking to dealers on the '54 trip to Hawaii. While the article does mention the Tupperware line reaching close to one hundred "polyethylene plastic houseware items including

On horseback with Jerry at Water's Edge, ca. 1956. Jerry said it was not easy for Wise to pose or ride because of a back injury she suffered during a fall.

dishes, refrigerator storage containers, salt and pepper shakers, combs, even fly swatters," there are no product photos. There is only one mention of Tupper, and it's similarly dismissive, as in the breakthrough *Business Week* cover story. "Brownie's title indicates she isn't the top rung on the company ladder, in reality Earl Tupper is the president," the article states, "but, he has given Brownie free rein, and she runs the whole show of selling the product that's fast becoming a household word."[22] Earl Tupper, the now nearly invisible man dropped further into the long shadow of "What a Woman!"

What's not clear is whether the Tupperware Home Parties' new public relations department headed by Charlie McBurney was feeding the press these stories, or whether it was Wise herself. "It was our idea to promote Brownie because she was so well thought of," said Don Hinton. "The more we did for her, the more the gals thought of her."[23] Given the considerable demands of her career, her son said Wise was not a big fan of the demands reporters and photographers put on her personal life. But in a history of THP that Wise penned herself, the emphasis is clear: "On magazine stands across the nation appeared more recognition for the success of Tupperware, as shown through the success of Brownie Wise."[24] Even if the articles focused solely on THP's charismatic female chief executive, it appeared obvious Wise felt that Tupperware would also benefit. Up until that point, the explosive expansion of Tupperware across America made that belief hard to dispute.

In January, one hundred distributors and managers from across the country gathered at THP headquarters for another conference. Don Fuhr had done his part by securing new steak-knife and kitchen-tool sets for THP's premium program to lure more Tupperware Party hostesses. The THP team also introduced to its product line what would soon become the "wildly popular" Jumbo Canister.[25] Wise introduced a new Star Demonstrator contest in which dealers across the country could compete for an array of fabulous prizes like diamond rings, diamond wristwatches, and mink stoles. Each distributor was issued a magic slate scorecard on which to judge who gave the best demonstration and was deserving of an award. Seven distributors were inducted as charter members of the Lantern Club for having the highest per-capita sales: Pat Brown, Bill Segraves, Ed Drey, Una and Art Osrud, Eli Schofield. and two top Tupperware distributor/power brokers from the start: Rose Humphrey and Peter Block.

In Rose Humphrey, Brownie Wise had an obvious ally among the ranks of powerful distributors. But in Peter and Elsie Block, she did not. The Blocks felt that they had thrived with Tupperware despite their flow of merchandise being cut off by the Hostess Division. Then they had to endure supply problems that Elsie Block claimed were caused by the autocratic ways of Brownie Wise. There were other examples that Elsie Block claimed showed a lack of experience and integrity on Wise's part. Despite that, Elsie Block claimed they were directly responsible for recruiting two of Wise and THP's most valuable staff people: Jack Marshall and Hamer Wilson.

The couple's Poly Sales Company of Pasadena had become so successful that, by 1954, the Blocks were the only distributors in the nation ordering their inventory by the train car load. There's a famous picture of the Blocks posing with dozens of their dealers in front of a huge banner heralding the arrival of that first train car load of Tupperware. "What a relief," Elsie Block wrote. "At the time Tupperware had no major warehousing anywhere in the United States between Massachusetts and us. We were it."[26]

This was at the same time that Tupperware dealers were signing up in record numbers. Because of their success, Block claimed Wise often made "urgent" phone calls to her asking if she and Peter had new distributor candidates to take over virgin territories.[27] In one early case, Jack and Jean Kelly were promoted out of Poly Sales to take over Cincinnati. Despite all the positive press

Brownie Wise was earning over her training programs and distributor conferences, Elsie Block said new distributors acquired all the tools they needed in their own sales regions. "Those were the days when new distributors learned everything from their promoting distributors," wrote Elsie Block. "Tupperware Home Parties had nothing to do but sign an agreement to supply them with Tupperware."[28]

But that's where Brownie Wise and THP retained power over the distributors. The heads of various sales regions did not work for THP, nor did they draw benefits or a pension from the Tupperware Corporation. That saved the company a fortune. But as their lines shrunk from selling several products to exclusively Tupperware, the distributors had to maintain some sense of subservience to THP and Brownie Wise. If they did not perform well in the contests and make sure their dealers and unit managers were giving their all, they could have their distributorship yanked. Despite the good times and big-time sales of those early years, some distributorships were not renewed. That's when Brownie Wise had to put away the carrots and bring out the stick. In 1955, as the positive press kept rolling out and Brownie Wise was in demand for high-profile public appearances, behind the scenes it got very ugly among her, the THP staff, and a group of distributors who decided they deserved more power than the company was giving them.

According to Wise, a pair of former distributors, Dot and Bill Henry, circulated to many other dealers and distributors a letter with "a number of derogatory statements about Tupperware as a product and the policies of Tupperware Home Parties Inc."[29] According to Gary McDonald, distributors were unhappy about pricing and product lines. Competing vendors, recognizing how successful these distributors were, would "take them out to dinner, wining and dining," in an attempt to get them to carry their products in addition to, or in lieu of, Tupperware.[30] "They talked about them representing the strength of the business," McDonald said. "They were really not getting a fair shake with the discount they were getting, and they didn't have a voice to approach management."[31] Tupperware Home Parties, on the other hand, had the most power when their distributors carried the least amount of competitor products. This argument resonated in particular with some of the early distributors who felt they had been successful on their own, before and, perhaps, despite Brownie Wise and Tupperware Home Parties. "The men of that group wanted to have more control," McDonald said, "even though they were making more money than you can imagine doing it the way we suggested."[32]

Tupper sent Wise a confidential memo responding to the Henrys' letter. "It is not good but I see nothing that we can do to stop it now," Tupper advised. "Your dealers are going to at least listen to the offerings of the other side now."[33] Wise responded with a lengthy open letter to all Tupperware dealers and distributors. "Every day I receive letters from enthusiastic dealers voicing their gratitude for the good things that have come their way—new cars and homes, education for their children, pianos, surgical and medical treatments, added insurance and savings accounts or security," Wise wrote. "Of the many advantages realized by what we do, all of us feel, I am sure, that the greatest pleasure comes to us and to the distributors from watching the growth and development of people."[34]

A small group of powerful distributors agreed to a meeting in Philadelphia with the idea of forming a distributors' union. If there was one thing the THP staff knew Earl Tupper loathed from the outset, it was unions. And here you had a handful of his most prosperous distributors considering the possibility of forming a partnership, carrying another line of product, and moving elsewhere. According to McDonald, when he, Wise, and the rest of the THP management got wind of what was afoot, they knew they needed to act decisively to quell the revolt. When they found out which hotel in Philadelphia the distributors planned to use for their clandestine meeting, Jack Marshall went to work.

Through "a friend who had a friend," Marshall managed to get a microphone placed inside the room where the distributors were meeting.[35] Unbeknownst to them, members of the THP management team found out who the key players were. "When we had that recorder in the hotel room listening to them," McDonald said, "you could hear them vying for position to be the one who was going to be the strength in the organization."[36] According to McDonald, the man jockeying to head up this powerful proposed union was none other than their biggest West Coast distributor, Peter Block.

Following up on that information, a group of THP executives flew out to Southern California to confront "ringleader" Peter Block.[37] In his office, the nation's largest distributor told THP executives that he could do a better job running the company's sales operation than Brownie Wise. In the corner, not saying very much, was the new PR guy, Don Hinton, wearing a hidden microphone and recorder. "He thought he could take the business over," Hinton recalled. "He tried and didn't win."[38] They had the evidence they needed and soon would take decisive action against the Blocks' operation.

Meanwhile, THP executives had to work quickly to build bridges with the other distributors. "You are the organization," Wise and her staff assured them.[39]

"That wording stung," McDonald said, "because we knew it was going to the people who were going to defect as well." The real target audience was distributors who had prospered considerably from selling Tupperware. "Helping you is the only way we can build our organization," the THP top brass assured them.[40] After the letters were sent, THP dispatched representatives to different cities to make personal follow-ups. They argued that no product had the kind of backing or growing national reputation that Tupperware did. In other words, where you go, Tupperware dealers and dollars may not follow.

In the end, some did choose to leave. But, according to McDonald, they learned the hard way that as distributors they were not bigger than Tupperware. "Fortunately, the product they got involved with was not much in the way of a product," McDonald said. "It wasn't even a knockoff, and it did not succeed, and they did not succeed."[41] Two of the distributors who decided to take part in the revolt were eventually welcomed back into the Tupperware fold without recrimination. The same could not be said for Peter and Elsie Block. They were stripped of their distributorship in what Elsie Block referred to as the "Tupperware Raid."[42]

"Seven men from Tupperware Home Parties Inc.," Block wrote, "arrived at our warehouse to finish destroying our business."[43] The two men running the operation, whom Block painted as henchmen for Brownie Wise, were none other than Jack Marshall and Hamer Wilson. Their intent was to remove all the product from the Blocks' massive Pasadena warehouse. What wasn't thrown in a truck, Block said, was heaped in a corner like broken toys. "My grief over the sickening, immoral act perpetrated against our Poly Sales Company," Block wrote, "consumed me more than all else."[44]

In her book *My Tupperware Party Was Over . . . and I Sat Down and Cried,* Elsie Block claimed she and Peter had had no idea why such an act was being perpetrated against their business. "We desperately tried to find out what was going on at headquarters," she reported. "When Peter tried to get information, his calls were not accepted. The General Manager, Brownie Wise, instructed her receptionist to tell the caller that she didn't know anyone by the name of Peter Block."[45] Nowhere in her book does Block make mention of her husband, Peter, spearheading the drive to unionize Tupperware distributors. Peter Block, the star distributor awarded a gold lantern in 1955, a winner of Cadillacs and other performance-based premiums, and a Tupperware insider who helped grow the ranks of dealers and THP executives, was out in the cold—cut off for good.

If indeed Peter Block had made the power play just as Gary McDonald and

Don Hinton described, it cost the Blocks all they had worked for since their days of selling Stanley products in Detroit. "After the Tupperware crew finished with what they were sent to do and left our warehouse," Elsie Block lamented, "Peter and I stood together at the shipping gate as the last truckload pulled away. We turned and stared at the long lines of conveyers that would no longer roll. We went to the back gate, looking at the empty train track, knowing another freight car full of Tupperware would not come. The profound silence was awful."[46]

In a long letter to Tupper, Wise did not acknowledge any kind of "raid" on the Blocks' operation: "I'm not gloating, nor do I tell you this in a spirit of viciousness, but I think you will be interested to know . . . the Blocks have disposed of all their merchandise, hostess premiums and sale merchandise, to the discount houses, and are apparently clearing out the business completely."[47] While she admitted to Tupper that "the fight got pretty dirty,"[48] she did not acknowledge in her correspondence the bugging of the distributors' hotel room or wiring Hinton for the meeting with Block. If those orders were given, it appears that the highest level they could have come from was Wise. She blamed the revolt on THP'S "ultimatum on handling other merchandise along with Tupperware on our party plan."[49]

Whatever the core reasons for the revolt of long-time, top-performing distributors like the Blocks, the shock waves it sent were undeniable. Because of what Wise referred to as the "holocaust" of 1955, sales figures for the rest of that year and the next started to disappoint. "We worked and worried our way through an almost unbearable stretch of disappointing sales totals, month after month," Wise told Tupper.[50] It seems clear from the amount of explanation Wise offers in this later document, dated May 27, 1957, that whatever happened between THP and its defecting distributors went on with only cursory input at most from Tupper.

Distributors could have understandably felt some pangs of jealousy reading all the praise and press being heaped upon Brownie Wise while they and Tupper remained all but invisible. Most, if not all, of them were not privy to the fact that Tupper had signed off on the public relations strategy of building up Wise as long as Tupperware shined in the process. The rocky relationship Wise endured with the distributors did nothing to deter the growing cult of personality and devotion she was developing with thousands of Tupperware dealers—many of whom felt as if they enjoyed a one-on-one relationship with her. Letters poured in. Always a prolific note writer, often working well into the night with a typewriter on her bed, Brownie Wise made sure the correspondence kept going back in return. She kept up the practice of using a ruler or stylus when signing her name so the signature came out perfectly straight.

"What she was doing was helping people accomplish things beyond *their wildest* imaginations," McDonald remembered. "They never thought of working, let alone making more money than their husbands."[51]

As another dealer incentive, Wise would give away the clothes she wore to rallies all across the country. "When she would go out to rallies in the field," McDonald reflected, "people would have thousand-dollar weeks to get the outfits she was wearing. They would lose fifty or sixty pounds in a short time to make it fit."[52] In spite of everything dealers would have happening in their personal lives, what seemed to haunt many of them most was letting down Brownie Wise.

In a personal letter to Wise, one unit manager from San Diego confessed that, "I'm afraid I've been a disappointment to the company after they've been so good to me." She didn't want her letter to be an "excuse," just an explanation of "the reasons why." After attending one of the Tupperware jubilees, "my mother suffered a stroke. I returned to find she barely knew me and since she has steadily grown worse. As I write this she is expected to pass at any minute having been in a coma for 6 days." Because of all the adversity she had "*barely been a dealer since.*"[53]

In another letter, a woman who called herself one of Wise's "Tupperware Children" described holding twenty Tupperware parties in one week: "I had to date 31 parties to have the 20. I had three postponed in one afternoon. But I kept pushing on. I was determined to prove your faith in me if I had to knock on every door in Evansville to date the 20 parties."[54] The letter came from a mother of four children, one of them an infant. "So the big week came, the third day I took the flu along with a lot of other people, and my husband had to go out on three parties for me. I broke him in right, he didn't know a thing but hearing me talk around the house. But as always he did a wonderful job. But I had to go out and have my day parties and in the mean time my four sons and Mother (who had come down to stay with my baby while I had the parties) came down with the flu. I would Dr. them up and go on a party, come back and see about them and go on another party. So we had quite a week."[55]

"Thanks to Tupperware," another dealer wrote Wise, "I sent my son a round-trip ticket and he is home for Christmas first time I've seen him in three years, two months, eight days."[56] In her letter she also mentioned that as a prize for having the highest monthly sales, she was awarded a Brownie Wise dress: "It's all over lace with satin ribbon inserts and bow in back, sorta rose shade. It fits me."[57] It was that kind of flourishing dealer motivation and drive, perhaps more than any other factor, that was the real key to Tupperware's early success. That and the avalanche of press that Brownie Wise and her public relations machine kept generating.

To almost 3 million readers in the March 1955 edition of *Coronet* magazine, travel writer Ludwig Bemelmens recounted experiencing "the true dream of Paris" while accompanying the Tupperware prize winners in September 1954. "Mrs. Wise is a party giver," Bemelmens wrote. "Perhaps the greatest of them, bigger than Elsa Maxwell even. At her parties—thousands of them throughout America every day—women demonstrate and sell polyethylene wares. They play parlor games and shop from the same arm chair, an amazing phenomenon."[58] In that same time period, Wise scored an admiring cover story written by Charles B. Roth for *Salesman's Opportunity* magazine. For *Woman's Life,* Roth penned an article about Wise entitled "She Planned Her Way to Success."

In March, the Central Florida Sales Executive Club asked Wise to be one of the headline speakers at a motivational rally held at Orlando's Municipal Auditorium. Wise shared the bill with Elmer Wheeler, whose "sizzlemanship" concepts she had used to motivate her early dealers in Michigan. Wise was thrilled to address a crowd of 2,500 people, having been introduced as one of three "most outstanding sales authorities in America." In 1955, in that same non-air-conditioned arena that locals used to called "the hotbox," nineteen-year-old-phenomenon Elvis Presley wowed the crowd as a last-minute warm-up act for comedian Andy Griffith, famous in those days for his comedy record album "the Football Monologues."

At Tupperware's fourth anniversary jubilee the following month, as a new way to reward the hardworking ranks of twenty thousand dealers, Wise dedicated what was known as "The Garden That Loyalty Built." To the assembled group of one thousand Tupperware faithful, Wise gave an inspired address capturing the unique, people-helping-people aspect of their business: "The success that we have had and the milestones we've checked off are the achievements of all of us," she told them. "How near we always are to each other in spite of the miles between. Who would be willing to guess the number of new thoughts that will be awakened, the ambitions that will be fired, and the goals of personal achievement that will be reached, as the spirit of this Jubilee. I hope that we may always remember that our interest is common and that any real eminence that we attain as a company will always rest in the personal growth and achievements of our people."[59]

On Tuesday, April 19, 1955, visiting speaker Dr. Norman Vincent Peale underscored the positive thinking, all-for-one-and-one-for-all Tupperware doctrines. "Fill your mind with positive thoughts," Peale preached. "Think in terms of success and you can achieve whatever you set out to achieve."[60] Especially when that successful frame of mind is backed up by people willing to give Tupperware parties while they and their whole families are sick with fever, or when dealers will work until they drop just to have the privilege of losing fifty pounds to fit into a Brownie Wise prize dress.

The THP team unveiled the Vanguard shield, crest of the company and "badge of high honor" to the highest-performing managers. As an added motivator, those managers would soon start receiving their own *Vanguard* magazine. Not forgetting distributors, a spring and summer "777" contest would send seven winners to London and Paris and would award seven runner-up winners a trip to the glamorous Mexican Riviera. Wise wrote that there were so many top-performing dealers that, for the first time, runners-up would be added to the list of those who received National Merit Award trophies.

For the four-day 1955 jubilee, the grounds of headquarters were transformed into "Tupperware Gulch." On Wednesday, attendees were treated to a county fair highlighted by a show from the Silver Spurs Riding Club. Each person also received $1,500 dollars in "bogus money" to spend on items inside the line of old western storefronts. At Tupperware jubilees, meetings were always preceded by a recitation of the Lord's Prayer. Drinking and dancing were not allowed. Staff members planned the events with a kind of calculated, but professional corniness for a very specific reason. Many of the women who paid their own way to the jubilees came alone; how would it look, in the America of the 1950s, if midwestern housewives in for training and motivation were seen drinking or even dancing in public? Tupperware Home Parties took great stock in the wholesome image that executives, dealers, and distributors projected. It was also an important recruiting tool when convincing a reticent husband that it was OK for his wife to become a "Tupperware Lady."

Wise and George Reynolds had been busy plotting out new attractions at headquarters for tourists and visiting members of the Tupperware family. On the so-called Isle of Cypress, paths were laid out and a new statue added. In the Garden That Loyalty Built, dealers who had done such a superb job recruiting others during the 1954 Top of the World drive, had their names put on a plaque and added to a long, gold chain.[61] And Wise wrote that THP hosted a Florida Symphony Orchestra concert in the Garden Pavilion for one thousand Osceola County schoolchildren. The headquarters' unofficial landscaper, M. J. Daetwyler, resigned all of his other work to devote his full-time attention to maintaining all of the gardens and greenery on the THP grounds.

On the cultural scene, THP continued to be well ahead of its time, for the first time sending on a nationwide tour, the thirty-nine top-ranked paintings from the first annual $2,500 Tupperware Art Fund competition. When the director of the Tupperware Art Fund, Ernest Fiene, announced the 1955 competition, Wise wrote that "200 entries poured in."[62]

The company's forward-thinking attitude about art in the workplace was recognized by *Arts Digest* magazine. "It is all too rare that big business steps out into the arts. When it does, the steps are often cautious and temporary. For this reason," the editors wrote, "we are delighted that Tupperware Home Parties Inc. is continuing and expanding its art program."[63]

For his part, Earl Tupper had continued to commit the capital necessary to keep pace with sales' successes. The four-story Blackstone facility was now operating at full capacity. To complement that effort, in 1955 Tupper purchased a massive plant at North Smithfield, Rhode Island, which he planned to use as his new hub of research and development. As his rank-and-file kept growing, Tupper too found interesting ways to reward and motivate his workers—though they certainly could not compete with the mink coats and Cadillacs his sales division bestowed on its people.

On July 19, 1955, Tupper sent out a notice to his "fellow workers," about a drawing in which the grand-prize winner would get a trip to tour the Home Party team's Kissimmee headquarters.[64] "The first draw will be an all-expense-paid trip there," Tupper wrote. "The second draw will be a very poor second. The winner can spend a day as my guest at the laboratory. It won't be exciting but it will be interesting and show you what makes a business tick. In both trips you will draw your regular pay just as though you had worked—so you can't lose." The grand-prize winner would be flown from Boston or New York City to Miami. The winner would get a night's stay and fifty dollars to spend on clothing in Miami Beach. "Then you will be flown to Orlando and at the airport given a special flight over the beautiful city of Orlando (the Venice of America)," Tupper wrote. A taxi would then shuttle the winner through Orlando to a daylong tour of the Tupperware Home Parties facility. "Then you will have to come back here and live like the rest of us," Tupper deadpanned. "The above lucky drawing will be available only to the people at Blackstone and Farnumsville plants who do not work in the offices or who do not have supervisor's jobs—because if we let them draw and they should happen to win you would figure the deal was rigged."[65]

For a man who avoided social situations, skulked around as "Mister Esty," and said little more than "good morning" when touring one of his myriad operations encompassing factories and offices in Massachusetts, Rhode Island, Florida, New York, and Canada, Earl Tupper was witty, folksy, and usually to the point when forced to write to his workers. Here are some examples from an August 1955 memo:

Benefits is not the word for us to use. RESULTS is the word we all like—if we do a good job in a good place, we get results.

There are no politics here to hold you back. No one will envy you if you grow and fill a better job—because you will be helping everyone in our plant to do a better job and make more money.

Many mills in New England for the last few years have been letting their plants run down with the idea of moving out. Thus they have been able to yield temporarily to demands for higher wages until close down of plants. We have come in and spent a lot of money to replace the results of long neglect. Our money was well spent for your future here and our future here.

Safety is important. Special triple safety devices on our machines for your safety cost a lot of money—and result in slower production and uneven and faulty production unless you are alert and cooperate to make the machinery produce efficiently.

If one of our people is struck by a death in the family, we can't do much to help. We do what we can with such things as flowers and three days off with pay to cope with the problems that arise. Flowers are sent if you are sick so that you know you are missed.

Once in a while, a surprise gift of Tupperware is given to every employee. A summer vacation with pay is standard and then comes Thanksgiving and usually a turkey on the company. After that soon comes Christmas with little gifts and then the second week of vacation with pay.

We are not bragging about all this, but we do think that for a new company in a new place with a lot of problems to solve, and tough competitors to cope with, well we think we have a right to hold our heads up just as we like to see you hold yours up.[66]

The front page of the August 1955 issue of *Tupperware Sparks* featured photos of the winning distributors in the "777" contest. As the distributor revolt simmered, only the familiar names of Rose Humphrey and Corliss Levitt were among the Europe-bound winners. Underneath all of her usual cheerleading, Wise felt pressured. "We knew all the other distributors were watching on the sidelines, some of them wavering. That hurt," Wise wrote Tupper.[67] "There was intense pressure for about a year from these renegades, as well as their suppliers who thought, at first, that this motley little crew constituted a gold mine for them."[68] Though that didn't happen, Wise was clearly bothered that big-dollar producers like the Blocks were rebelling against her authority through THP. "It simply didn't make sense," she wrote, "that a bunch of prospering distributors would pull out of a good thing."[69] But in her soul-searching letter to Tupper, Wise never considered that it could have anything to do with her management style or tactics.

This first serious bout of growing pains for Tupperware Home Parties and Brownie Wise manifested itself in the annual sales numbers. Despite triple- and double-digit increases in 1953 and 1954 respectively, and despite the Tupperware dealer numbers at record levels, in 1955 the gross sales of Tupperware to its distributors dropped 8 percent for the year. That shocking turn of events could be tied directly to losing players like Peter and Elsie Block, who had ordered Tupperware by the train car load. This was arguably the first time during her rapid ascent in the world of direct selling that Brownie Wise got a clear message that she was not infallible and that all was not coming up Beauty Roses in the house of Tupper.

Twelve

New Players in Place

You're not gonna grow by accepting what is; you're gonna grow by accepting what can be. And then doing something about it.
—Pat Jordan

While much of the early history of Tupperware has been written with an emphasis on Earl Tupper and Brownie Wise, by the end of 1955 many of the people were in place who would shepherd Tupperware and its distributorships after those two giants departed. More hardworking and ambitious self-starters were coming on board every day. One of them was a young South Florida mother who was told she was "too qualified" to become a Tupperware dealer.[1]

Sometime near the end of 1955, Pat Jordan got interested in selling Tupperware for the same reason so many others did—money. Jordan had grown up in a poor family where money was always tight. Her husband, Phil, resigned his commission in the navy and had to work two to three jobs to put food on the table. "*That* was motivation," Jordan remembered about what drew her to selling Tupperware. "It was money; it was gifts. It was everybody was for everybody. I'm not going to step on you to get ahead; I'm going to take your hand and help you along. It was a big family affair."[2] It was that Tupper feeling, as the song went; it was the new religion that seduced even wary executives like Tony Ponticelli.

For whatever reason, despite having a baby at home and a genuine need for the income

Tupperware could provide, Jordan's history as a professional woman made her recruiter cautious. "She said, 'I'm sorry Pat, I don't think this is something for you,'" Jordan remembered. "I don't know what that meant. Time went on, and the more I thought about it the madder I got. I thought to myself, 'I can do anything I want to do.'" She called Rose Humphrey's Orlando distributorship, told them she'd love to sell Tupperware, and finally got the response she'd hoped for. In return for shelling out the $35 she described as "a lot of money," a big cardboard box containing a suitcase arrived—a case filled with Tupperware.[3] In 1955, the average American household made $4,137 a year; gas was twenty-three cents per gallon. You could buy a first-class stamp for three cents. Pat Jordan was embarking on a thirty-year road through adversity and success and a career climb from dealer to manager to distributor.

"I was always going where angels fear to tread. I guess I still do," Jordan chuckled. In the early days, Jordan knocked on a lot of doors and made a lot of neighborhood cold calls hoping to date Tupperware parties. There were occasional nasty dogs to contend with, doors shut in her face, but more times than not, people were receptive. "You know, women were home during that era; there weren't many women working," she said.[4] And there was always encouragement coming from higher up to do more than you thought possible. For Jordan, the person that offered that encouragement was Jean Conlogue.

Conlogue and her husband, Jack, had come out of the Blocks' Poly Sales Company. According to Jordan, the Conlogues helped recruit Hamer Wilson, who had emerged as one of the top conduits between the sales force and THP's home office. Having left St. Louis, the Conlogues took a distributorship in South Florida and developed promising young recruits like Jordan. "Jean was a teacher; she was a motivator," Jordan recalled. "Jean took my hand and said to me, 'If you want to be successful in this business, you come with me.' And you didn't say no to Jean Conlogue." Together, the distributor and her new dealer headed south to what Conlogue called "the end of the world"—Homestead, Florida.[5] Later famous as ground zero for Hurricane Andrew in 1992, in the mid-1950s Homestead was just another in a string of South Florida outpost towns; single-story cinder-block homes within easy reach of U.S. 1, hotter than blazes in the summer, ripe as a tangerine and ready for picking.

"I used to do some strange things," Jordan admitted. "I used to knock on the door with bags of lettuce and carrots. This is the way we got in the door asking people to put them in the refrigerator—one in Tupperware, one without; then I'd come back in three days. The piece of lettuce not in Tupperware would be wilted, the one in Tupperware would not, and that's how we dated parties."[6] It's a method that harkened back to when Wise and McDonald told their Detroit customers to throw away the shower caps. With simple, yet effective examples, would-be hostesses could see that the product really worked. It was the same all across America—parties were held, products were sold, businesses were grown, and dealers like Pat Jordan moved up the ranks.

Conlogue promoted Jordan to Tupperware manager. "Then I got pregnant and had another baby, number two," Jordan recalled. "I went to a Tupperware party the night my water broke and went immediately to the hospital and had my second child. That's what you did."[7] But Jordan's charmed life as an up-and-coming Tupperware sales rep took an unfortunate turn. Her second child, Susan, came down with a serious bout of spinal meningitis. She told Conlogue it was unlikely she could continue. Jordan had a sick baby at home and only one car, which husband Phil needed. Despite all the adversity, Conlogue asked her to hold on. Very slowly, baby Susan started to recover from what could have been a fatal illness. Once she was well enough, Jordan soldiered on.

"I begged a car from everyone I could think of," she said. "And everybody in my neighborhood knew what was happening and helped me. Sometimes I would put the kids in the car and drive Phil to work in downtown Miami and I would drive back. I had a wonderful neighbor who helped watch my children so I could make my parties. Phil did almost all of my bagging and delivering of Tupperware on his way to and from work because I was too busy holding parties."[8]

The Jordans were similarly resourceful when looking to recruit new dealers. Pat took the lead, identifying woman after woman to bring into the distributorship. The talkative ones were an easy sell, but Jordan would also go after a wallflower if she saw potential. "I would look at her and say, 'Honey, you need me,'" laughed Jordan. "'You're sweet and darling and all you can talk about is your love of children, which is fine, but there's a big world out there.'" It was that kind of woman who often told Jordan the idea would never fly with her husband. That's when Pat brought Phil into the game. "I would say to them," Jordan remembered, her tone turning a bit conspiratorial, 'I'd like to bring my husband and talk to your husband.' They'd say, 'It's not going to do any good, but okay.' Phil and I would drive up in our shiny car. Phil would have on his suit and tie and I would have on my five-inch heels. And he would talk about what he did in the early days, how much pride he had in the things I was doing for the family. It was always the family."[9]

After more assurances that they weren't trying to take the man's wife away, that she could do this during the day, and that she wouldn't need a lot of clothes or extras to get started—and couldn't your family really use the extra money?—the Jordans had burped up another Tupperware recruit. But that was

Headed for the 1954 jubilee, Pat Jordan is the mouse in the back row, third from right. Jean and Jack Conlogue are on either end.

only the beginning; often a shy person would have to be reassured that they were capable of giving demonstrations, of running both a business and a family. "How do you know if you don't try?" was the mantra Jordan said she passed on to her own recruits. "I was on the training team and traveled all over the country. In places like Utah, [I would say,] 'What if you could be one of the most successful people in your community and you never tried? What if this would bring so much happiness to your family and you never tried?'"[10]

Along with the Conlogues, Jordan credited Wilson's mentoring skills for helping people like her up the ladder. "When Hamer came into the business," she recalled, "he would sit cross-legged on the desk or table, and he would know your name, your children's names, where you came from. It was all family. It was such a wonderful thing to be remembered." It was Wilson who offered the Jordans a distributorship in Norfolk, Virginia. For Phil, it was a tough proposal. He'd just returned from Norfolk, where he still remembered signs that read, "Dogs and sailors keep off the grass." Wilson just laughed, and eventually the Jordans went. As the Jordans and people like them grew in their businesses, there were no 401Ks or IRAs. Yet there was never a thought about what they would do about retirement. "Never thought about it, never thought about it," Jordan said flatly. "We invested our money in our product."[11]

During this time period, another towering figure in the history of Tupperware was so short she had to stand on a Coke box to reach the microphones—someone who started much like the wallflowers Pat Jordan was so skilled at recruiting. After joining Tupperware Home Parties as its first hostess demonstrator, Elsie Mortland was also credited with helping instill "a sense of family, loyalty and leadership."[12] Women could always count on Elsie to hold their young children in her lap. The same was true whenever Earl Tupper made a new product out of his baby, Poly-T. Since Mortland was also director of the experimental kitchen, she became the first person to test any one of his prototypes. It was all done in Tupper's typically clandestine style.

"He had to be very careful about other plastics companies stealing his design," Mortland said. From time to time, a carefully packaged container would arrive at THP headquarters. "He had them sealed with tape, of course, and written on the outside [was], 'To be opened by Elsie Mortland only,'" she recalled.[13]

Mortland and the PR man Charles McBurney were the two principals on a crucial trip to New York. Mortland met with directors from the highly influential publication *Good Housekeeping*. Just as Brownie Wise gave a pivotal demonstration to assembled members of the press in 1953, Mortland's successful demonstration led to Tupperware receiving the all-important Good Housekeeping Seal of Approval. It was all pretty impressive and at the same time intimidating for the shy housewife from Deland, Florida. Mortland had one very simple key to all of her success as a Tupperware demonstrator: "I was always very honest; I didn't exaggerate," Mortland said, "so when people got their Tupperware they weren't disappointed with it."[14]

During her own move up through the ranks of Tupperware Home Parties, in the early days, Mortland could get her inspiration right from the top. In 1955 and into 1956, Mortland and her family lived in the caretaker's cottage behind Water's Edge. She became part of the after-hours brainstorming sessions: "Everybody had their department they were responsible for, but there wasn't any definite dividing line between responsibilities; everybody worked together." Elsie Mortland had become a key member of the executive team striving to keep the Tupperware juggernaut moving forward, and the only other woman with any kind of executive influence. "If I had any problem, I'd go to Brownie and get it straightened out. She was very willing to help me in any way she could. And if she could push any of her responsibilities on me she would," said Mortland with a chuckle.[15]

Gary McDonald had also come a long way since packing up his sea bag for Massachusetts in 1951. A wide array of responsibilities fell under McDonald's job description: promotions, recruiting, running the office. He played an important role in THP's handling of the distributor revolt, and he was often the man at the microphone helping motivate the dealers. If someone came up with a promotion or gimmick, it was often McDonald where the buck stopped as far as pulling it off. Though he was a full five years younger than his director of special events, Tony Ponticelli, the respect Ponticelli had for McDonald ran deep. "I always admired Gary. He got up there and did things he'd never done in his life," Ponticelli said. "His neck was on the line all the time."[16] He had studied the way Wise was able to motivate a crowd, internalized that skill, and put it to his own use. Unlike some of the other male THP executives who had come on board after him, McDonald had given Tupperware parties and demonstrations, adding that important skill to his institutional knowledge.

To help women like Pat Jordan, who often had transportation conflicts, McDonald and Don Fuhr came up with an idea that ranks as one of the great incentive programs in THP history. McDonald worked a deal with Ford to provide a Fairlane 500 to Tupperware managers, but that's not how it was announced at one of the early jubilees. In the Garden Pavilion, McDonald told the audience that the company had decided on a car program for Vanguard managers. That might have caused a stir, but not a big one, considering how long and often THP had given away cars. But, McDonald told the audience, it wouldn't be for just the top ten managers—how about the top sixty? That caused a great deal more excitement in the crowd. Then, for what McDonald called "the coupe de grace," he announced that they had decided to take it another step, and that THP would give a Ford Fairlane 500 to every Tupperware manager in the world to use.[17]

Pat Jordan, who was in the audience, attested to the reaction: "You talk about screaming, hysterical women. It was the biggest thing that anyone could ever imagine: To be able to get a car free by doing your job that you loved while you were earning money and earning gifts and earning trips."[18] At least two women in the crowd fainted at the news.

It earned McDonald the kind of adoration to which Wise was accustomed, and then some. "They tore the sleeves out of the suit I was wearing," he laughed.[19] Decades later, TV talk-show host Oprah Winfrey took a page from the Tupperware playbook, giving a car to everyone in the audience, and, just like Gary McDonald, brought the house down. The idea of giving something to everyone in the audience has been mimicked again and again.

All the Tupperware faithful could take that kind of electricity back to their own home distributorships and re-create it there. At Monday morning meetings, they regaled dealers who didn't make it to Kissimmee with stories of how incredible the jubilee had been. That would stoke the competitive fires of those who promised themselves they would do what it took to make it down to Florida the following year. "That's why we kept growing," McDonald said.[20]

The major players to take Tupperware Home Parties into the 1960s and even greater heights were in place: affable Hamer Wilson had a good way with distributors and the sales force from behind the scenes; Elsie Mortland could demonstrate the product and pass on her knowledge to neophytes in a friendly, low- pressure way; and Gary McDonald had the same flair for razzmatazz, showmanship, and motivation as the woman from whom he'd learned it, Brownie Wise. The man who would lead the manufacturing side for almost thirty years, John Ansley, also came on board in 1956. Other key players like Joe Hara, Jon and Sylvia Boyd, and Li Walker were still working as dealers, managers, and distributors.

According to Tony Ponticelli, McDonald's emergence at such a young age was no accident. Both men credited Wise and her considerable skills as an executive for bringing those kinds of traits out in the people around her. "It takes an executive to know the talent you have and bring out the best in that talent. So you gotta give her that," Ponticelli offered. "Then she had a belief in the religion she was trying to teach, which was direct selling and party-plan selling. And I would say that she knew how to work with men where other women did not."[21] Public relations man Don Hinton had done stints with United Press and Pan Am and, before Brownie Wise, had never interviewed for a job with a female executive. "I was impressed because she was sharp, she was intelligent, and asked the right questions," he recalled, "After thirty minutes, she asked me, 'Can you start tomorrow?'"[22]

Beginning in 1956 and more so in 1957, Wise had more and more difficulty and disagreement with the most important man in her professional life, Earl Tupper. As those years unfolded, their relationship became increasingly strained. In previous years, as profits and new dealers rolled in, the two could handle most of their business, and their differences, during long one-on-one phone calls. During that time, Tupper kept a "totally hands-off" approach to Tupperware Home Parties.[23] A string of events took place that made it obvious that Tupper felt the need to rein in Wise. The personal communication started to evaporate. The distributor revolt was the first serious cause for concern. Then profits for the year dipped. Flattering publicity kept coming that seemed to focus more on Brownie Wise than on Tupperware, and not at all on the other key THP executives who could rightly claim to have helped make the young company what it was.

Thirteen

THE FOUNDATIONS SHAKEN

I think it is an absolute miracle, in more ways than one. It is certainly a miracle of nature that it was created in the first place . . . a miracle that it has been left untouched. And still another miracle that it now belongs to me!
—Brownie Wise

For Brownie Wise and the THP team, the end of 1955 proved to be far more subdued and less celebratory than the year before. In *Tupperware Sparks*, there were no screaming headlines about sales records smashed or dealer numbers skyrocketing like in '54. As winners of THP's Star Demonstrator contest, June Clark claimed her mink stole and Marjorie Bowser her diamond ring. Distributors who won the "777" competition were shown posing in front of the Eiffel Tower in Paris. To illustrate the distributor revolt's detrimental effects on their ranks, not one of them had been among those initiated into the Gold Lantern Club at the beginning of the year. For Wise, there wasn't much time for introspection; Tupper had all that new production capacity to keep busy. As always, that meant the pressure was on to create more contests, recruit more dealers, and spread the good news of Poly-T.

The public relations department had done its job, scoring a write-up in the January 1956 issue of *McCall's* magazine. In an article entitled "Mrs. Carmony Goes to an All-Girl Convention," writer Eleanor Pollack examined through the eyes of a typical Tupperware dealer, Margaret Carmony of Portland, the experience of traveling to Florida for THP's unique brand of motivation by way of the heartstrings.[1] That write-up helped boost the company's ongoing "Red Carpet" campaign to recruit new dealers. "The first person to call as a result of the *McCall's* article was recruited and held her first Tupperware party only four days later," wrote distributor Jack Gibson from Atlanta, adding, with a generous dollop of hyperbole, "The Red Carpet campaign is the most stupendous thing that ever happened to us."[2] Across the country, distributorships held so-called Red Carpet assemblies where loyal foot-soldier dealers promised to work toward making manager and bring in new recruits to take their places.

Back at the home office, Wise manned the bank of phones on her desk, taking calls from distributors. Her secretary, Mary Frances Babb, brought in telegrams from around the country. "Mary Frances just brought this telegram in from Mildred Schaefer and the news is so hot the paper is scorched," Wise recounted in the February 1956 issue of *Sparks*. "It says "18 Red Carpet recruits.'"[3] Deep down, Wise had to be hoping that the enthusiasm that met this campaign throughout the country could help turn around the disappointing sales numbers of 1955.

On February 27, 1956, *Newsweek* featured a prominent photograph of Wise and a quote from her in an article about the trailblazing women starting to emerge in top corporate jobs. By that time, the magazine reported, 3 million American women carried union cards. Retailer Montgomery Ward had 65 percent women on its payroll. Every single one of its 568 store managers across America was a man. It could be argued that Wise kept the glass ceiling for women in place by promoting men to the key executive positions around her at THP. But that could also be attributed to the lack of women qualified to fill key roles. "The discovery that women are people," RCA's chairman David Sarnoff told *Newsweek*, "is being extended and opportunity for women should expand with it."[4] The article noted that men often were not chivalrous toward women in business dealings—quite the opposite; traditional antagonism toward women in the workplace was common. One former THP secretary during this era noted that attitude at the Kissimmee home office: "Men resented Brownie's position and resented working for a woman."[5]

From Earl Tupper himself on down, the men of Tupperware Home Parties knew that if you took issue with Brownie Wise, you did so at your own peril. Tony Ponticelli noted a "certain look" she would get on her face when you were "treading on thin ice."[6] When Hamer Wilson ordered some landscaping changed without her consent, she put a stop to it. Then, to emphasize her unhappiness with him, Wise took Wilson for a walk. "She cut him down real bad," Jerry Wise recalled. "When they came back, he didn't look so good."[7] During one of the brainstorming sessions at Water's Edge, a disagreement between

Wilson and Wise became so heated that Jack Marshall all but carried him out of the house.

According to her son, Brownie Wise thought Wilson was arrogant, to the point that she didn't even like the way he walked. "Like he had a post lying across his shoulders, like a little prize fighter," Jerry Wise recounted. "Brownie hated that."[8] Those who knew him said Wilson resented Wise because she "started believing her own publicity."[9] The friction could have also come from the fact that Wilson's star was on the rise and that he got on well with distributors, which Wise could have seen as a potential threat to her own position.

As he grew closer in business dealings with Wise, Ponticelli said he tried to warn her not to take all the positive press and ego gratification too seriously. It came after Wise and the public relations men finished courting a writer from *Redbook* magazine. "I'm listening to what I call ego inflation," Ponticelli recalled. "I said, 'You know, Brownie, I hope you don't believe those things that you see. Coming from New York, you have to do that for the public and the press . . . but don't ever believe what you read,' and left it at that."[10] Part of the reason Ponticelli said he was hesitant to go further was the "thin ice" look Wise gave him in return. Her son insisted Wise only put up with the publicity because it was a necessary tool to help recruit dealers and publicize Tupperware. Because of the great benefits and business the coverage reaped, Gary McDonald said Wise could be forgiven if her ego did get inflated: "I'm not sure I know of anybody who would be so selfless that [if] they were subjected to that much adoration, praise, and publicity that they would not start believing it."[11]

For her part, Wise often wrote and spoke of forsaking personal gratification for the good of the whole, and remaining humble even in times of great success. To remind herself of that point, Wise liked to climb into Jerry's small motorboat and steer it over to an undeveloped island in Lake Toho. "I have christened it, *Isla Milagra*, the Miracle Island," she wrote.[12] Local legend had it that hundreds of years ago the Seminole and Calusa tribes had stashed their women and children on the island during times of war. Wise envisioned building a homestead on the 130-acre expanse, planting citrus, and raising cattle and chickens. Strolling alone in the evenings through the untamed flora and fauna, Wise could marvel at the foreboding thunderheads that rolled in over the lake.

Wise wrote: "Lightning streaks across the great dark bowl of sky ripping it open with a gash . . . then a ponderous roll of thunder will crash against the land and water . . . continuing one roll upon the other. Powerful, echoing notes of nature's wildest music. It does me good to watch a storm on the island. To listen to it. For in the midst of it I am always reminded of God's strength and man's frailty. It is good sometimes for us to be reminded!"[13] And it was in that moment, Wise wrote, that she recognized the limitations of her own existence: "I stand under the great umbrella of night sky, on which a million stars are twinkling, and I stand there long enough to absorb the vastness of the universe. I feel small again . . . and it is good that I do!"[14]

Wise had an abiding faith in God, her son said, but her spiritual nature didn't stop there. According to Jerry, his mother would walk through cemeteries and actually thought she could communicate with the dead—people like her grandmother, who'd been so influential molding young Brownie's strong work ethic, her practicality, and her fierce independence. Her grandmother had instilled the notion of giving something back, "paying for our room on Earth."[15] Wise had big plans for her island paradise: "It is my special wishing place that I expect to share with the working wishers of the world."[16] She embarked on an effort to buy the secluded property from Dick Makinson, owner/operator of Florida's oldest hardware store, located in downtown Kissimmee.

The mood among THP brass brightened further in April when Florida governor LeRoy Collins agreed to speak at the company's fifth birthday celebration. To mark the important milestone, Wise commissioned the baking of what was thought to be the biggest cake ever baked in Florida. Looking like a replica of the headquarters building, it measured 3½ feet by 10 feet and weighed seven hundred pounds. A special tank made to look like the reflecting pond in front of headquarters served as the punch bowl.

After the U.S. Supreme Court struck down segregation in 1954, historians credited Florida's Governor Collins with being "cool while the rest of Dixie appeared to be burning."[17] Like Wise, Collins was an expert communicator and the first Florida governor to actively court the press. On April 19, 1956, Wise introduced him to a crowd of five hundred invited guests, dignitaries, and Florida Tupperware dealers, managers, and distributors. After posing for photos and cutting the massive cake with a beaming Brownie Wise, Collins congratulated the company for its success. PR man Glen Bump led the crowd in a rousing rendition of "Happy Birthday." Collins then moved to the Garden Pavilion, where his speech was carried live on local radio stations. Despite the high honor and validation a visit from the governor brought, Earl Tupper did not attend.

As a companion contest to celebrate the fifth birthday month, Wise encouraged all dealers who held five parties in a day to call collect and let her know. If that wasn't frenetic enough, some held seven daily parties. In Silver Springs, Maryland, homemaker Myrtle Scharfenburg held five in one day—with six children under twelve at home. THP had come up with another powerful incentive to spur on the sales force. The 1956 jubilee would be in July, and the company had already secured big-name talent like crooner Rudy Vallee. "Outstanding achievements by dealers and managers will be suitably rewarded by the presentation of awards, trophies and prizes" read an article in *Tupperware Sparks*.[18] "You'll thrill again to a brilliant fireworks display as the sky explodes in beauty. You'll be in the movies too. Yes, there'll be another Jubilee movie made this year. And the highlight of everything will be wish granting! Such excitement, such suspense! There's never been anything like it!"[19] All the dealers had to do to gain entry to such an extravaganza was recruit one new person between May 1 and June 9.

Back home at Water's Edge, seventeen-year-old Jerry seemed to take a special pleasure in goading his mother with practical jokes and salty language. It was all Tupperware's photographer Jack McCollum and Brownie could do to get Jerry to pose for publicity photos: in a bathrobe shaving, tooling around the lake in a boat with his mother, watching admiringly as she pulled something delicious from the oven, sitting opposite her on horseback. After Wise injured her back, her son says she had to wear a brace and often found such photo sessions painful. "They wanted it to look like she oversaw everything," Jerry remembered.[20]

Late at night, as his mother sat on her bed typing letters and talking into her Dictaphone in a nightshirt or some other form of undress, Jerry liked to creep in and threaten to snap a photo of his own. "She said, 'Don't you know how to knock?' I said, 'No, I sure don't; can I take the picture now?'" Jerry reminisced.[21]

"Here I am in all my glory," she groused, "and my only child comes sneaking in to my room . . . NO, and that's final!"

Jerry snapped the shutter anyway, prompting his mother to chase him all the way out of the house. She finally caught up to her son, retrieved the camera, and popped it open.

"Where's the film?" she demanded.

"There wasn't any in it. I was just kidding," he replied.

Jerry chuckled, "Oh, she was mad, and she said, 'I want a hot cup of coffee with half and half, and I want it now!'" Only a woman with the energy of Brownie Wise could drink coffee late at night as a sedative. "Oh, she loved it," her practical joker son said.

Wise had a practical-joker side of her own, once having a pair of newly dead timber rattlesnakes brought into the house and placed on the table just to scare the hell out of her dinner guests. "She loved to eat rattlesnake, especially fried," said Jerry, "but she hated to clean 'em."[22]

Months before the July jubilee, Wise was able to make one of her own special wishes come true. At a law office in downtown Kissimmee, she signed her name to deed papers making the Lake Toho island her own. Wise was elated. "You don't just buy an island like you do a bag of groceries or a keg of nails," she remarked. "Bells ought to ring. Flower petals should drift down from somewhere. Banners should unfurl. Something besides signing a paper should open the door to the magic of owning an island!"[23] True to her word, Wise populated the island with a small herd of purebred Brahman cattle. Jerry and a buddy named John Smithell took charge of the animals and thirty-five acres of citrus already growing there.

Tupper and Wise exchanged ideas about using the island property for Tupperware functions. In lieu of paying Wise an increase over her $31,800 annual salary, they considered the possibility of the company compensating her $10,000 per year to lease the property. That way any improvements she made to the island for possible company use could come out of that pot of money. It's not clear if the two ever came to any formal conclusion; as was their custom up until that point, they often carried on phone conversations rather than putting anything in writing. The same murky business arrangement was true of the Water's Edge home and property. Wise would come to regret not getting important business matters between herself and Tupper in writing. For the time being, she had many other ambitious ideas on her agenda.

In 1956, Wise embarked on the idea of writing a kind of inspirational self-help book she could use as another promotional vehicle. She contracted with a writer named Robert Froman to help her ghostwrite the book she planned to call *Best Wishes*. She asked Norman Vincent Peale to write a foreword, and he agreed. Wise planned to send the book to some of the biggest newsmakers and newsmen of the day.

What woman in 1956 could be more qualified to write a book about wishes coming true? Through boundless ambition, tireless work, and endless travel, Brownie Wise had transformed her life into what Hibiscus had always written about—minus a loving man with whom to share her home. In a decade, she had risen from a government secretary with limited education to a tycoon in June Cleaver pearls. And she had done it in what was decidedly a *man's world*, 1950s America.

She could be forgiven the presumption of wanting to gain the publicity a book would bring, even more than the substantial amount she was already getting. Brownie Wise had plenty to say, and with her considerable skills as a writer and communicator, this book could tell people a lot, women especially. She had drawn up the blueprints for feminine success on no one's terms but her own. That was her legacy to the untold number of women who would follow a similar path in the latter half of the twentieth century. After Frank Stanley Beveridge tried to throw water on her ambition, Brownie Wise now had the brass ring; the hands-off confidence of Earl Tupper, glamorous luxury cars, a spacious estate, a movie star's persona, the admiration of thousands, and a miracle island to call her own. Yet she retained her old-school values and never forgot the things her grandmother taught: the love of music, culture, and creativity; a forward-thinking attitude about race relations; and an indomitable spirit. In myriad ways, Brownie Humphrey Wise was far ahead of her time. These days, some sort of biographical book is all but expected of someone who has a significant following in fields like business, media, or entertainment.

In 1956, the *Houston Post* writer Napoleon Hill wrote this about Wise in his Science of Success column: "It has been estimated that Brownie Wise has helped more women to financial success than any other single living person. Moreover, she has proved that no matter what problems face a woman, there is a way to solve them through courage and humor."[24] Those words may well have been regenerated straight from a THP press release, but it was still a sign of how writers of the day were beginning to see the significant role Wise had already played for women in American business.

On May 25, 1956, Brownie and Jerry celebrated their birthday. At eighteen, Jerry was living a kind of idyllic life, parts of which he would look back on with great fondness. At times, he had to deal with his alcoholic father, the boredom of playing Tupperware poster child, plus his mother spending a lot of time away. Nevertheless, at eighteen Jerry enjoyed being a young rancher—riding by the compass for miles on the plentiful central Florida rangelands, looking after a herd of cattle and some of the day-to-day operations at Water's Edge. Anywhere, he was instantly recognized and treated by many as a celebrity. Jerry Wise was also around to witness the birth of an extraordinary company and all the things it did to wow its sales force and the American public.

"When you live it, you don't think it's unusual," he reflected. "It's just what happened during my life. There were times when Tupperware was very exciting."[25]

In June, Jerry and his friend John Smithell signed on for a six-month stint in the army, followed by seven-and-a-half years in the so called "ready reserve." The program, available to young men between the ages of seventeen to eighteen and a half, meant Jerry would ship out for eight weeks' training at Fort Jackson, South Carolina. He had graduated from the Seese School and hoped the military training would come in handy. Brownie was sad to see her son go, but she made sure his enlistment grabbed headlines in the Kissimmee paper.

"From the employer's point of view," she told them, "it's much more desirable to hire a young man who has served his time in the Army than one who may be drafted at any time."[26] He would ship out just after THP's jubilee. For some unknown reason, in two articles of that time period, Wise referred to both Jerry and his friend as her "two sons."

Wise continued the wishing theme for the first-ever July jubilee, calling it "Treasurama." In advance of the event, Tupperware dealers and managers had been sent a questionnaire that asked, If dreams were for sale, what would they buy? Seven of the wishes from those questionnaires would be granted. A young beauty queen, Diane Tauscher, was even hired to play the part of Tupperware's wish fairy. A wishing well would also be dedicated in honor of the six thousand people who reportedly sent back answer cards. At the jubilee, they would be asked to line up and drop their dreams down the well inside tiny Tupperware midget containers. Besides the singing of long-time matinee idol Rudy Vallee, NBC radio commentator and reporter H. V. Kaltenborn signed on to speak. Both would be carried live on local radio station WORZ. As always, a spectacular fireworks display was sure to draw people from all over the Orlando area. In what became a long-standing summer tradition, for miles, parents and children would pull alongside the Orange Blossom Trail near headquarters and watch.

At 8:30 on Tuesday morning, July 3, 1956, Wise blew the trumpet on the opening of Tupperware Home Parties third annual jubilee, the first held in July. Coming from as far away as Hawaii and Canada, 1,200 dealers and managers had again paid their own way to attend. Greeting the Tupperware pilgrims were twenty-two-foot poles with silk banners, giant tents, pavilions, marquees, and knights on horseback. "Even Mrs. Wise's two sons," noted writer Mari-ellen Kauch, were dressed as "costumed gentry astride gallant stallions."[27] Eight hundred treasure chests were filled with Treasurama prizes: mink stoles, diamonds, coffeepots, and toasters would be given out based on the level of sales achievement. "Two women will be crowned queens," Wise announced, "and they'll get their weight in Tupperware."[28] The seven big winners wouldn't know their wishes were coming true until the moment was just right, and the ecstasy of the person chosen could be maximized.

"Tupperware people take a vacation and talk Tupperware," Wise told the audience in her welcome address:

We *need* work as we need food, human companionship, and divine compassion. Work that is the greatest blessing is that work which we like. Work with people we like, work with things and thoughts and objectives that we like. To this work, we come well. This work blesses us. It gives us confidence. It points a way to growth. That WORK is food and tonic for our spirit and our bodies.[29]

In the spirit of the unity their unique line of work created, hundreds of Tupperware people from across North America recited the company creed:

In the unity of our ideas and our ambitions lies our greatest strength. No exchange offers so rich a compensation as the exchange of thought. A drop of water contains but an infinitesimal molecule of strength . . . powerless in itself . . . but the merging of billions of drops of water produces the tremendous power of Niagara Falls. There is no process, mechanical or mental, that can measure the power our united effort can create.

As a plane flew overhead, pilot Charles Deck gave the "OK" for a thousand cards to be dropped from directly above Tupperware headquarters. Each one had the name of Tupperware's first lucky wish winner. Dealers and their families raced over to where the cards were still fluttering down. A *Life* magazine photograph showed other dealers raising their hands and pointing to Mabel Best, her mouth wide open in amazement. THP had granted the Kansas City Tupperware dealer's wish—an all-expense paid, seven-day trip to help her marine son celebrate his twenty-second birthday in Tokyo. Tupperware included enough birthday cake for the young sergeant's entire company to celebrate. The *Life* spread in August showed Best and her son having just visited the Buddha at Kamakura—a mother and son unexpectedly reunited through the magic of Tupperware.

There were other wishes granted in similarly creative ways: Doris Stewart of Moline, Illinois, saw her name spelled out in fireworks. Her five-year-old daughter, Susan, had dreamed of their entire family taking an air trip to Disneyland in California; now that was coming true. San Diego dealer Kay Tilden watched a Correct Kraft Atom Skier come tearing up the reflecting pond, not knowing it was picking her up. She had wished for an inboard motor boat for her husband. A highway patrolman handed a summons to Mary Smorse of Granger, Illinois. It carried the unexpected news that she was about to have two more rooms added to her home. It had gotten too small for her family of five, and she remarked, "I need more room for my Tupperware."[30] Another dealer watched an hour-long fashion show, only to find out it was all clothing for the new wardrobe she'd requested for her husband. Peggy Allison found out she was getting her wish of a new car, and then the submerged vehicle came floating to the surface of THP's Poly Pond.

All of this razzle-dazzle took long, hard hours to plan and perfect, much of it the handiwork of Tony Ponticelli, Gary McDonald, and George Reynolds. Jerry Wise watched as Reynolds sweated the logistics of submerging an automobile and, when it bubbled to the surface, having it driven up onto a platform. "The pond had to be deepened," Wise remembered, "so the car couldn't be seen."[31] Then, with a wave of Reynolds's hand, the entire display would happen with flawless timing. Pat Jordan was among the young dealers who experienced the wonder of the 1956 jubilee: "I thought wow, wow, there isn't that much money in the whole world because it was all very impressive. It was all show, it was all glitz, it was all glamour, it was all wonderful, wonderful, wonderful."[32] When storms brought heavy rains, Jordan remembered fondly slogging around in the mud with the attitude, "rain or shine, it was just fine."[33]

From a business side, according to McDonald, the big boss Earl Tupper had no problem with the expense of putting on jubilees. "He didn't give a rap about that because it didn't factor," McDonald insisted. "It didn't come out of the profit he was making, and he was making *tremendous* profit. It was like a rocket going off from what he had. It was beyond his imagination and expectation."[34] The rocket ship that was his sales operation would help Earl Silas Tupper realize his wish of becoming a millionaire. "He wasn't that much about money," McDonald said. "I never got the impression it was the important thing. Success was. He wanted to make a mark in life."[35]

Tupper took the fruits of his company's success and made an unusual move. Ever the pragmatist, Tupper looked to diversify his holdings by buying a shoe-heel factory in Maine. Add that to the 67,000-square-foot lab at Branch River, Rhode Island, that Tupper used as a base for all research and design of his products. To meet the demand of his sales division, Tupper invested in fifty more molding machines for the Blackstone plant, making it the "largest injection molding facility under one roof in the world."[36] Despite the "tremendous profit" Tupper was still able to make, he lived frugally, true to his Old World ways.[37] In 1955, he bought two farmhouses in Smithfield, Rhode Island, and connected them, by building an addition, to form one larger homestead. Despite that, biographer Neil Osterweil reported that a typical Saturday night dinner at the Tupper household for himself, his wife, and five children "might consist of a large bowl of baked beans and nothing else."[38] As time went on, the holdings and money Tupper was able to amass became a source of considerable worry. If something were to happen to him, government estate taxes could devastate all he had worked to build.

At the same time, Earl Tupper's product was helping the thousands selling it to achieve success and realize their own dreams, albeit on smaller terms. "I reached my goal[,] which was owning our own home," Rae Frank wrote from

Rochester, New York," in one year, four months. I think that is wonderful."[39]
Lavon Weber of "Wheatheart Sales" in Wichita, Kansas, wrote that working
in the business with her husband, Bob, had brought them closer together and
improved their marriage. More important, with the money they earned, it was
possible to adopt two children. "Bobby is 4 and Fran is 2 and saying everything," wrote Lavon Weber. "For them we are so thankful."[40]

On fun night at the jubilee, the rain poured down as hundreds of Tupperware
people dined on food catered from Morrison's cafeterias. "You would laugh
and slide around in the mud," Jordan reminisced. "We didn't care if we were
wet and slimy." Elsie Mortland ran the long training sessions teaching dealers the best ways to demonstrate the product, date parties, and sell multiple
Tupperware sets. "I remember taking these copious notes," said Jordan. "I
wanted to get everything down because I was anxious to get home and try all
of these new wonderful ideas."[41]

With all the Treasurama loot passed out, the inspirational talks given, copious notes taken, and memories made, graduation marked the end of what
Wise called their most successful jubilee to date. It had been an emotional
week for Wise herself: preparing for Jerry's army send-off, dealing with the
endless details, and listening to the speech from Reverend James B. Grambling,
a Methodist minister who preached at the church she attended as a young girl.
Now it was time to say good-bye to busloads of Tupperware "family." As staff
members stood assembled on the front steps of headquarters, the Tupperware
choraliers sang "Aloha" across sparkling Poly Pond. From *Tupperware Sparks*:
"Tiny lights on masts of sailboats on Tupper Lake blinked a fond 'til we meet
again.'"[42]

As a final, brilliant piece of recognition for new Tupperware graduates, Don
Hinton typed out press releases and sent them to the hometown newspapers of
every person who'd graduated from the jubilee training programs.

In July 1956, President Dwight D. Eisenhower signed a resolution making "In
God We Trust" the official national slogan. The upcoming election was shaping
up to be a replay of 1952 with the incumbent war hero taking on Democratic
challenger Adlai Stevenson. On August 8, Elvis Presley played two shows to
seven thousand screaming fans at Orlando's Municipal Auditorium. Dressed
in a red sport coat with an upturned collar and a white shirt open to the navel,
his hips gyrating to the music, Elvis represented a threat to the conservative
values of the Old South. In Jacksonville, where Presley played two nights later,
a juvenile court judge warned against his "obscene burlesque dance" and demanded it be toned down. In defiance, Presley wiggled his finger. That same
day, August 10, *Life* magazine hit the newsstands featuring its latest spread on

Tupperware. In full color, readers were treated to the fireworks, frenzy, and sizzlemanship that went into the 1956 Treasurama.

In September, THP kicked off what Wise called "the biggest training program in Tupperware History."[43] The so-called Opp-Hop program would ensure that every dealer could put on the most effective demonstration possible. "Let the SOUND of Tupperware speak for itself," Wise urged, "as you *snap* the Square Seal into place and as the air *hisses* out when you *burp* the round containers! A good demonstration includes these things and a *good demonstration* SELLS Tupperware!"[44] To keep sales on the rebound, Tupperware launched its first national advertising campaign with a full-page color ad in *Woman's Home Companion* and other publications.

In a piece so close to the Farnumsville operation that it was sure to catch Tupper's attention, the *Boston Traveler* afternoon newspaper ran a front-page article on Wise. In what was typical of the flattering, but also sexist, articles of the day dealing with women in business, Wise was heralded as "the housewife's dream come true."[45] Perpetuating the unstated notion that any strong woman in business had to be some sort of man-hating shrew, the article's author noted: "Being one of America's top-flight women executives hasn't turned Brownie's pretty head. She has a sunny disposition that makes people like her as much as she likes them."[46] In October, Wise traveled to Boston to accept the Greater Boston Chamber of Commerce award as "the most outstanding salesman of the year, 1956." A rally crowd of three thousand people watched inside Boston's Symphony Hall as Wise accepted the oversized gold trophy.

"Put your wishes to work," Wise told them, "and you will find your passport to happiness."[47]

"We have heard a great deal about Brownie Wise," remarked the awards chairman, "and feel she has become the nation's leading sales personality."[48]

All of this good news was dutifully written up by THP's public relations man Don Hinton and reprinted under his byline in the *Kissimmee Gazette*. It was a welcome bit of good local news. For days, a deluge of 16.23 inches of rain had left much of downtown Kissimmee underwater.

The honor in Boston became another example of how Brownie Wise the sales personality was starting to compete with and overshadow Tupperware. And that's where Tupper had a problem. "If it didn't have the product and the organization as the major element," remembered Gary McDonald, "that was the thing that bothered him because it was promoting her as opposed to promoting the organization and his product."[49] And that was the crux of what Tupper had told Wise in his 1954 note after the *Business Week* cover story. The photos he liked most showed her holding *Tupperware*. If she was more interested and intent on promoting herself and her own interests, could she be neglecting those of Tupperware?

Her writings suggested Wise was passionate, to say the least, about turning around the sales slump caused by the 1955 distributor revolt. As Wise wrote Tupper, "1956 was a disturbing year for us."[50] But in the fall of that year, Wise told him she felt THP and its distributors experienced a "real settling down" thanks to the company establishing a uniform retail price policy,[51] and a program of prepaying the freight for product shipment. Just because of the distance, some West Coast distributors had to shell out considerably more for freight, causing disagreements about the amount of discount they should receive and the wholesale prices they had to pay. "This was perhaps the biggest single step forward THP has ever taken," she wrote Tupper.[52] Then came the national advertising program for which distributors had been asking. "You could almost *see* the distributors settling back," she observed, "and saying to themselves, 'Well, now, this is going to work after all.'"[53]

Yet behind all of the cheerleading, promotions, and PR, Wise and her staff had to deal with the very real problem of replacing a small but powerful and experienced group of distributors who had left on their own or, like the Blocks, had been kicked out for trying to unionize. That meant trying to squeeze new blood out of the fragile network that remained. "We did everything we could to get the distributors to recommend perspective [*sic*] distributors to us from the manager ranks," Wise recounted, "begged, threatened, cajoled, praised, browbeat. We got more than we had before, but not as many as we needed." Despite sluggish sales during the 1956 Christmas season, Wise sensed "a better spirit in the family. Things were looking up. There was a different feeling, hard to explain or describe, but there."[54]

In a roundabout way, Wise acknowledged that her focus on the dealers and managers who adored her, at the expense of the distributors so vital to the company's growth, had been a huge mistake. It came during one of the executive brainstorming sessions at Water's Edge. "Through the step-by-step process of retracing our history, considering all we had on all levels," Wise wrote to Tupper, "we made a discovery so shockingly stupid it is shameful." What they discovered was that the THP team had gotten away from offering any substantive incentive program to the distributors—those on the highest rung of the actual selling food chain. "We were so involved in fighting the runaway distributors," she reasoned, "out of disgust, perhaps, we discounted the personal (and basically human) needs of all distributors. We simply forgot."[55]

In short, as vice president and general manager, Brownie Wise had forgotten where she'd come from. She had forgotten the angst of leaving Detroit on that snowy morning for Florida and an uncertain future. She had forgotten what it was like to have to hand over the reins of all she'd built there to someone else, in essence making the venture in her new home a do-or-die proposition. Across America, people like Pat and Phil Jordan, Jean and Jack Conlogue, Howard and Anna Tate, Peter and Elsie Block, and many others were pulling their children from school, selling their homes, leaving behind a sales network—another family, really—and heading for parts unknown, to places like Wichita, Cincinnati, Spokane, and Norfolk, to start all over. Perhaps because Wise had been so caught up with the accolades, the island, and the book deal, besides the day-to-day business, she had taken her eye off the ball and forgotten all she had had to endure to make a go of selling Tupperware in South Florida. Perhaps those distributors felt she and THP were leaving them flapping in the breeze, just the feeling that had prompted a furious Brownie Wise to call Earl Tupper that very first time.

For someone as detail-oriented and thoroughly devoted to Tupperware Home Parties as Brownie Wise, this was a most disturbing revelation. She confessed to Tupper:

"Believe me, we were a shocked little circle that night in my living room. I was so dumb-founded that later I couldn't go to sleep. I walked the floor and the garden paths until almost dawn, wondering how we could have been so stupid. Inexpressibly stupid. I discovered the next morning that I hadn't been the only one to do that."[56] While Wise used the word *we*, this was as close as she could come to admitting she was responsible, that when it came to the sales side, the buck stopped with her.

Wise had not forgotten the distributors; she had made a conscious decision, a serious and expensive tactical mistake, to downplay their importance and concentrate on the dealers. She confirmed this thinking in a November 1953 memo to Tupper. "Our customers are actually not our distributors at all," Wise wrote, "but the total number of dealers operating in the field." Her acknowledgment of their role within the growth of the company came only in passing. "It is true that we depend upon our distributors, as other companies depend upon their managers, for general over-all supervision and leadership of the selling, training, and recruiting program," Wise relented, "but our real stock-in-trade is the dealer force itself."[57]

In typical Brownie Wise fashion, she threw herself into building better relationships with the distributor network: "I made telephone calls, I sent complimentary wires, I followed their goals week-by-week, I kept in close touch."[58] It's unclear how much Wise's admission may have weakened her position with Tupper. And who knows what those under Brownie Wise were telling him?

If one thing was certain, Earl Tupper was all business, and the Tupperware distributorships were the heart of that business. The dramatic drop in 1955 sales proved it. In 1956, sales had increased 16.3 percent. That was an obvious improvement from the year previous, but it was clearly not good enough for anyone involved.

That set the stage for all of the dramatic developments of 1957. The revelation that kept Wise up all night would not deter her plans to move forward with a book, or the work she wanted done on the island. She would find time to do the interviews, stay in the spotlight, and steer the company back to healthy profitability. At least one of the executives around her was already starting to see Brownie Wise heading toward professional burnout. To make matters worse, in 1957 Earl Tupper decided he needed to be a lot more hands-on with the Florida operation. The informal phone calls between the two morphed into long, contentious memos. Was Earl Tupper feeling the need to build a paper trail? Despite the problems in 1955 and 1956, Wise had enjoyed the freedom to do pretty much as she wished. When that started to change, she pulled hard at the reins. Deep fissures started to form in the unorthodox business relationship of these two widely disparate personalities. As Brownie Wise had forgotten in 1956 who and what was the heart of the business she loved so passionately, in 1957 she forgot with whom the buck really stopped—who was the ultimate boss, who held the keys to the kingdom of Tupperware. The storm clouds would roll back in, this time unexpectedly.

Soon after, things started to crumble.

Fourteen

Hibiscus, the Sunshine Cinderella

All in all, I feel GOOD about our prospects. I'm not looking forward to a problem-less future for our business; the only business without them is a dead one.
—Brownie Wise

At the beginning of 1957, Tupperware had less than half of the twenty thousand dealers the company still claimed to have in newspaper and magazine articles. In January, the exact number was 8,816, and by February it had dwindled further to 8,391.[1] The numbers showed why there was so much pressure on Brownie Wise and the sales division to seek publicity, recruit, hold contests, and, in essence, keep the workforce interested in selling Tupperware. If those numbers didn't turn around, it would be a pipe dream to expect sales figures to grow. For January 1957, sales totaled $404,360.50 versus $335,919.66 for January 1956. That momentum was tempered by the loss of dealers in February, resulting in a $60,000 sales deficit for the month compared to February 1956. Things were moving in the wrong direction. Tupper asked Wise what he could expect for 1957. "I BELIEVE we WILL do between ten and twelve million," she predicted, "and believe me we're working for twelve or over . . . and I realize full well that this is what we should have done, and what we expected to do last year."[2] Gross sales for 1956 were just over $8 million.

Wise was risking her credibility with Tupper by forecasting a minimum 25 percent increase in sales for the year. THP hadn't done anything close to that since the record expansion year of 1954. In February 1957, her dealer numbers were at the lowest point they'd been in years, and the monthly sales figures reflected it. Wise was going to have to dig in and work harder to prove to herself and Tupper that she could right the ship. She hoped that a particularly brutal stretch of winter weather up North was in large part to blame for canceled parties and dealer drop-off. After making the soul-searching discovery that she had neglected THP's legion of distributors, Wise had come up with a thirteen-point incentive plan to get them back on board. She hoped sales figures would blossom along with the spring thaw.

Wise forged on with plans for her inspirational book *Best Wishes*. In January, she cofounded the Podium Publishing Company in Orlando with PR man Charles McBurney. Wise signed on in the company in an "advisory capacity"[3]; she was putting up her own money to publish the book and planned to donate the proceeds to the local Heart Fund. On her other pet project, Wise discussed ideas for a flag to fly on her new Isla Milagra. The Connecticut artist Jon Whitcomb sent her five pencil sketches: "By the 25th doodle," he wrote, "I decided the ingredients here could be reduced to your initials, one palm tree and an island."[4] Wise had been mulling over a plan to hold at least part of the July jubilee on the island; if that were to be accomplished, a lot of work would have to be done to get it ready.

In the middle of all that, Wise and her executive staff were obligated to fly all over the country for regional Tupperware seminars and jubilees. To congratulate winners of the Opp-Hop campaign, Wise flew to Chicago to celebrate with dealers from Par-T-Wise Sales and their distributor, Joe Hara. Hamer Wilson did the West Coast swing, awarding a Pontiac Catalina to Salt Lake City dealer Rita Richardson and a mink stole to Peggy Graves in Los Angeles, and doing more handshaking and backslapping with Joe and Maure Solari in Portland. Former sales counselors Jack Marshall and Jack McCall had left for the more lucrative job of running their own distributorships. By the time he left, Wise felt her former right-hand man, Jack Marshall, had developed "a superiority complex."[5] Despite the fact that "he was making the same salary I am, a distributorship looked awfully good," Wise noted.[6] Marshall opened "Tropical Sales" in Miami. Jack McCall started "McCall Enterprises" in Fresno.

In Florida, Tupperware employees were coveted by other businesses putting down roots. Just five miles up the Orange Blossom Trail, the Martin Aircraft Company bought five thousand acres on which to establish a new manufacturing facility. That led to a feeling around THP known as "Martinitis." With the lures of higher pay, a thirty-six-hour work week, and other attractive, company-paid benefits, there was always a threat THP employees might choose to leave for greener pastures. "We haven't lost anyone to them yet," Wise assured Tupper, "but there are the usual rumblings."[7]

Brownie Wise had worked hard to expose locals to art and classical music, with mixed results. She opened up Tupperware's Garden Pavilion to hundreds of schoolchildren for a concert by the sixty-piece Florida Symphony Orchestra—believed to be the first symphony concert ever in Osceola County. Entries in the 1956 Art Fund competition garnered little interest during a one-week stand early the following year at the Tupperware Museum. The apathy led Kissimmee's newspaper to run the headline "Culture Comes to City, but City Won't Come to Culture." In a time when influential painters like Jackson Pollock were redefining the parameters of modern American abstract art, entries from like-minded artists left the locals a little puzzled. "Some are inspiring," the Kissimmee newspaperman Max Norris wrote, "some are disturbing, some confusing, some pleasing, and at least one, I found downright uncomfortable."[8]

For yet another incentive campaign, Wise promised to plant a pine seedling on the east end of THP grounds "for each dealer who has opened the new opportunities of Tupperware to a new dealer" during the upcoming April birthday-month celebration.[9] The Orlando photographer Fred DeWitt was hired to photograph Wise as she planted the dealer trees. "She talked to some people on the phone with a shovel in her hands," DeWitt remembered.[10] Though Wise was used to putting in marathon days, it was obvious the long hours were taking their toll. "She seemed very tired," he observed.[11]

Besides doing the pencil drawings for Wise, Jon Whitcomb was a writer responsible for one of the most memorable pieces of journalism and puffery Wise received as head of Tupperware Home Parties. As usual, Wise was able to charm the writer to the point he appeared to be smitten with her, hence the title of the piece, "Sunshine Cinderella." The April 1957 *Cosmopolitan* magazine focused entirely on "Fabulous Florida, America's Lush Playground."

"I was expecting to meet a lady tycoon of the type Rosalind Russell used to play in the movies—brusque, clipped, and dominating," Whitcomb noted in the typical male, let's-size-up-this-career-gal way. "She is small and feminine, a 'charm girl' in the words of one of the prosperous-looking, tanned executives who soon strolled in and joined us. Most of Brownie's aides are males, all singularly well adjusted to taking orders from a woman."[12] Or at least that's how it appeared on the surface. As was also typical of THP publicity, neither the writers nor the company made much effort to shine a little of the spotlight on some of the other key executives who helped grow the company during its "democratic" strategy sessions—or on any distributors who had their own success stories. It was all Brownie, Brownie, Brownie. Whitcomb did make a good attempt to boil down how dealers moved up in the ranks and made better profit margins along the way:

> The dealer persuades a hostess to give a party, for which she receives a present, and the dealer gets a commission. The hostess often winds up as a dealer herself. When a dealer shows her ability to recruit and train others, she becomes a unit manager thereby collecting an additional overriding discount. With still more dealers under her wing she may become a branch manager. Next in line is the franchised distributor, who gets a bigger discount but must warehouse the goods. Dealers buy from the distributors; distributors buy from Tupperware Home Parties Inc. And T.H.P. is the client of the Tupper Company.[13]

Tupper had to appreciate a photograph of Wise with Tupperware showing Whitcomb how to perform the now-famous Tupperware "burp." Whitcomb also made mention of the fact that the Tupperware line at that time exceeded "one hundred different sizes and shapes in several pastel colors."[14] In reviewing how Wise convinced Tupper to switch to home-based parties, no mention was made of the other home-party distributors like Ann and Tom Damigella, who did business directly with Earl Tupper before Brownie Wise came along. In Whitcomb's rewrite of THP history, when Tupper was sold on the home-party method, he told Wise, "Show us how, you're the boss."[15]

There were fawning descriptions of Sunshine Cinderella's home and work lives: "'The boss' sits at a king-sized desk in a luxurious office roughly the size of a basketball court. When I walked in, she was taking calls in rotation from three telephones on her desk." And without a quote to authenticate his assertion, Whitcomb concluded that Wise's secretary, Mary Frances Babb, "feels strongly that her boss is a goddess who can do no wrong." Whitcomb reported that Wise had been offered jobs with six-figure incomes by other companies, "but she plans to stick with the company she built from scratch." Whitcomb credited Wise with designing the headquarters that arose out of a vision Wise described to Tupper. "I looked toward the far side and there it stood," Wise told the interviewer, "It was real to me."

At home, the "boss" and "goddess" was still a regular gal who spent free time polishing stones into rings and earrings, and raising cattle with her hot-rodding, teenaged rancher son. To go along with the Horatio Alger flavor of the article, Wise reportedly got into Tupperware in the first place because Jerry was sickly and Brownie needed money to pay his medical bills. Both Jerry Wise and Gary McDonald said that wasn't true. Wise also received a nice plug for the

Wise loading into the car for one of her many business trips, ca. 1955.

soon-to-be-released *Best Wishes* book. "Wishing," the article quoted Wise, "is the art of reacting to the opportunities your ambition uncovers every day."[16]

Wise and her latest writer/promoter even floated over to Isla Milagra on a power barge, taking with them a truck and a station wagon. "We floated into a landing," Whitcomb noted, "beyond which live oaks dripping Spanish moss formed a tall backdrop." Wandering through acres of old citrus groves and below oak limbs wrapped with tangled growth, Wise remarked: "Isn't it still? I feel secure here."[17]

"Sunshine Cinderella," for better or worse, was another milestone in the ascent of Tupperware and the promotion of Brownie Wise as its star sales personality. More important, the month the article was published, THP picked up 840 new dealers, bringing the total to more than 9,400. The sales numbers followed. In April 1957, THP did $1,029.271.77 in sales, more than a quarter-million dollars better than the year previous, offering arguable proof that puff pieces like the *Cosmo* article reaped high-dollar sales in return. Undoubtedly, some of her underlings at Tupperware who had put in similar hours and days on the road had to bristle at the notion that their success was all due to Brownie Wise. Earl Tupper no doubt would find it hard to swallow that THP was the company Wise built from scratch, and that she was the boss. He was still the president. If anyone was to blame for signing off on putting Brownie Wise on the public relations pedestal, it was Tupper. He had agreed to the idea in 1953 after she convinced him it was the way to go.

The *Kissimmee Gazette* had become a virtual public relations arm for Wise. The local paper dutifully noted the *Cosmopolitan* article, lauding Wise as "our most famous citizen."[18] Commonly referred to only as "Brownie," she made front-page news with civic activities like lighting the Heart Fund torch as publicity chairman for the campaign. Her decision to donate book royalties to the drive brought another article and a glowing quote from her "publishers." "With a heart as big as the company she heads," said the unnamed publishers, "Brownie Wise has become synonymous with 'sincerity' to her constant desire to contribute good to the world about her."[19]

The paper ran a review of *Best Wishes*, but the article had no byline identifying its author. With no mention of Earl Tupper, the piece cast Brownie Wise as a fairy godmother spreading seeds of Poly-T prosperity across the nation: "Beginning with a handful of dealers, Brownie scattered her stardust into the living rooms of America. Her merchandising methods proved sheer magic for the increasing numbers of dealers who saw fantasy fade from wishing and a bright new business emerge."[20] Wise said she compiled *Best Wishes* "because I wanted to share my thoughts on wishing with everybody, and because a number of people had asked me to put them in writing."[21]

Besides the irritation of reading the revisionist history about Tupperware in publicity pieces, Tupper was growing angry that Brownie Wise was spending too much time promoting side projects, like herself, and not Tupperware. In an April 29 memo to Wise, he told her he was embarrassed to read about her book in the *Orlando Sentinel* newspaper seeing as he had not received a copy. "Nor have you seen fit to discuss with me how you wish to handle its promotion through T.H.P.," he complained.[22]

Wise shot back, "NO ONE HAD RECEIVED A COPY."[23] Though the *Sentinel* had mentioned the book was near publication, it was late coming out. Wise explained further that she was trying to have a copy sprayed with a fine gold leafing to send to him. "I wanted to have a copy of *Best Wishes* done like that for you," she told him. After two tries, the company she hired to do the job told Wise the binding wouldn't stand up to that kind of treatment. "An hour after that, you were asking Mary Frances to have a book sent to you," Wise recounted. "I'm sorry. It meant a great deal to me to get that special one for you, but it doesn't matter now."[24]

Her sense of disappointment about *Best Wishes* ran deeper. Wise found the manuscript "disconnected and disappointing."[25] She had hoped to make an inspirational statement with the help of writer Robert Froman, but the two had gotten into a legal dispute about the "interpretation" of their contract. Early in the year, that dispute was the subject of several staff meetings at headquarters. Wise decided to pay Froman $4,000 to make the matter go away.[26] Given that she also cofounded the publishing company under which her book was launched, *Best Wishes* had become a deep money pit. "The book does not have any particular sparkle," Wise confessed to Tupper. "I did not have time to do it myself. It is made up of talks I have given, and therefore it lacks continuity."[27]

Tupper also quizzed Wise on how she planned to spend time promoting the book. Wise told him she had turned down offers for television interviews in Jacksonville, Miami, Saint Petersburg, and Tampa. She did admit signing books for an hour and a half on a Saturday afternoon at an Orlando department store. "THAT CONSTITUTES MY PERSONAL TIME DEVOTED TO THE PROMOTION OF THE BOOK," Wise argued, her tone obviously defensive.[28] "Did you have in mind that I was spending a lot of time on the promotion of something personal?" she quizzed Tupper in her reply memo; "That I was planning to get rich on this book? That I was using the machinery and sales force of THP to increase the book's sales? If so . . . and it sounds that way . . . I'm surprised at you."[29]

From the star-studded list of people to whom Wise wanted complimentary copies of her book sent, she clearly had *something* ambitious in mind for *Best Wishes*.

"I appreciate your sending it to me and your kind inscription," Eleanor Roosevelt said in a thank-you note to Wise.[30] Other copies went to Walt Disney, Edward R. Murrow, actress Jane Russell, Dale Evans, Roy Rogers, Steve Allen, Kate Smith, and Billy Graham. If Wise was looking for a way to increase her profile and fame through publication of her book, these were the people who could help her do it. Contrary to her negative rumination to Tupper, Wise

Brownie Wise at her Water's Edge home, Hibiscus personified, 1957.

obviously felt enough pride in her book to send it to a long list of famous, influential people.

With good reason. While the book may not have carried the "sparkle" of Brownie Wise in person, the text does reflect why she was so good at motivating and relating to the everyday dreams and desires of her workforce. "Believe me, there can be no better thing in life than the ability to wish, sincerely, to improve the world about you," Wise wrote.[31] She lamented that "time saving devices" had not made the world easier, just the opposite: "The key of tension is constantly turning," she wrote, "winding the nervous fibre tighter and tighter, until it frays or snaps completely."

Yet, in *Best Wishes*, Wise testified that she had found her key to happiness: "If you have set a course for yourself and know where you are going—where you should go—you can write your own ticket and find, as I did, that your work is your passport to happiness." She preached patience, determination, curiosity: "You can salvage success," she assured, and get caught in "the quicksand of security." Brownie Wise told the thousands of Tupperware dealers and other women she hoped might be inspired by her words that "a 'working wish' for you is now just the matter of laying out a program. It's simply the practice of taking a goal and breaking it down into the little workable steps of every day, every week, every month, and sometimes even every hour."[32]

One of her motivational mentors, Dr. Norman Vincent Peale, added his endorsement in a foreword to the book: "She loves people and all who work with her share a sense of oneness with her. Having visited Brownie Wise's organization I sensed a pervasive spirit of good will and joy and friendship in that beauty spot in Florida—a business headquarters ostensibly—but in reality an inspirational center as well."[33]

At the time people were reading Dr. Peale's words, the "good will and joy and friendship" Wise had felt toward Tupper and THP staff toward her was starting to show signs of change—for the worse. Wise wrote that she was finding Tupper "edgy and irascible."[34] The once-democratic brainstorming sessions at THP were no longer that way, with Wise turning more autocratic. "She just considered the whole thing her responsibility," Elsie Mortland observed, "and she could do whatever she wanted."[35] For the first time, Brownie Wise saw her leadership undergoing questions and scrutiny. One of her closer associates in the company during that period. Tony Ponticelli, felt Wise was becoming more defensive. For the first time, "doubt was creeping in."[36] Pat Jordan was more blunt. She thought Wise less the fairy godmother that she was portrayed to be in so much adoring publicity and more like the jailed 1980s New York hotelier Leona Helmsley, to many the archetypal female autocrat.

In an attempt to reassure Tupper, and herself perhaps, Wise typed out an impressive thirty-page, double-spaced memo to Tupper entitled "The Business." The epic communiqué dealt with every aspect of THP dealings—her analysis of sales figures, distributor problems and solutions, evaluations of current and former executives, civic activities, and future prospects. It also gives a glimpse into how Wise could adopt a demeaning attitude toward Tupper, yet show him the respect he demanded from other employees. Perhaps it was her attempt to show him she was just as tough as he was. "I should explain first that this is a personal job of typing," Wise told him, "and that I expect to receive the courtesy of having errors over-looked . . . yes, even taken for granted."[37]

Yet her tone softens considerably when bringing up the evolution of the product line the two had dedicated their lives to creating and selling. "I am still amazed every time I go into the consumer's lounge," Wise remarked, "and see the east wall, covered with Tupperware . . . a beautiful sight. . . . I'm still amazed at its beauty, even after a love affair that's eight years old . . . but I'm still amazed at the richness of our QUANTITY, too, every time I see it. How the line has grown! And to think I used to make a living from 16 or 18 Tupperware items. (I don't want to forget that either.) It's a beautiful array, Mr. Tupper. I have never seen a work of art in any museum with more beautiful lines than some of our bowls here."[38]

She talked about THP's public relations program and some of the press suitors to whom the company said no. "We have had the singular good fortune not to have ever been 'panned' in any story," Wise bragged. "Of course, we've been extremely cagey; we've turned down *Fortune* twice; steered clear of *Time* and *Newsweek*, and turned thumbs-down on some TV tie-ins that were tempting in some ways."[39] THP executives felt Lucille Ball creating a madcap situation with Tupperware on her wildly popular *I Love Lucy* show had the potential to be demeaning to the product.

Wise told Tupper her ultimate goal was to be in *Reader's Digest*, a publication of which she had been fond for years. Getting in the magazine proved a lot more difficult than she expected. She remained hopeful, confident, and perhaps a little falsely modest: "I'm told that we'll probably be ripe for it within the year. We found out two months ago that the *Digest* editorial board had been compiling a file on us, and that the *Cosmopolitan* article was particularly impressive to them. Why, I don't know."[40]

Wise ended her long letter on a note of optimism for their sales prospects, but sadness that the nature of their own business relationship had changed. "I miss talking with you on the phone occasionally," Wise lamented, "not about a specific something that demands attention, but just to bring you up to date on how things are going."[41]

Home at Water's Edge, despite all of the friction at Tupperware, Wise had a lot to celebrate. Sales for 1957 were up 23 percent over the year previous, well within reach of her annual projection. A dozen new distributors had already been appointed, bringing the total number to 117, with plans for 15 more by the end of the year. Jerry was back home from his stint in the reserves, and "Tiny Hands" was about to turn nineteen. "My love for you that cannot be measured or defined," Wise wrote her son, "surely it will surround you and warm you every day of your life. The greatest gift of *my* life is that you call 'mother' the woman others call 'Brownie Wise.'"[42] Despite his flair for practical jokes, his salty language, and his rebel attitude, Jerry clearly returned that love for the only parent he'd ever known.

The upcoming July jubilee promised to be the most spectacular yet, with an around-the-world theme. Wise decided to move forward on plans to host a Hawaiian-themed luau on Isla Milagra for many of THP's key distributors, managers, and visiting press. George Reynolds and his work crews spent considerable time clearing land, taming the wild environs enough to make it inhabitable for the big event. There was no running water so teams had to dig deep to create thatch-roofed, outdoor latrines. Transportation would be a problem. Because there were no roads to the island, everyone would have to be brought there by a so-called power squad of local boat owners.[43] Jerry would take others back and forth on the company barge. Special events man Tony Ponticelli was wary of the idea of depending on outside people for transportation. "I didn't approve of the barges and boats. You can't take that many people back and forth," he recalled. "I didn't want anything to do with it."[44]

Wise should have trusted Ponticelli's instincts. But by that time, he and others were cautious about telling her she might be wrong about anything. This would be her chance to share with Tupperware people and the press the untamed jewel that was her miracle island. In the end, it proved to be her Waterloo. Forces out of her control came into play that actually put people's *lives* at risk. Tupper could put up with Brownie Wise questioning his authority or dressing him down in front of others. That's when times were good and money was rolling in. The events surrounding the 1957 luau on Wise's island became by far the biggest blunder of her THP tenure.

Tupper was livid.

JUBILEE
NIGHTMARE

This was a disaster.
—Gary McDonald

During the spring of 1957, Earl Tupper often vented his frustrations about Brownie Wise through conversations with her secretary, Mary Frances Babb. Without the one-on-one phone contact between Tupper and Wise, problems and confusion between the two seemed to become amplified. At the end of May, Tupper told Babb he was upset that Wise was taking so long to give him any feedback on a proposed teething and baby spoon. On May 17, the prototype had arrived in Florida with Tupper's instructions for Wise to give her comments and then return it immediately. "If we move quickly," Tupper advised, "the mold could be completed in about ten weeks."[1]

"At the time the spoon came in, please believe me," Wise wrote back, "we were involved in things that had to be done—right THEN—and it was two days before we got into an actual discussion about the spoon."[2] If this had been some test of her acumen in sizing up a product's usefulness and marketability, Wise appeared, in her memo, to be very much in control, providing detailed analysis of the product's strengths and weaknesses. But it's clear she found Tupper's impatient inquiry troubling. "After all this time," she questioned Tupper, "why do you get annoyed because we keep the sample spoon for a week, trying to make as good a decision on it as possible?"

Surely you must realize that while I don't know a great deal about your production picture, I DO realize molds are expensive . . . and that I, in fact all of us down here, feel a responsibility about advising you to go ahead on a mold without feeling as certain as possible that we can do a good sales job on the product? Don't you want us to look at it that way?[3]

By June, Wise had to turn her attention to readying THP's new "world." For the fast-approaching July jubilee, the theme would be "Around the World in 80 Days."[4] Each Tupperware dealer and manager would be assigned a different destination, depending on the amount of sales achieved. Reynolds and his team produced an ornate Japanese section complete with footbridge, windmills to evoke the flavor of Holland, and grass huts found on the road to Zanzibar. Each port of call had corresponding prizes like fine Irish linens and Hong Kong pewter. For the so-called Around the World Day, attendees would be encouraged to dress in clothes typical of the country for which prizes they had been chosen eligible. "If any of them come into town in their costumes," the *Kissimmee Gazette* noted, "Kissimmee may take on the appearance of a small United Nations gathering."[5]

The grand finale of Around the World Day would be kept a secret. Of course, the local newspaper played along: "The Tupperware crowd will be coming into town on that day to embark on a mysterious boat excursion to some foreign land nearby. Full details have not been divulged, but boat clubs throughout central Florida have been alerted and pressed into service to help transport the crowd."[6]

A new lake and surrounding park would be dedicated on the grounds of headquarters along with a plaque commemorating Tupperware's leading Vanguard Club managers. The Osceola High School band drum and bugle corps would accompany the flag-raising ceremony, and a dedication would be given by Dr. William Kadel of Orlando's First Presbyterian Church. Fireworks would light up the night and draw parents to park their cars along the Orange Blossom Trail in front of headquarters, to watch the bursting colors and wonderment reflected in their children's eyes. As always, the jubilee would be the highlight of the steamy central Florida summer, and the atmosphere promised to be electric. Tupperware's best of the best across the country were bringing the sales numbers back to where Wise and Tupper expected, and they were shelling out their own money to come celebrate. It was a time for motivation and learning—a four-day sales convention celebrating the unconventional. It was wholesome, all-American, and spectacular in a way only Tupperware seemed to know how to do. In many aspects, the nighttime fireworks and around-the-world theme foreshadowed the Magic Kingdom and Epcot, long before Walt Disney put down his own roots on Irlo Bronson rangeland.

Brownie Wise, with her trim physique flattered by tailored summer dresses, perfectly appointed strands of pearls and matching earrings, coiffed pewter hair, and the beaming smile the cameras loved so, would again assume the roles of ever-present First Lady and fairy godmother of Tupperware wishers; she was the Queen of Kissimmee, the Matriarch of Isla Milagra. And, of course, the press would be there to capture it all for the local front pages and the more coveted national publications. William Campbell, publisher of *Cosmopolitan*, was high on the guest list, as was *American Salesman* publisher Michael Gore, and Glen Fouche, vice president of *Parade* publications. With all that star power, tons of attention to detail, and Brownie's island surprise, how could the '57 jubilee be anything but spectacular?

From as far away as Puerto Rico and Alaska, 1,200 dealers, managers, and distributors streamed into headquarters on July 1, to be greeted by such eclectic around-the-world attractions as a five-person human totem pole. "Distributors, costumed with the wings, eagle beaks and horns of such totem poles," commented one writer, "mounted the special telephone totem pole and sat on the perches with remarkable stillness."[7] In the Garden Pavilion, the radiant hostess Brownie Wise engaged in a little horseplay with Herb Young.

"Pay me ten bucks," she ordered. "You bet there wouldn't be a man of distinction at this jubilee and there he is."[8]

It was sales counselor Jack Mann dressed in a mustache and goatee for an occasion as auspicious as the jubilee's opening day. Forced to acknowledge that this was indeed a man of distinction, Herb Young surrendered a ten spot to the woman who always seemed to come out on top. With that, Mann gave Wise a victorious peck on the cheek.

"It tickles," she sparkled as her adoring followers laughed and applauded.

Much of the first two days of the jubilee brought a steady stream of motivational speeches and award presentations. William H. Alexander, an Oklahoma City preacher and host of a nationally broadcast radio show, spoke to the Tupperware faithful about his *Life's Quiz Program*. Arthur Motley amazed the crowd with details of hosting the world's largest sales convention ever carried on closed-circuit television. Other speakers hammered home the secrets to sales success, business philosophy, and advertising. Before too many eyes could glaze over, the next important event in the jubilee was the awards program. Each of the three categories had its own special recognition: leading distributors became part of the Tupperware Lantern Club, managers were welcomed into the Vanguard, and dealers received Merit Awards and $1,000-a-week recognition.

After the speeches and awards, on Tuesday afternoon Tupperware guests fanned out into the nine around-the-world stations to marvel at the exotic handiwork created by George Reynolds and crew, and to collect the gifts they'd labored all year to earn. Charley McBurney assumed the role of cobra-coaxing fakir at the East Indian booth. The human totem pole, in honor of those who had traveled from Alaska, proved to be one of the most popular draws. Amidst the joy and merriment, busses rumbled onto Tupperware grounds to take attendees to their mystery trip. The atmosphere was heavy with anticipation and the ever-present humidity of a sultry July day in central Florida.

The long bus procession rolled five miles south down the Orange Blossom Trail to the Tohopekaliga lakefront, arriving by three in the afternoon. An armada of boats from the Winter Garden Boat Club, the Tohopekaliga Yacht Club, the Orange Boating Club, and other private owners waited to perform transport duty. Dick Makinson, the man who sold Isla Milagra to Brownie Wise, hauled his boat out of retirement. *The Venture*, long a fixture in the Kissimmee Boat-a-Cade, got a fresh coat of paint for the big affair. Jerry Wise was there to take people to and from the island on the Tupperware power barge. At least fifty rumbling boats in all were needed in the "power squad" to get the large assemblage of Tupperware guests to their mystery destination.

McDonald, Reynolds, and Glen Bump had done a great deal of research into how to transport more than a thousand people on the water. The Coast Guard in South Florida told them they were too busy to participate. The executives even looked into whether a landing craft, like those used by the marines to transport troops, could do the job. That didn't work out either. Finally, the Tupperware team sent out invitations to dozens of Kissimmee-area boat owners. In return for participating, the boat owners would get to take part in that evening's mystery gala event.

In the steamy temperatures hovering past ninety degrees, the cool breeze and occasional water spray were welcome relief to the hundreds of guests, many of whom had already been out in the heat for several hours. Hamer Wilson, who had spent ten years as a meteorologist for Eastern Airlines, took note of a bank of thunderheads off in the distance. "The storm was well away from there," Wilson remembered, "considerably so."[9] Isla Milagra sat toward the south end of the 23,000-acre lake. As the island grew closer, revelers could make out stands of bald cypress, Carolina willow, and red maple trees. Shades of deep green from the tropical overgrowth reflected in the water.

A line of homegrown, faux-Hawaiian hula girls shook their grass skirts and showed off the dance prowess they had spent weeks perfecting. More girls welcomed each guest with a paper lei and the traditional Hawaiian "aloha" greeting. It promised to be an over-the-top Tupperware night; guests sipped punch and watched entertainment and hijinks on a thatched stage, the cooking operation already in high gear. Morrison's had been planning for months how to feed a small army in such a remote place. The barge had been used to haul in tons of ice. Eight hundred live, wriggling lobsters were flown in from Maine; there were just as many baked chickens and fresh pineapples, as well as two thousand ears of baked corn. The low tables were decorated with bananas, tropical mangoes and papayas. In true Polynesian fashion, a suckling pig was prepared in a ground oven. For their meal served under the stars, guests were encouraged to feast in island style, with no spoons, knives, or forks.

Resplendent in her aqua Hawaiian *holomuu* decorated with purple figures, a flowered skirt dusting the ground, and two orchid leis adorning her neck, Brownie Wise was finally living the dream of sharing her island with the Tupperware family. "Isn't it wonderful?" she asked. "Each year is the best and each year is better."[10] Most of the THP top brass were there, too, including Wilson, McDonald, and Mortland. Tony Ponticelli decided he wanted nothing to do with crossing such a big lake on someone else's small boat. Two photographers often used by Tupperware, Jack McCollum and Fred DeWitt, trudged off boats with their camera equipment. With so many people to feed and the luau already starting late, it would be a challenge to keep the affair on schedule.

The crowd of hundreds indulged in the food by hand and then mopped themselves up with warm towels. Following the hearty meal, grand prizes were awarded to some of Tupperware's top performers of the year. With the partygoers enjoying the family spirit, good times, and great food, the hours slipped past quickly. "Nobody wanted to go home," remembered McCollum.

This event was unusual because it was not on company grounds per se and so many people outside the Tupperware family were included. THP had asked the boat drivers not to drink during the party, but there was no way to enforce that request. As they waited for the party to end and their passengers to return, some drivers in the so-called power squad were drinking. McCollum, who had driven his own boat to the luau, felt some of the drivers were drunk.[11] All had been instructed to drive in a large, counterclockwise circle around the island to keep the water route safe and the departure orderly. The THP team handed out maps.

When the atmosphere inland is rich with humidity, and the cooler, late-afternoon sea breezes start to blow in off the Atlantic, the meeting of those two

forces can quickly produce very large thunderheads. It's a summer phenomenon in central Florida by which you can almost set your watch. If it happens
in the middle of the night and you're sitting on an island with no cover, it can
be dangerous. That worst-case scenario came true on the night of July 2, 1957.
Storms brought with them wind, lightning, and rain. There weren't enough
boats to get people off the island quickly and back to safety.

"At first they were anxious to get off the island," remembered Wilson, "and
when we found out they were going to have to wait for the boats, a great number of them sat down on logs and visited."[12] Some, still infused with the spirit
of the evening, broke into Tupperware songs. As the night gave way to deep,
dark early morning, the number of boats returning from shore grew fewer and
fewer. Anxious to get people to safety, McDonald considered a small house and
two cabins on the island for cover: "We contemplated the possibility of having
them bunk in the three houses over there if things were such that it was impossible to get them back."[13] By several estimates, there were 1,200 people on the
island and not nearly enough boats to get them to dry land.

Jack McCollum put Wise and her secretary on his boat. Passage was so slow
and the water so choppy that he was practically idling. Storm clouds had obscured the moon, making the water route almost pitch-black. To help guide the
way, McCollum gave another passenger a flashlight and instructions to stand at
the front of the boat. Of Wise, McCollum said, "I think she was concerned, but
she didn't show it."[14] A long line of guests and Tupperware employees remained
on the island, waiting their turn.

Boat owner Bill Boyd had room for four passengers but was taking as many
as nine. "The people were crowding in and the boats were way over loaded,"
Boyd said. "That is one advantage of that bailer on there, it kept the water
pumped out, we had quite a bit of water coming over one time with seven people and one time with nine."[15] The effects of the alcohol they had drunk, along
with the elements, caused the boat drivers to stray from the longer, circular
route they had been instructed to take, making the dark waters more dangerous. "We could see some lights on the water which indicated there was some
so-called hot rodders," Glen Bump said, "driving their boats in an irresponsible
fashion."[16] Some drivers decided there was too much risk and went home, putting even more pressure on those remaining to help get stranded people off the
island.

Gerry Croxton, a forty-four-year-old shop manager at Autrey Motors, continued to make runs in the darkness. He'd lived on the lake for thirty years and
his wife, Thelma, said Gerry could "run it blind," if need be.[17] The rain came in
showers, with flashes of lighting and occasional thunder. Despite the danger,

this night was so dark that Croxton insisted on his wife accompanying him back and forth. "I needed her eyes," Croxton recalled.[18]

On the west side of the island, Croxton and his wife picked up two older women and began to depart. Croxton stood to the back of the boat, steering with his left hand, steadying himself on the boat's awning with the right. The three women, including his wife, sat at the front. Gerry Croxton said later he spied another boat headed right for his stern, and there was no time to avoid it: "I tried to go with it is all I could do."[19] The boat plowed into the back of Croxton's craft, tearing the engine to pieces and catapulting him into the water. "I don't remember him [the other boat driver] ever hitting the boat," Croxton said later. "I remember him coming and the next thing I knew I was in the water."[20] The women passengers were not thrown from the boat, and Thelma Croxton tried unsuccessfully to throw her husband seat cushions.

As Bill Boyd drove by, it was only by "a sudden flash of lightning" that he saw Croxton in the water.[21] Boyd jumped in. "I just held him up and he was moaning and groaning," Boyd remembered. "I tried to talk to him but he was out of his head."[22] Another boat came along whose driver helped Boyd hoist the injured man aboard. It was Kissimmee's chief of police, Bob Best. Boyd treaded water into the reeds, where he was able to climb back on board his own boat.

When Croxton was brought to the dock in Kissimmee, Dr. M. L. Jewell triaged him. "He had a puncture wound of the chest and bleeding," the doctor said.[23] Jewell sent the seriously injured man to the hospital via ambulance. Croxton wasn't the only person injured that night. Jewell remembered routing as many as twenty-one people to the hospital because of accidents and other issues related to the luau.

"You could hear all this crashing, and you knew what it was," remembered Jerry Wise, "There were some real seriously hurt."[24] As Wise piloted the barge back to the city dock in Kissimmee, he saw an ominous sign: two ambulances waiting on shore. One had been there on standby the whole night; Jewell had ordered the other brought down to deal with the excess patients. Unaware of what was going on, Wilson and McDonald had stayed behind to get people off the island. Brownie Wise had already headed home.

Boyd finally picked up his wife, Mary, and the last load of island passengers at three-thirty in the morning. Croxton had serious internal injuries to the chest and leg. Another man who worked at a local boat dealership, Rudy Crews, was suffering from internal bleeding. In the wake of the accidents, both underwent surgery.

Once the shock of the events started to wear off, McDonald realized this could also be a public relations nightmare. For a teetotaling, family-oriented, all-American company that prided itself on no negative publicity, it could all be washed away in the events of Tuesday, July 2. How would it look if the local and national press spun the story that several people had been injured after an all-night booze bash at the Tupperware Queen's personal island? "We did everything we could to make it go smoothly," McDonald remembered, "and unlike other times when we had people go into town and it turned out great, this was a disaster."[25] Tony Ponticelli's instincts had been right. "These are individuals with their own boats, and you have no control over them except they're doing you a favor," he said.[26]

Elsie Mortland had been stranded on the island with her sons, John and Larry, until two in the morning. She was angry at Wise. Why did she let the party go on so long? Couldn't she tell a big storm was brewing? With all of the planning and expense that had gone into throwing the elaborate luau, why had she chosen to ignore the weather? And where was she while all hell was breaking loose on her island? On Jack McCollum's boat heading for dry land long before many of her guests. It seemed as if Brownie Wise had ignored her better instincts and chosen her own needs before those of friends and coworkers. She left to others the job of deciding how to get the rest of her guests off the island and to safety.

According to her son, Wise was wracked with guilt over what had happened. Croxton was an acquaintance with whom she had spoken many times when taking vehicles to the Autrey Ford dealership for service or repairs. She knew his participation in her party had left him seriously injured. Jerry Wise, in a voice cracking with emotion, remembered how responsible his mother felt. "Oh sure she did. . . . That was bad times."[27] Her attitude at THP was another matter entirely. Of the luau and the accidents that resulted, Tony Ponticelli said, "She wouldn't admit that was a big mistake."[28] According to Elsie Mortland, "She wanted to sweep it under the rug and let it be gone."[29] Don Hinton said Wise didn't find out about the accidents until the next day. He blamed drinking boat drivers for the accidents rather than the weather or lack of foresight from Wise. But ultimately, her former public relations man and strong ally acknowledged that that buck stopped with Brownie Wise.

For the first time, McDonald and the PR staff would have to attempt to do damage control. George Reynolds, a gregarious and popular personality, went to the Kissimmee newspaper. Don Hinton appealed to editors in Orlando. It was time to call in some of the bargaining chips Tupperware had earned through all of its goodwill and good deeds in central Florida. According to McDonald, their appeal boiled down to this: "We would appreciate if you don't sensationalize because it was an unfortunate accident. We know it has to be in your paper, but as little space as you can give to it, we'll appreciate it."[30]

The approach worked. The July 4 edition of the *Kissimmee Gazette* read like an issue of *Tupperware Sparks*. Photos splashed on the front page showed the human totem pole, the hula dancers on the island, Charles McBurney and the girls at the East Indian booth, Brownie Wise beaming like a prom queen next to one of the jubilee VIPs, and Dick Makinson's newly unretired boat, *The Venture*.

Coverage of the luau painted it as a smashing success: guests had feasted on a traditional Hawaiian meal and sipped "non-alcoholic" punch.[31] The Tupperware magic was intact, its reputation unsullied. Buried within the body of the newspaper were the articles making mention of people who'd been hurt in a boat accident. But the incident was in no way connected to Brownie Wise and Tupperware. The one-inch story about Rudy Crews undergoing surgery was dwarfed by an article and photo of local teen Jack Crum headed to a baton-twirling contest in Binghamton, New York.

In a large ad that ran one week after the accidents, while the victims were still recovering from their injuries, Brownie Wise said this about the 1957 jubilee:

TO OUR FRIENDS AND NEIGHBORS IN THE KISSIMMEE AREA:
Thank you, most sincerely . . . for helping us make our homecoming Jubilee the most enjoyable and successful ever!
Because of your cooperation, participation and the genuine enthusiasm of our community, we were able to display to the nation the kind of hospitality for which Central Florida has become famous.
Once again . . . the kindness and generosity you continue to show our people has made the members of the Tupperware family feel proud and happy to call this part of Florida their second home.
Thank you each and every one!
Best Wishes,
Brownie Wise

Wise had gotten her own wish; the miracle island blunder didn't become fodder for the press she was so adept at courting. And the goodwill Tupperware had built in central Florida helped keep the company image intact. "We were good to both cities; I mean, we did all sorts of things," reasoned Gary McDonald. "I ran the first million-dollar United Appeal Orlando ever had. We had people in Kissimmee doing all sorts of things. We were good citizens."[32]

Wise would not get off so easy with Earl Tupper. He came to Florida to assess the impact of the accidents, and what insurance coverage might be needed if the company planned to continue to have an association with the island and transporting people to and from it. Elsie Mortland witnessed his fury and disgust over a picture that showed a boat on the way to the luau, overloaded and listing dangerously to one side. "You see the foolish things people do?" he asked Mortland. Tupper pointed to the photograph. "See all those distributors? We could have been out of business."[33]

On Tuesday July 16, 1957, the Kissimmee city commission adopted a new boat-speed ordinance. Kissimmee police chief Bob Best, who had also driven during the Tupperware luau and had helped get Gerry Croxton to the hospital, asked the city to provide a boat and motor to his officers so they could enforce it.

Brownie Wise had given Earl Tupper another reason to look more closely at the sales operation and to question her decision making and commitment to the business. Their already testy relationship was deteriorating. After the 1957 jubilee boat accidents, their own collision course was set.

Sixteen

THE BREAKING POINT

Earl was either high on a person or very quickly wanted to pull the rug out from under them.
—Ed Creiger

After the July boat accidents on Lake Toho, Earl Tupper decided he needed to keep closer watch on the Florida operation. "He was very, very suspicious of Brownie," said Tupper's longtime accountant Ed Creiger. "Once she started to divert her attention away from business, he never knew what was coming next."[1] Some of those who were close to Wise felt Tupper's problems with her weren't about business at all but, rather, ego. "He was jealous of her," said Don Hinton, "because she was the queen of Tupperware and he was nothing. He did not get publicity because he didn't want it."[2] Despite the boat accidents, Wise felt she had built a tremendously successful sales operation with little or no help from Tupper, and who was he to come in now and start making demands?

From his Branch River Lab in Woonsocket, Rhode Island, Tupper wrote Wise, "You may feel that all of a sudden I'm asking a lot of questions about a lot of things."[3] He went on to list four reasons: a need to be better informed on the "financial end"; a need to reduce expenses "that do not directly bring in sales"; a general reduction in "all liability risks" in the wake of the boat accidents; and his constant worry about the "probability of increasing income tax rates."[4] Since Tupper owned all the stock in the Tupper Corporation, his tax experts told him the government considered it a "one-man" business.

179

"If I had died," Tupper wrote, "then the government would have arbitrarily valued my estate for at least 20 times earnings and it would have been taxed at 77 and-a-half percent. It would have destroyed my entire estate."[5] Tupper's solution was to quietly start shopping his company to interested suitors.

Wise felt the source of Tupper's edginess was that all his time, effort, and expense were being spent on a newly acquired plastic shoe-heel manufacturing business in Maine, Footwear Plastics Corporation. "This necessitated his moving equipment, personnel, and material to that location from Woonsocket, and during several months he spent considerable time back and forth between the locations," Wise wrote. "The shoe heel business folded in August, after much dissention with the people he had in charge." Wise did not or would not acknowledge Tupper's problems were also with her. "He was edgy and irascible during the months from April to September or October when I spoke to him on the 'phone," she recalled, "but not especially about anything concerning the Florida operation."[6] That was the same time period in which Tupper had been concerned about Wise's ability to bring sales numbers back around and had been infuriated about her book, the luau disaster, and the resulting legal exposure.

In September and October, Tupper and Wise seemed to enjoy a relative thaw in their frosty relations. THP continued its push to reach the ambitious sales goals Wise had outlined to Tupper earlier in the year. Thanks to the company's relentless recruiting programs, for the first time all year the number of Tupperware dealers once again surpassed ten thousand. At the end of October, Tupper made a scheduled visit to Florida. "He was not at all unpleasant to me on the occasion," Wise remembered.[7] Tupper made the trip to see if he might be able to recoup out of the ever-profitable sales side the $85,000 he had lost on the shoe operation. Wise and THP no longer enjoyed carte blanche on their own expenses. At the end of October, accountant Dave Seraphine reported to Wise that expenses for 1957 were up $22,000 over the year previous, not an unreasonable increase. For all THP did to promote, reward, recruit, train, and advertise, Wise was known to refer to the amount spent as "hairpins and Kleenex money."[8]

The final rift between Tupper and Wise started to form in November 1957. Tupperware had skirted responsibility for the boat accidents in the public eye, but not in courts of law. Gerry Croxton sued Tupper and Tupperware for $150,000, claiming he had suffered permanent injuries to his kidneys, ribs, hip, and lungs. He argued that there had been no lights in the water at the time of the crash, the company had done no screening of the boat operators to determine if they were fit to be entrusted with the lives of their passengers, and there had been no specific and enforced directions for the boat drivers to take. His suit also claimed that the boat operators operating under the auspices of Tupperware Home Parties Inc. failed to have their boats under control, failed to keep lookout for others in the water, failed to give warning signals of their approach, and failed to follow proper rules of navigation. To make matters worse, during the seven weeks Croxton spent in the hospital, he earned no money. Upon his return, Croxton was so hobbled by his injuries that he was essentially demoted from service manager to mechanic. The suits also alleged that for some unknown reason, prior to the luau, Tupper had canceled the insurance policy intended to provide coverage for the boat excursions.[9] That became a major point of contention as the suits wound their way through the courts.

William Boyd, along with his wife, Mary, filed a similar suit for $151,000. Boyd claimed he suffered back problems and "a great decline in his health" due to his efforts to get Croxton out of the water.[10] The legal action held Tupperware Home Parties responsible for failing "to keep their guests on the said island during the storm, but directed boat operators to continue to take passengers into a violent rainstorm at night when there was practically no moon, and when they knew, or should have known, that said transfer was very dangerous."[11]

For Tupper, this was big trouble on many fronts, and Wise knew it. For a man so bent on keeping his secrets and his business away from prying eyes, these personal injury suits could bring the kind of scrutiny he could not avoid, the kind of attention he detested. "Tupper has had, as long as I have known him, an antipathy to any action that would force him to bring his books into court," Wise observed. "He hated being cross-examined he said. He can be made to blow if he's prodded or needled enough, and when he blows it's an all-out thing; he explodes."[12] Those who had been around Earl Tupper during times of extreme stress could attest to the accuracy of Wise's observations.

After the seemingly uneventful October visit, Tupper told Wise he'd be back in November. When it came time for that Florida trip, he arrived without giving Wise notice as to the exact time and date. She felt "his attitude was strange during this visit."[13] Inspecting the building and new gardens around headquarters, Tupper seemed to have little to say. "He was not actually disapproving . . . not approving either," Wise wrote of Tupper's demeanor. "It shook morale among some of the executives who were left with the feeling that perhaps he felt they were beneath his dignity, or that he was leaving something unsaid."[14] Wise had a lengthy list of issues she had hoped to discuss with him, including the company's lease of her island, but Tupper was "evasive," instead going on and on about problems on the manufacturing side. Before Wise could get into her list, Tupper informed her he was being called back to Woonsocket, and that he needed her to make arrangements for an earlier flight.

In the ensuing days, a stream of memos started coming from Tupper. Wise found them "cross and unpleasant and [that they took] a completely different slant to any mail I had ever received from him before. Several were complete reversals of his previous attitude."[15] It could be something as seemingly trivial as an idea Wise had for a nonsliding dog dish. Earlier in the year, Tupper had talked about producing a prototype and then did a sudden and stern about-face. In a November 12 memo, Tupper chided Wise for the idea. "I hate to be critical, but I thought you followed my thinking about the use of Tupperware for a dog-feeding dish," Tupper remarked, "when it's a dish that is normally associated with human food storage and serving. I think it scars the mind of any user or potential user who sees it. It's bad, at your house of all places. Don't you agree?"[16]

That week, Tupper made another move Wise found curious and unsettling. Seemingly out of the blue, Tupper informed her he was exerting his authority as president of THP on personnel issues. "I believe that all salary changes and discharge of personnel should be done only after we have both agreed as to the proper course of action in each specific case," he told Wise. "I have a deep personal interest in the people at THP whom I know and I expect to become better acquainted with the whole group."[17] For years, Tupper had gone to great lengths to make sure as few people as possible knew who he was when he came to Florida. Now, all of the sudden, he had "a deep personal interest" in them?

Wise had issued a revised sales estimate for 1957 at $10 million—a 25 percent increase over 1956. But on November 16, Wise sent Tupper a memo explaining why she thought they were going to fall just short. "We stated that the current run of flu was resultant in cancellation or postponement of many parties and as a result of this our yearly projection would necessarily be affected."[18] Not being a woman used to coming up short on goals, Wise and her team pushed distributors to finish the year strong in a "Wind-Up week"[19] promotion for December 2. Sales counselors were in the field doing what they could to cajole peak performance and "keep their personal enthusiasm up." Wise sounded a hopeful note to Tupper: "We're pulling out all the stops in the *hope* that if we can't actually make it, we'll come as close as possible to the projection figure given you."[20]

Tupper's response to the revised numbers stung. He suggested Wise and her team needed to have a "sober re-evaluation" of the "causes of failure to produce."[21] He told Wise he did not feel they were doing a good enough job of sales management. What THP needed, Tupper said, was more "standard operating procedures and planning," more "controls."[22] The critique seemed to be a little over the top given the fact that Tupperware dealer numbers had continued to rise in November, past the 10,500 mark. And sales for 1957 still promised to be at least a 20 percent improvement over 1956. Perhaps Tupper had gotten spoiled with years like 1953 and 1954, and increases of 102.5 percent and 71.9 percent respectively.

"You spoke of sales *management* as if it were a term we were unfamiliar with in this organization," Wise shot back. "I would like very much to have your ideas on what we should do differently. We have felt all along that we were on the right track . . . we're rather shocked at this point to see that you do not feel we are doing a job of *sales management*."[23] In a critique of her own, Wise told Tupper, "We have long felt there should be a closer relationship between what we (from our miles of travel and thousands of contacts in the field) found the consumer wanted and what was developed by Tupper Corporation in the way of new products." Taking an obstinate tone often apparent when her abilities were questioned, Wise wrote: "We wonder what 'controls' you mean. Do you mean something to 'control' sales?"[24]

By that point, the sales numbers were becoming just another brick in the wall in Earl Tupper's attitude toward Brownie Wise. His longtime accountant Ed Creiger had seen a lot of employees come and go in the Tupper Corporation. "Earl was either high on a person," Creiger said, "or very quickly wanted to pull the rug out from under them."[25] Then again, Brownie Wise wasn't just any employee; she and Tupperware were all but synonymous. But therein lay the problem for Earl Tupper. "It was clear there was a competition between Tupperware and Brownie," Gary McDonald observed, "and Brownie was pushing Brownie as far as his view. I'm not sure it was true."[26] But it didn't matter if it were true or not; what mattered was what was true in Earl Tupper's mind.

Suspecting something was clearly at hand due to the change in Earl Tupper's attitude, the five top THP executives—Wise, Wilson, McDonald, Young, and Reynolds—signed a letter asking Tupper to come to Florida and meet with them. "What we are greatly concerned with *right now*," Wise complained, "are the bumps between the sales organization and the manufacturer . . . both of whom are presumably interested in the same thing . . . *BUILDING SALES*."[27] Since he had made two trips to Florida in recent weeks, Tupper told Wise to come to his office in Providence and meet with him on December 9 or 10. Wise wrote back that she was booked solid with long-distance calls from dealers and managers and with a sales award that was part of a big final push for 1957 called "One to Grow On." Tupper moved the timeline for their meeting to December 19 through 21.

In mid-December, Wise took a fall at her office that resulted in a concussion. It was the last thing she needed as the pressure was building for a face-to-face meeting with Tupper. She'd once again injured her lower back, this time in the third and fourth vertebra. Her doctor informed Wise she'd be unable to travel for seven to ten days. Tony Ponticelli witnessed George Reynolds carrying her into her office. "I said to myself she must be really ill or coming down with a breakdown," Ponticelli remembered.[28] The stress of 1957 was taking a serious toll on Wise. In the early days, addressing crowds of adoring dealers used to be a joy for her; now Wise was canceling meetings and no-showing at out-of-town commitments. That left Gary McDonald and Hamer Wilson to pick up the considerable slack. "We would have to go on without the star," McDonald said, "and that was tough."[29]

Whether he deserved it or not, Hamer Wilson had lost favor with Wise. The two had an arrangement where they both had to agree on candidates for new distributorships. That led to more friction between them. Others have spoken of Wilson's easygoing and friendly demeanor, but something about him seemed to spark a deep, visceral dislike and distrust in Wise. In late 1957, Tony Ponticelli was on a flight with Wise coming back from a rally in Chicago. She made it clear to him that his THP star was going to rise in 1958. "She said to me, 'I want more from you than I've asked from you before,'" Ponticelli recalled.[30] Part of the reason for a new opportunity, Ponticelli said, would be the vacuum created by her plans for Wilson. "She said, 'I'm going to fire him the first of the year.'"[31] Perhaps Tupper had gotten wind of her plans, and that's why he inserted himself in the hiring and firing process. For whatever reason, Wise never made good on her intention to fire Hamer Wilson.

As 1957 drew to a close, Earl Tupper and Brownie Wise—Tupperware manufacturing and sales, the yin and the yang—were at a stalemate. Each was resentful toward the other for a lack of accommodation and respect. Earl Tupper, through his inventive genius and considerable perseverance, had laid the sturdy foundation upon which Brownie Wise and her committed, energetic, and creative staff had built a powerhouse sales organization. But when push came to shove, each was so singularly convinced that they and they alone knew the right course of action that any criticism became a deep, personal attack. Both had poured their lives into making the Tupperware machinery work right, but now nothing was as easy as it had been. Success and expansion had brought with them considerable rewards. For Tupper it was millions of dollars in the bank; his baby Poly-T—the young veteran back from war—twelve years later was now a household name. For Wise, it was the kind of fame and recognition her Hibiscus alter ego had dreamed of on those cold, snowy nights in suburban Detroit.

But by this time, the Tupperware juggernaut had taken on a life of its own. It had become gigantic to the point of being unwieldy for the Tupper-Wise twosome. Brownie Wise was suffering physically, and it looked to her staff like she was heading for a nervous breakdown or burnout. Tupper also was feeling the strain. Many years later, Tupper wrote of this time period that it felt as if "somebody was squeezing soap suds or bubbles" through his heart.[32] By this time he had already decided, for tax reasons, to sell the Tupperware Corporation.

It was Christmas of 1957. Contrary to his image as a joyless fuddy-duddy, Earl Tupper always had Christmas parties for his employees and their children, awarding prizes and maintaining a familial atmosphere. At home on the farm, Tupper loved music and made tapes of his family singing and playing musical instruments. He and Marie had been married for twenty-six years. Their oldest son, Ronnie, was twenty-five. Myles, who recalled his father's long days of experimentation refining Poly-T, was twenty-three. Glenn and Mark rounded out the four Tupper sons. The breach baby Tupper himself had had to deliver, his daughter, Starr, was nineteen years old. It was their last Christmas as a family.

At Water's Edge, Brownie and Jerry Wise carried on a Christmas Eve tradition of leaving the lights off and lighting holiday candles in all the downstairs rooms. Her father had had another tradition of sprinkling ashes from the old Christmas tree upon the new one. Legend had it that it could help assure folks of a long life. With Brownie, Jerry, and Rose Humphrey gathered 'round, they opened all of the Christmas cards they made a practice of saving until Christmas Eve. On Christmas morning, the three always brought their stockings into the dining room at breakfast. After seeing what goodies were inside, and with full stomachs, they took turns opening gifts packed under the tree. It was their last Christmas at Brownie's dream home.

On New Year's Eve, Earl Tupper made a last attempt to try to get his relations with Wise back on track. His letter came to Wise on the familiar stationery: "Tupperware Home Parties Inc." was at the top, and below was the company slogan, "Buyers of Quality Buy Again . . ."[33] Tupper marked it "*PERSONAL*" in bold capital letters and reverted to addressing her with the more familiar "Dear Brownie."

"This is a personal letter that is intended to be friendly and helpful," Tupper began. "First of all, I hope that your concussion difficulties are sufficiently cleared up so that you can wire me an early date after which you will be able to come up here. I'll then give you a date to come."[34] He continued in this cordial tone: "I'm looking forward to seeing you and going over with you the many things that have piled up which you and I alone have to cover."[35] Soon after, Tupper mentioned plans to come to Florida to meet with her lieutenants about their concerns. Then came the real gist of why he was writing:

> From your recent conduct you seem to resist coming up here. There can be no justification for refusal or unreasonable delay, since I'm the President of the corporation and no business can be conducted unless there is respect for authority. Won't you please recognize that fact? Unless you can give me whole-hearted, friendly cooperation, representing my interests fully at THP and in a way to win friends for me there, then you are not doing and cannot do the job that must be done. You are the key person to carry out my wishes and give the organization good tone. If you quarrel with the person above you, then you weaken yourself with those under you.

After signing his full name at the bottom of his air mail letter, Tupper tried to sound a more upbeat and friendly tone, "P.S. Let's go!—For a Happy New Year."[36]

What Tupper received in return was the full-force fury of Hurricane Brownie, in written form, reminiscent of the first time she let Tupper have it over the telephone in 1951. Wise began with full-on, in-your-face insubordination, "This letter is about as 'friendly' as a mad dog, and about as helpful as a first-class case of leprosy. I have read this letter over a dozen times; it is unbelievable. I can't help but wonder if you read it over, even once, before you sent it?"[37] For six double-spaced pages, Wise dissected Tupper's letter and let her own pent-up feelings flow.

"Please look at the facts clearly and tell me where I have failed to respect your authority. Let me make something plain; I have always respected your authority, and I believe my actions for six and a half years speak with a louder voice than either your words on paper or mine," Wise countered. "You have [not] taken a telephone call from me in the last eight weeks. (Even the telephone operators in Winter Park are aware that I cannot get a call placed to you.) Do you consider this good public relations—and how about inter-company relations?"[38]

Clearly what upset Wise the most was Tupper's intimation that she was not cooperating with him:

> Look back over the last six and a half years. . .and bring yourself right up to date. . . give serious consideration to the last eight weeks. It's been quite a pic-

ture. Because it's full of action. And action speaks louder than words. The past six and a half—or it's closer to seven—represent a lot of giving, and a lot of giving UP for me. Mr. Tupper, many many people recognize that I have given you much, much more than the "wholehearted, friendly cooperation" you speak of, representing your interests fully as you put it. . . . The fact that you could actually use such words in speaking to me, after the way I have worked for THP and devoted myself so wholly that I have been criticized for it is an absolutely astounding fact. In the fact of your insistence that you would have nothing to do with the active management of this corporation, I HAVE made friends for you among the distributors, the managers and the dealers.[39]

Tupperware had been her life—what more could he want? "I felt from the very beginning and told you so," Wise declared, "that I was working for something I believed in, and could devote myself to with no reservations. And that's the way it's been. This business has had my time, my thought, whatever creativeness I have, my energy, my plans and my dreams . . . that takes in what physical stamina I have; there has been nothing left over from my interests in this business to use in any other way. . . . There's been no time for six years for any outside interests or any social life."[40]

Wise also adopted a personal tone, but only to describe to Tupper how deeply his letter had hurt her:

I take strong exception to what you say in this letter—because it is not true. I HAVE given you one thousand percent of wholehearted, friendly cooperation—and I have given it to you, without much cooperation in return. I HAVE represented your interests full at THP (to the sad exclusion of my own) in such a way as to win friends for you. . . . AND THIS HAS BEEN DONE WITHOUT ANY HELP FROM YOU. I don't believe you can be so blind as this letter sounds. So you must have written it to either annoy, anger, or wound me. It has done all three—and much more, because I am not a machine, though I have worked for you. I am a human being.[41]

Earl Tupper must have had one of two motives for writing his December 31 letter. Either he really wanted to try to put out an olive branch and had failed miserably, or he was throwing out a noose and letting Wise put it right around her own neck.

Seventeen

PICTURES OF DESPAIR

1958 will be the year of *real*
Tupperware history.
—Brownie Wise

After the two had a chance to blow off some steam in letter form, Tupper's response to Wise was brief. "My first concern is your health," he reassured her in a telegram.[1] "Please let me know the earliest date your health will permit you to leave to come up here."[2] In mid-January, along with her secretary, Mary Frances Babb, Wise made the trip to Providence.

For a day and a half, Tupper and Wise met alone, face-to-face. On the second day, in the presence of his accountant Ed Creiger, Tupper told Wise he wanted to cancel the lease on her island. Tupper assured her they would compensate her with a salary increase to make up for the loss of the island arrangement. The two agreed to write a letter. "I brought up that it would have to be more than that," Wise wrote, "since no written lease had been given to me, and Tupper outlined a letter, to be signed by both of us, he and I, stating that such a lease existed."[3] Tupper informed her he was concerned about the amount of insurance necessary to cover personnel visiting by barge or boat. Only approximately $7,000 in improvements had been made to the island in 1957. Since the agreement was $10,000 a year, Tupper assured Wise they "would make up to me in some way" for the difference.[4]

At that meeting, the two also discussed the possibility of Wise buying Water's Edge. "He said that it might be awkward for the corporation to let me have it at book value," Wise recalled, "if the actual market value had increased considerably."[5] Certainly, with all the improvements Wise had made to the home and its notoriety in the Kissimmee area, the value had to have increased a great deal in the five years Wise had lived there. That discussion was also put off, and no decision was made about ownership of the home.[6] For the second time, Wise had met with Tupper in person and had come away feeling like she had accomplished little. "I tried to bring him back to the list of things I needed to talk about," Wise complained. "He was concerned about Russia getting the jump on us with Sputnik, and went into detail about how poorly prepared New England was for a possible invasion.... He pulled a map out of his desk drawer, and showed me how a couple of bombs dropped on strategic points in the NY area would paralyze utilities and highway access."[7]

Tupper wasn't just being eccentric or paranoid; he was stalling, formulating his own answer to her tirade memo of January 3. By the end of the month, other things were bothering Earl Tupper. He had gotten wind that Wise and several of her top executives, frustrated with his new hands-on approach and meddling, might be plotting some sort of takeover of the sales division or a mass departure to another company. (Two THP supervisory executives, Gary McDonald and Don Hinton, denied any plot ever took place.) How would it look to those interested in buying his company to have such a headstrong woman at the helm of such a crucial division? And worse, how would it look to the public and the press if Wise really was plotting some sort of mutiny? By then she had developed such a wide cult of personality among the dealers that Wise just might be able to take a huge chunk of his business with her. It was time for Earl Tupper to take back the reins of his live-wire sales division once and for all. It was time to come up with an airtight and permanent solution to the Brownie Wise problem.

On his journey to cut ties with Wise, Earl Tupper would be accompanied by the other person most responsible for helping him amass all that wealth. When he boarded a Florida-bound flight one blustery late January day in New England, he had at his side his trusted CPA of thirteen years, Ed Creiger.

After checking into the Angebilt Hotel in downtown Orlando, the two stayed up most of one night plotting strategy. They were planning "not so much that he wanted to get rid of Brownie," Creiger said, "but who would succeed her."[8] Tupper summoned the successors whom he hoped could take THP through the rocky transition from Brownie Wise to the next phase in its history: Hamer Wilson and Gary McDonald. Wilson, because of his age and varied business experience, would be top man. The two had been aware of the friction between Tupper and Wise, but Tupper's pronouncement of his intention to get rid of Wise hit Gary McDonald like a concussion grenade. Despite his young age, his awe of Earl Tupper, and the risk that he might be thrown out with Wise, McDonald pleaded with him.

"I said, 'You gotta understand, she worked her heart out building this company,'" McDonald said with great emphasis. "'You cannot just go out there and summarily say you're done, good-bye.' And I said, 'You have to recognize her in some way for all she has put in to it. Regardless of how you feel about what she has been doing, what she is doing is building this company and we all picked her as the person we would publicize. That's what we've done. That's not her fault.'"[9]

And what about the dealers, many of whom saw Brownie Wise as America's very first Tupperware lady and the First Lady of Tupperware, their role model?

"I said, 'Their life is built around Tupperware and all those people are our people. To them Brownie is exactly what she was publicized to be and she is the image they're striving for and she is on a pedestal. What you're doing is removing her from that pedestal,'" McDonald argued. "'They're not gonna understand it.'"[10]

"That's what your first job is going to be," Tupper ordered, "enable them to understand it. She's done. Enough of that. She's done."[11]

At their Angebilt Hotel meeting, McDonald said, Tupper expressed his intention to fire Brownie Wise and not give her a dime of severance, no golden parachute, no chance to leave with a semblance of dignity. Earl Tupper wanted Brownie Wise expunged from Tupperware as if she had never existed. According to McDonald, he said, "That's it. No pay. No nothing."[12]

It would not be that easy.

On Wednesday, January 29, 1958, just before lunch, Earl Tupper and other key THP executives met with Brownie Wise. Someone had finally convinced Tupper that firing her immediately was not the way to go. They presented her with the notion of a two-year personal services contract under which she would continue on at $30,000 a year, but take "an inactive part" from that point forward.[13] Like the queen of England, her new role would be ceremonial, attending events like jubilees and seminars but no longer having day-to-day managerial duties. The contract called for a one-day-per-week commitment—a fifty-two-days-a-year "semi-retirement."[14]

Later that afternoon, Mary Frances Babb saw Wise in her office, stacking papers and crying. "I'm going home to write my resignation," Wise told her.[15] Babb helped her to the car and Wise drove home to Water's Edge. She summoned her friend and confidante Charles McBurney, her former PR man with whom she had published *Best Wishes*. "Tupper said I'm fired," she told him. "You know, there goes my life. I'm through with life."[16] She told Jerry she'd quit.

The next day, Tupper composed a short letter to Wise, making official what they had informed her of the day before. "Dear Mrs. Wise," he began, "The following action was taken to clear the way for re-organization of Tupperware Home Parties Inc. operations. A meeting of the Board of Directors was held on January 27th, 1958, and it was voted to cancel the appointment of Brownie Humphrey Wise as Vice-President and General Manager of Tupperware Home Parties Inc. This letter is to serve as notification of same."[17] That was it. If Tupper expressed any personal gratitude for all the years of work Wise spent building the sales operation and helping him reap a fortune, it came elsewhere, if at all. It was cold, impersonal, and permanent.

"He couldn't get rid of her fast enough," remembered Ed Creiger.[18]

On Friday, Tupper convened a lunch at headquarters with his THP executive staff including Hamer Wilson, Gary McDonald, Don Hinton, Herb Young, Don Fuhr, George Reynolds, and Dave Seraphine. With the men assembled who he hoped would carry on THP and not let it fall apart in the absence of Brownie Wise, he announced the promotions of Wilson and McDonald. Tupper also made a blunt ultimatum, "You're either with me or with Brownie."[19] Office manager Herb Young, who had been with the company since its early days in the Orlando airport hangar, stood up.

"I'm with Brownie," he said, and walked out.[20]

Gary McDonald chose to stay. Ever since his discharge from the military, Tupperware was all he'd known. Now the pressure was on him to take all he'd learned and, along with Hamer Wilson, shepherd the company without the very formidable personality and underappreciated management acumen of Brownie Wise. Elsie Mortland happened upon McDonald sitting at a table with his head down. "He looked like the absolute picture of despair," Mortland recalled, "and I just went over to him and said, 'Don't worry, Gary, we'll stick by you.'"[21] Not only did McDonald feel new pressure to perform, but there was the guilt of choosing to stay rather than following Herb Young's lead. After all, Brownie Wise was far more than just his boss. In Detroit, they had helped bring Earl Tupper's invention out of obscurity. McDonald had been like a father figure and big brother to young Jerry, and Brownie Wise like the mother McDonald lost at sixteen. In Massachusetts, they poured the foundations of the Home Party Division and then brought it to Florida, introducing Tupperware to the world, transforming the lives of thousands of dealers and their own. Now, so abruptly, their seemingly endless journey together was over?

McDonald soul-searched: "I felt that she felt that I had betrayed her. And I guess I ask myself, by being willing to stay and run the company, was I betraying her?"[22]

Wise dictated a letter that would serve as her official notification of what she had "chosen" to do. It went out as a *Spark-O-Gram* to Tupperware distributors on Saturday, February 1:

> Well, this is the day . . . the day of glad thoughts and with sad thoughts. I have enjoyed the long hours, the long days and the not-so-long years that I have spent working with all of you, but of course, I have always felt that I would like to spend more time with my son, Jerry. There are many personal creative things that I have often wished for time to do. (Writing, for instance . . . and many of you know I'm a "rock hound.". . . I love working with the various stones . . . cutting polishing, shaping . . . and I certainly appreciate the rocks that you and your dealers and managers have sent me from time to time).
>
> From now on, I'll be working with Tupperware on a part-time basis. . . . I'll still be part of the Tupperware family . . . and of course, at every Tupperware get together my thoughts will be with you. I'll still be attending some of them in person, too.
>
> I will act as an advisor to the staff . . . though you know the boys . . . sometimes they don't go along with my thoughts and opinions . . . but that's why it's been fun.
>
> You know, I'll miss all of you . . . miss the telephone jangling Constantly . . . miss your letters and your wires.
>
> This year will be a great year, as they all have been, but this one greater still . . . and I'll be watching closely . . . watching all of you, because now, as always, you're very close to me.
> Best Wishes,
> Brownie Wise[23]

Wise decided to work with Tupper on the contract offer rather than rejecting the proposal for what it really was: a cynical attempt to give her false hope, placate the dealers, and minimize bad press and doubts from potential buyers of his company. At the Friday lunch meeting, Tupper had made clear his true attitude toward Wise. On Monday, February 3, Tupper had a press release sent out with the heading, "Brownie Wise Goes into Semi-Retirement." Tupper assured those who read it that Mrs. Wise "is still an important member of the Tupperware family."[24]

Not surprisingly, when Wise received the written contract offer, it little resembled the agreement she thought she had reached with Tupper on January 29. For a ceremonial position at a good salary, Tupper was still requiring the kind of exclusivity and loyalty Wise had shown when she ran the place. During the proposed two-year period, Wise would have to get Tupper's written permission before pursuing any other sales venture. While the job was supposed to involve only fifty-two days a year, Wise would be required to "render herself available at any time for the performance of such duties."[25]

While Wise was still "an important part of the Tupperware family," the contract required her to turn over "all papers, records and other property of any kind or description, real or personal, in her possession or control, which are the property of the Employer and give the Employer any information which she has relative to the location of any records or papers relating to the Employer's affairs."[26] This open-ended mandate seemed to require Wise to relinquish any and all information she had accumulated over the years to Tupper or his officers at their whim.

The contract also called for an audit of THP's books and records. If Wise didn't agree with the results of that audit, she could, at her own expense, order one done by a CPA of her own choosing. Despite any earlier conversations Wise and Tupper had about her interest in buying Water's Edge, his position on that had changed too. "The Employee shall be allowed the use of the Employer's house where she now lives for a period of sixty days," the contract stated. "The Employee shall remove herself and her personal belongings from such property on or before the expiration of said sixty days."[27] It was another devastatingly clear message from Tupper: *Congratulations on your new semi-retired role. You now have sixty days to get out of the house.*

Not only was she required to move, but if Wise failed to live up to any requirements of the contract, it could be revoked immediately. Tupper shrewdly included another proviso that stated that even if the agreement was revoked, "paragraph 3b of this contract shall nevertheless survive."[28] That paragraph effectively banned Wise from getting involved in any other sales activity for two years without Tupper's permission. And he certainly would have no intention of letting her do any such thing if she were no longer on the Tupperware payroll.

On February 25, 1958, Wise wrote her last letter to Earl Tupper, outlining why the agreement was unacceptable. "This contract bears very slight resemblance to the contract outlined at THP on Wednesday, January 29, when you, Herbert Young, Gary McDonald and Hamer Wilson were present," Wise wrote.

> It was quite specific that ample notice was to be given me about personal appearances. I was to be free to sell real estate, insurance, or any product or service excepting items competitive to Tupperware, on the home party plan. I

was not, in any way, to be restricted against using my own ability or my experience except as it conflicted with the specific interests of Tupperware.[29]

No mention was made of the island lease arrangement on which Wise estimated she was owed $3,000. No mention was made of the verbal agreement she thought she had with Tupper on buying Water's Edge. She would not sign the contract without a resolution of these questions.

Dave Seraphine's audit gave Wise another indication that the company was drawing battle lines. The probe questioned her on everything from $49 dresses to 1,880 copies of *Best Wishes* she had given away to people "not associated with Tupper." Her reply was defensive. "Yes, I bought 6,000 books for THP without any OK," Wise wrote in her answer to the audit, "OK from whom? I also built the pavilion, designed and contracted for the lakes, for the garden wall, wrote purchase orders for $35,000 worth of silver from International Silver etc. without any OK."[30] Wise went on to say the quantity of books had been determined with input and knowledge of other members of the THP staff. A more legitimate company concern about *Best Wishes* came from the fact that Wise had expended $1,261.90 in attorney fees stemming from her failed ghostwriting arrangement with Robert Froman.[31]

But her point in all this was that she enjoyed a certain amount of privilege that came from being a chief executive of the company, America's Tupperware Lady. Tony Ponticelli agreed: "I would argue any day, I'm using that from experience out of Madison Avenue, all the executives had unlimited expense money, clothing, vehicles. You want me to be that character. I'm in a movie for you. I need the money to play the part."[32] As Gary McDonald had argued previously about the expenses of putting on jubilees and giving away lavish prizes, it didn't factor because the company was making enormous profits in return.

Correspondence between Wise and her "Employer" soon dwindled to letters between their lawyers. The line in the sand was being drawn over the differences between what Wise perceived was their verbal agreement back on January 29 and the demands the company was making in the written personal services contract she refused to sign. More than a month had gone by. Wise had already been eased out. "The position of Tupperware Home Parties Inc," stated a letter written by a company lawyer dated March 7, "is that her employment must be considered to have terminated."[33]

"We have to move," Wise informed her son with no explanation.

"Do we have to move this fast?" Jerry asked, bewildered. "I can't get my horses out of here this fast."

"You're going to have to," she told him.

"I left five head of cows at Water's Edge," Jerry recalled. "I kept thinking, why don't we own it?"[34] Wise always thought she'd be given the chance to buy Water's Edge, her dream home. But once Tupper decided to "pull the rug out," there was no way he would allow her to stay in the house and keep the glamorous trappings of the job from which she had been removed. She very quickly purchased a three-story home at 309 Clyde Avenue in Kissimmee.

Brownie Wise would not take her unceremonious ouster without a fight. In response to being terminated, she filed suits totaling $1.6 million, naming Tupper Corporation and THP as defendants along with Tupper, McDonald, Wilson, Seraphine, and Creiger personally. Wise claimed she had been "boycotted and blacklisted"[35] from getting other jobs as well as being "accused of embezzlement."[36] During the process of leaving the company, Wise was accused of taking proprietary information—a list of dealer names. George Reynolds explained that he'd gone to Water's Edge on Thursday, January 30—while Wise was still on the payroll—and retrieved the list from a box of old magazines. After that, Reynolds said, Tupper seemed satisfied: "He thanked me for my cooperation and Brownie's cooperation."[37] It seemed this was another key issue Tupper used to get rid of her.

To the newspapers, Earl Tupper said the Brownie Wise lawsuits came from out of the blue. "I was shocked and bewildered after receiving the information by telephone about the suits, because she hasn't had anything but kindness and consideration from us."[38] This was the last thing Tupper needed as he looked toward trying to sell his company and solve his tax worries.

As the legal battle wore on, Wise tried to put on a brave face. She poured out her feelings in private: "This has been the most painful experience of my life . . . I couldn't begin to describe to you how shattering it's been, and will, I suppose, continue to be for some time." Wise wrote her attorneys: "The most serious mistake I have made during my 7-years' association with Tupper and Tupperware, is that of being naïve. ('Stupid' is the better word I suppose). Otherwise I would have on hand documents to support what I claim; there would have been contracts and leases and written 'O.K.'s' and I would be in the driver's seat, where I should be, after these years of blindly putting Tupperware and its interests ahead of Brownie and her interests."[39]

It was obvious that Tupper and his lawyers also planned to take the gloves off if it became necessary to wage a court battle with Wise. In the discovery phase of the suit, records show they demanded Wise produce evidence of how she had been accused of embezzlement, and how their actions had left her blacklisted. They also wanted Wise to produce her tax returns dating back to 1954 for possible scrutiny in open court. Without written documentation to back up her claims, legal action would be fruitless. Wise eventually settled everything for $30,000 and walked away. After all the years that Brownie Wise had lived in her fashionable lakeside home, earned a handsome salary, took on a movie star's persona, and earned the adoration of many, her Hibiscus dreams at Tupperware were coming to an end. For his part, Earl Tupper never willingly gave her anything in the way of severance pay, despite all she had done to put money in his pocket.

At THP, orders were given for a big hole to be dug on company grounds and the hundreds of copies of *Best Wishes* still on hand to be dumped in it. "It wasn't until later I found out about the books being buried. I was kind of pissed," remembered Gary McDonald. He felt the only reason they'd been disposed of that way was "just because they said 'Brownie Wise.'"[40] That wasn't all the company was burying—Earl Tupper wanted the name *Brownie Wise* erased from any and all of the company history. He gave McDonald strict orders on what dates and information to include when handing out company information to the press. For decades after Brownie Wise departed and filed suit, her name was never associated with the company. "You couldn't mention Brownie any more," remarked the man who'd gone to such pains to promote her, Don Hinton. "There was never such a person."[41] The annual Tupperware catalogue no longer featured Brownie Wise, Tupperware's "First Lady." In 1958, her name was nowhere in *The Fabulous Tupperware Story*.

To bolster morale and retain employees, Tupper sent roses to the wives of executives like Tony Ponticelli and took on the role of cheerleader. He wrote a memo to Wilson and McDonald, "I am getting more and more enthusiastic about the future of THP now that B.W. is out."[42] He went on to describe seven products featuring "new type black polyethylene handles which I believe will send the whole housewares industry agog." Tupper anticipated a move by Wise to try to derail his efforts. "BW will, of course, be out for any kind of a deal that can be worked with a competitor," Tupper warned. "We can best upset their applecart and store competition by moving fast on a well-planned program with all these new items."[43]

There was no way you could simply erase Brownie Wise, like markings on a chalkboard, from the hearts and minds of the countless women across the country who still adored her and who weren't privy to all the intrigue behind her ouster. They were still of the mind that Wise was going to continue, though in her semiretired "advisory" capacity. Throughout 1958, she continued to get letters from dealers and distributors everywhere, inviting her to assemblies, wondering if they would still see her, and then questioning why she was no longer with Tupperware. "I was quite concerned thinking you were ill or that the company which you had really *made* had given you a dirty deal," wrote one Indiana dealer. "You see, you have been the symbol of things hoped for in my selling career. I think of your life with an ordinary beginning and how you took hold of the things at hand and have truly become a star for any saleswoman to use as a guide."[44]

Tupper and Wise had more momentous history to make in 1958. With Brownie Wise out of the picture, Tupper was on the verge of divesting himself of the other primary relationships in his life, both business and personal. For her part, Wise already had a new home-based selling venture lined up, but she needed the workforce to build it. She would try to do what Earl Tupper had feared; claim a sizeable chunk of Tupperware dealers. The showdown came at the 1958 jubilee, when those dealers would be forced to choose sides.

Eighteen

MOVING ON, SELLING OUT

Success in business depends on how much you do—Not when you get ready to do it—but how much you do when the business is ready to do it.

—Earl Tupper

Even before her departure from Tupperware and the lawsuits she filed, Brownie Wise was planning the next phase in her career: capitalizing on her notoriety in a real estate venture, Brownie Wise Developments. "The rivers and lakes at our doorstep are practically untouched," Wise told the *Kissimmee Gazette*, "as far as real estate development is concerned."[1] On May 2, 1958, Wise was back on the front page of the local paper, celebrating the sale of her first "Hearthside Home" to a former Kentucky coal miner and his wife.[2] The firm already had a half-dozen homes priced at $10,500 going up within the Kissimmee city limits.[3] Along with other creative hobbies like writing and working with rocks, Wise became enamored with pottery. She had her own kiln and entered the pieces she made in area competitions. Wise enjoyed crafts and collected wicker baskets. She put on a sales seminar and donated the class fees to the Red Cross.

When Brownie and Jerry celebrated their birthday at the end of May, it was a joyous surprise party. Her mother, Rose Humphrey, threw a big steak cookout for twenty guests on the Isla Milagra property. Friends brought dozens of cement blocks as presents to help in the construction of the new home Wise was planning to have built. That homesite was not far from the lake and within view of the island she was now thinking about developing. As a surprise, Grandmother Rose presented twenty-year-old Jerry with a new Nash Rambler. Jerry was happy with the notion that his mother would be around more and have time to spend on a "normal" life with him. She had more ambitious plans to get back into the world of home-based selling.

Once it was clear her career with Tupperware had ended, Wise accepted the post of president of Cinderella International Corporation, a home-selling concern with a line of cleaning products and beauty aids for men and women. Some familiar names from the Tupperware days joined her executive staff: Charles McBurney as vice president and Herb Young as administrative director and assistant treasurer. She also managed to lure some of her clerical staff away from Tupperware. Wise was saving her biggest power play for July, when Tupperware was planning to hold its first jubilee without her.

Mary Frances Babb wrote a memo to Earl Tupper assuring him that there would be no replay of the 1957 disaster; most of the jubilee events would take place on company grounds. Scheduled for July 1–4, the 1958 jubilee had a pirate theme, complete with a big, wooden pirate ship. The only off-site activity would be pirate "raids" planned for downtown Kissimmee shops.[4] For that, dealers would be bussed downtown. A cannon boom would announce the beginning and end of the contest. Then it would be right back on the bus and back to the Tupperware campus.

To coincide with the opening festivities, Wise took out a large newspaper ad announcing her new venture with Cinderella and invited Tupperware dealers to pay her a visit. Not only did Wilson and McDonald face the daunting job of putting on their first jubilee without Wise, now she was coming out as a direct adversary, pulling a pirate raid of her own. There was no way they could prevent people from reading the paper or seeing the ad, so they decided to do just the opposite. "We gave copies to people on busses as they arrived," McDonald remembered, "so everybody would see them."[5] Then they announced her plans to the large gathering of visitors. "We know how good Tupperware is, [but] we don't know anything about cosmetics, we don't know anything about Cinderella," McDonald told them. "We do know Brownie Wise and she's terrific. If you want to go see her, we want you to know that it's perfectly fine with us."[6]

No one left.

Wise herself extended a personal invitation to her friend and Tupperware's official demonstrator, Elsie Mortland. "I didn't have the belief or the faith in the products that I had in Tupperware. And I told her I just couldn't do it," Mortland recalled. "She said, 'Then we can't be friends any more,' and I said,

'I'm sorry.'"[7] That was that. The two never spoke again. Mortland once ran into Wise near her Cinderella offices in downtown Kissimmee. "I said, 'Hello Brownie,'" Mortland recalled sadly.[8] In response, Wise turned away and waved to a passing car, ignoring Mortland.

The same people she had trained to "surrender themselves" to Tupperware, Wise was now trying to convince to walk away from it.[9] But they had worked as hard as she had to build up their businesses and livelihoods through the product. Wise was trying to fight the enormous machine she helped build. Her own mother, Rose Humphrey, continued on as a Tupperware distributor. Tupperware was more than a product. It was people's bread and butter, the children's education, their retirement, their family, their future. Perhaps this was the moment of clarity for Brownie Wise; if she hoped to catch lightning in a bottle again, she'd be doing it with a novice sales force. The Tupperware family was closing ranks and moving on without her. "I think she had an idea the company would fall apart when she left," Mortland observed, "but it didn't. It didn't."[10]

Mortland knew something else was afoot when groups of strange men in dark suits started touring the Kissimmee headquarters. "This group of guys looked like they were in the mafia," remembered Gary McDonald.[11] In September 1958, McDonald was called into a meeting room at headquarters. On the table was an annual report belonging to the Rexall Drug Company, the new owners of the Tupper Corporation and Tupperware Home Parties. In a roller-coaster year for McDonald, this was an unquestionable low. Tupperware was going to be sold in drugstores? The distributors would never stand for it. They had worked so hard to keep Tupperware for sale solely through home-based parties, and that exclusivity was key to their success.

"I lost it," McDonald remembered.[12]

Tupper and Creiger had swung a $16-million deal with Justin Whitlock Dart Sr., the former "boy wonder" of the drugstore industry and president of Rexall Drugs[13]—$15 million for the company and another $1 million for potential liability Tupperware faced at the time from the Brownie Wise lawsuit. Dart was an heir to the Walgreen's drugstore chain, which his wife's father had founded. He took over the struggling United Drug Company in 1943 and rebranded it Rexall. The purchase of Tupperware was another step in turning the company into a powerhouse conglomerate.

Justin Dart had big plans for Tupperware, which he outlined to THP executives during a meeting at a famous south Orlando restaurant along the Orange Blossom Trail, Gary's Duck Inn. "I want you guys to know something," Dart said in a Tupper-esque tone. "I don't know anything about selling cups and bowls on party plan. You do that. But these guys will tell you I do tend to make suggestions. But it's like throwing mud against the barn fence. If they stick, fine, if they don't, that's fine, too."[14] But one suggestion on which Dart would not relent was his admonition, "You've gotta get overseas."[15] McDonald found his meeting with Dart reassuring because Rexall did not plan to come in and make wholesale changes. The sale of Tupperware would be left to the experts exclusively on the party plan. To further reassure distributors, at a meeting in Saint Louis where the sale was announced, each received a certificate for five shares of Rexall stock.

Tupper signed the sale papers in Worcester, Massachusetts, on September 28, 1958. On the way back, he told the new head of manufacturing, John Ansley: "This thing is going to blow up, it'll never last. Go out and get yourself another job."[16] Two days later, Dart and Tupper made a joint, public announcement of the sale. "In addition to serving as chairman of the Tupper board," Dart said, "Earl Tupper will continue research, designing and development of new materials and products."[17] For his part, Tupper announced his intention to carry on: "the development program will continue to employ the best polyethylene and polyolefin resins. As in the past, the line will continue to utilize other new materials as they are developed and effectively laboratory tested to meet our exacting requirements."[18] Tupperware also announced that their sales for the first eight months were up 25 percent over 1957.

The old taskmaster was gone. But the company would continue the meticulous standards of perfection he demanded. At every molding machine on every shift, they sampled the product for color and quality. Every piece had to be as close to perfect as possible. The castoffs were discarded, ground up, melted, and repoured.

Even before the sale, Earl Tupper was a very rich man. "I had 7 million dollars in the bank and was making another 7 and a half million for 1958," Tupper wrote.[19] But his fear of the possibility of a 77 percent government tax on his estate as the sole owner of all Tupperware stock forced him to sell his company at the $16-million "sacrifice price."[20] He also received 175,000 shares of Rexall stock and a seat on the board of directors. Hamer Wilson took over as president of Tupperware Home Parties, and John Ansley became president of the manufacturing division of the Tupperware Corporation. Now the top jobs on the sales and manufacturing sides of Tupperware—positions held by Wise and Tupper since the inception of THP—for the first time were occupied by others.

In Kissimmee, Wise continued to make a lot of noise about Cinderella. She posed her first eight Florida dealers for newspaper pictures. "Cinderella Hour" demonstrations anytime of the morning, noon, or night was her way of trying to re-create the famous Tupperware Party. She announced that the company was experiencing such "rapid growth" that it had to move into larger quarters.[21] Wise formed a Kissimmee chapter of the Florida Aero Club and started flying to Cinderella functions in places like Wichita and Cleveland. She adopted a new nickname, "Florida's Flying Cinderella."[22] The Cinderella holiday advertisement in the Kissimmee paper was the same size as Tupperware's.

As much as Wise tried to portray Cinderella as a company on the move, the glass slipper never fit. Regardless of how much energy, charisma, publicity, and sales know-how Wise poured into the new venture, the products did not hold the same allure as Tupperware. Time after time, Tupperware dealers would write Wise to tell her how much they missed her. She would write back and talk about a new opportunity with Cinderella. They would politely decline. On June 5, 1959, the *Kissimmee Gazette* carried the news that Wise and McBurney had resigned their positions. On November 1, the company relocated its headquarters to Orlando, with vice president Herb Young, the only executive holdover from the early THP team.

The most devastating blow for Wise came at the end of 1959 with the loss of her mother, Rose Stroud Humphrey. While others were getting ready to ring in the 1960s on New Year's Eve, Wise and a group of others mourned their loss at the Grissom Chapel in Kissimmee. Throughout the 1950s, Humphrey had played a lower-key role in shaping Tupperware's history, opening new markets in Florida and Puerto Rico. Humphrey was among the elite early distributors, consistently ranking among the top in sales. True to her Old World ways, the six or seven fancy Cadillacs she won never turned her head.[23] "She'd always go and sell it back and go down the street and buy a Ford," her grandson Jerry remembered fondly. "She said a Ford was fine."[24]

After relinquishing his active role in the day-to-day operations of Tupperware, Earl Tupper grew "restless."[25] He divorced his wife, Marie, after almost twenty-eight years of marriage and five children. According to Ed Creiger, Marie received only $50,000, a Ford Thunderbird, and $1,000 per month until she remarried.[26] When Marie found a new husband, Tupper said he had a right to pro-rate the monthly payment, but he chose not to. Tupper resigned his seat on the Rexall board and sold off his stock, so he could be free to travel and live abroad. Disillusioned with the political direction the country was taking, in 1965 Tupper purchased a home in Nassau, Grand Bahamas. In 1967, he relinquished his American citizenship. "I feel that since I'll never go back to the U.S.A. to live," he wrote. "I want to reorient my whole balance of life to the contented life and place where I now live."[27]

Tupper finally found the paradise he was looking for in San Jose, Costa Rica, settling there for good in 1973. In later life, Tupper became a very generous philanthropist, donating $10 million for the Earl S. Tupper Research Institute at Boston's New England Medical Center. He gave $4 million to the Smithsonian for a center for tropical disease research in Panama. From time to time, THP executives like Hamer Wilson and Gary McDonald would communicate with Tupper, but not often. When they did, it was memorable.

In the 1970s, while in New York for surgery, Tupper placed a call to Gary McDonald. "They wheeled me down on a gurney and by that time I had a whole bunch of notes because it wasn't nearly what it ought to be," Tupper had reported. "A guy gave me gas to put me out, and I said 'Before you do that, is that what you run the blood through?'"

The doctor said, "Yes, it is."

"You have a problem with condensation, don't you?" Tupper asked.

"Yes we do," the surprised doctor replied.

"I know how that could be fixed and redesigned," Tupper assured him.[28]

That was typical of Earl Silas Tupper, the farm boy who turned his inventive genius into plastic gold, the man who saw himself as a modern-day Leonardo da Vinci. "A mind like that is looking at everything without exception," McDonald marveled, "everything."[29]

On December 7, 1976, the Society of Plastics Industries inducted Tupper in the Plastics Hall of Fame for initiative and drive in creating useful, high-quality houseware, enhancing the image of the plastics industry. On Friday, October 7, 1983, newspapers worldwide reported Tupper's death from a heart attack. He was seventy-six. "The home parties through which Mr. Tupper sold his goods became a well-known part of American life and made him a millionaire," reported the *New York Times*. "The essence of Tupperware is a flexible, unbreakable and heat resistant blend of plastic that Mr. Tupper invented and called poly-T."[30] Tupper was buried in a cemetery near his home in San Jose, in his adopted country, Costa Rica.

The people whom Tupper entrusted to take Tupperware into the 1960s and beyond did not disappoint. Hamer Wilson became a beloved figure to distributors like Pat Jordan. "To me, it happened because of Hamer and Jean Conlogue," Jordan said. "They had the biggest influence on my life."[31] Wilson spearheaded the company's Cold War–era international expansion in 1960, picking former Chicago distributor Joe Hara to run the North American division. "Because the company was so successful," Wilson's wife of fifteen years and former distributor Marylin Mennello remembered, "Justin Dart let Hamer run the business his way."[32] Tupperware became a cash cow for Rexall and later Dart industries.

Elsie Mortland, the diminutive and shy housewife from Deland, flew all over the globe giving Tupperware demonstrations in England, Germany, Belgium, Holland, Italy, Costa Rica, and Guatemala, among other new international markets. In 1965, Mortland helped introduce Tupperware in Hong Kong. After the departure of Wise, Mortland became Tupperware's First Lady.

Gary McDonald, "Mister Stanley," outlived everyone else who was there at the beginning of Tupperware Home Parties Inc. Arguably, there was no one closer to the evolution of Tupperware itself: forgotten on the shelves of the J. L. Hudson department store in Detroit; a phenomenon at early Stanley parties; and a revolution when combined with the right sales strategy and the ambitious dealer force willing to preach the word of Tupperware to the world. Without question, in 1958 Gary McDonald had earned the right to stay on and ply his own considerable leadership acumen in the company he had played such a vital role building. Tony Ponticelli reflected: "Gary believed in respecting the public; the customer was always right. The gift of gab came from Brownie to him. He was able to inject his own personality into it and motivate people. I thought we had a good team."[33]

That leaves the considerable legacy of Brownie Humphrey Wise.

Nineteen

LEGACIES

It may be the most brilliant marketing scheme ever devised, for it is based less on sales pitch than on friendship.
—Morley Safer, CBS News, *60 Minutes*

If you take a drive to the very end of Aultman Road, there's no sign of Water's Edge, once the sprawling epicenter of Brownie Wise's reign as Tupperware's First Lady, Hibiscus personified. Through the magic of an Internet search engine's satellite photo program, the omnipotent view from above reveals a couple of remnants near the end of the peninsula. Beyond the cluster of private, pricey homes with a sandy beach fronting Lake Toho, you can still make out the channel Brownie Wise put in to accommodate her son's boat, and, gazing down from the heavens, you can still see the foundation of Water's Edge like a ghostly footprint. Fly over Isla Milagra, now known by its old name, Makinson Island, and you see that very little has changed since the 1957 luau disaster. You see a few animals on the land and a couple of outbuildings.

To tourists making the trip down South Orlando's clogged, congested Orange Blossom Trail, past the auto dealerships, strip malls, fast-food restaurants, and the old Florida attraction Gatorland, the site of Tupperware World Headquarters must seem awfully incongruous. The old building is long gone, replaced by a stately complex designed by the same architect who built the Kennedy Center in Washington, D.C. To the north, the land on which the company held some of its early

Pat and Phil Jordan being welcomed into the Tupperware President's Club by Hamer Wilson, 1979.

jubilees has been sold off for development. Pat Jordan said it's hard to go by there now without crying.

After Norfolk, the Jordans jumped at a distributorship back in Orlando and were doing $5 million in annual sales when they retired in 1987. At that time, they rented their south Orlando building known as "Little Tupperware" to tel-evangelist Tammy Faye Baker, just after the PTL scandal erupted.[1] When the Jordans' building sold, the money they made financed their retirement.

By the time she ended her Tupperware career in 1970, Elsie Mortland was a Tupperware legend. "It was very touching to me people had such a high opinion of me," Mortland, in her early nineties, said from her home on the western shore of Lake Toho. "I was very proud of it and very humbled by it."[2] She spoke with great respect and reverence for "Mr. Tupper" and her days with Tupperware. Mortland still has some of the earliest Tupperware Wonder Bowls from the "Millionaire Line."

Just days after celebrating his ninetieth birthday, Tupperware's erstwhile pho-tographer from the early days, Jack McCollum, held court at a buffet restaurant in the Kissimmee suburb of Saint Cloud. With wisecracking friends coming and going, McCollum retained vivid memories of working with Brownie Wise. "What a woman!" was his oft-repeated exclamation.[3] He proudly displayed a

Tupperware jubilee photo circa 1954 that showed him lying on his belly to take a picture inside the faux western town of "Tupperware Gulch."

The stories of some of the early Tupperware alumni didn't end as happily. Tupperware accountant Dave Seraphine suffered from serious financial problems. Former special events director Tony Ponticelli remembered getting a desperate phone call from him: "Tony, I need help, I'm in a hole."[4] Ponticelli had no idea how deep the hole was until he heard that Seraphine had walked in to a central Florida hospital emergency room, pulled out a revolver, and shot himself in the head.[5]

As he sat in a Maitland, Florida, restaurant talking about Tupperware, it was clear Ponticelli had far more good memories than bad. "You're telling a story I'm very proud of," he remarked. "We were the glamour boys, but we weren't the ones who did the work."[6] It was the legion of husbands and wives, the Tupperware teams all over the world, converts to the religion of home selling. Ponticelli takes great pride in the spectacular shows and jubilee wonders he and his team managed to pull off, often on a shoestring budget. "We were the first ones to put on conventions in Orlando," he asserted.[7] This is another way the Tupperware pioneers laid the groundwork for the tourism success Orlando enjoys today.

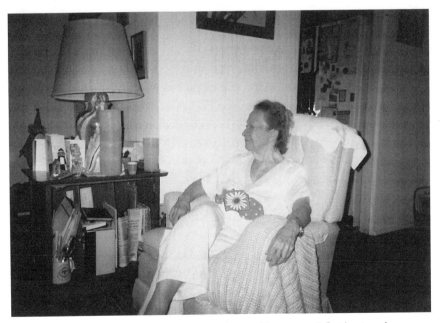

Elsie Mortland at her home in Kissimmee, March, 2005. Tupperware's first hostess demonstrator, Mortland brought the product to markets worldwide.

Jack McCollum, photographed near his home in Saint Cloud, Florida, July 2005, took many of the early Tupperware publicity photos.

Gary McDonald recounted his intimate knowledge of Tupperware's ascent from near his home in the Villages, a cluster of sprawling, active retirement communities situated about an hour northwest of Orlando. McDonald continued his association with Tupperware into the 1960s, then left to pursue other business, consulting, and teaching jobs. He is the last one alive from Tupperware's earliest days, and his friends have often encouraged him to write a book about his travels and travails building Tupperware Home Parties.

At a motel bar in Deltona, Florida, former Tupperware PR man Don Hinton recounted colorful stories of being on the road with the enormous personalities of sales counselors Jack Mann, Jack Marshall, and Hamer Wilson. Hinton was a main force behind the building up of Brownie Wise as Tupperware queen and felt she got a raw deal at the end. "She did a great deal for a great many people," he recalled, a portable oxygen machine at his side helping his deteriorating lungs breathe.[8]

In 1956, Brownie Wise described Tupperware as "a living drama of success—unequalled success of a product, a plan, an organization."[9] Beginning with Alison Clarke's 1999 book *Tupperware: the Promise of Plastic in 1950s America*, and gaining more momentum with Laurie Kahn-Levitt's 2003 documentary *Tupperware!* Wise's indelible contribution to that living drama could be buried no longer. Today the company recognizes that it can't possibly tell its own story without including her. "Wise was so successful demonstrating and selling Tupper's plastics," so goes an item from the Tupperware Web site, "that he brought Wise into the company in 1951 to build the direct selling system that has made the Tupperware party as famous as the products themselves."[10] The company literature recognizes her "genius for people and a flair for marketing."[11]

The product she spent a decade of her life traveling the world to grow and promote has become as commonplace to the American home as Band-Aids, Jell-O, and the Frisbee. People can't seem to resist poking fun at the blend of cornball kitsch and dealer fanaticism that Tupperware evokes. Humorist Dave Barry wrote "The Tupperware Song" and managed to earn an invitation to perform it before one thousand distributors along with his band, the Urban Professionals. "They gave us a standing ovation," Barry boasted, "although in the interest of accuracy, I should tell you that just before we performed, they also gave a standing ovation to a set of ovenware."[12]

In Kansas City, a sculptor and part-time demolition derby enthusiast named Mac Maclanahan heard the Tupperware Rock 'N Serve line was bulletproof. Also something of a gun aficionado, he helped put that claim to the test for a newspaper article. On a friend's farm in Lathrop, Missouri, with the help of an XKS sniper rifle, the two men proved that the Rock 'N Serve line should not be substituted for Kevlar. Another artist named Ryan Gale pierced a Rock 'N

Tony Ponticelli (shown here in September 2005) former Tupperware special events director, was a close associate of Brownie Wise during her tenure at Tupperware Home Parties.

Gary McDonald (shown in July 2005) is the last surviving executive from the earliest days of Tupperware Home Parties. McDonald drove the first truckload of Tupperware to Florida in 1951.

Serve Medium Shallow with an arrow. Yet, not a drop of raspberry Jell-O came out of the container. At the end of the merriment, Gale's grandma inquired, "Did you get all that Tupperware shot?"[13]

In tiny Pearlington, Mississippi, Kathleen Bello raced up to the attic with her eight-month-old baby, Hayden. Hurricane Katrina's storm surge was threatening to carry them both away to certain death. The boy's father, Frank, managed to pull his twelve-foot Boston Whaler up alongside the flooding home. But how could she get the baby down the steep slope of the home's steel roof safely, and into a boat that was rocking madly in the storm? In a flash, she grabbed a Tupperware clothes bin and emptied it. She put her child inside, sealed the top, and slid him down the roof and into Dad's waiting arms.

"I knew we were going to catch him," said one relative who helped steady the boat. "There was no choice."[14]

In August 2005, Tupperware struck a $566-million deal to buy the direct-selling beauty operation of the Sara Lee Corporation. As a way to underscore the company's new sales profile beyond burping bowls, the firm's name was changed to Tupperware Brands Corporation. With a worldwide sales force of more than 2 million, Tupperware sales hit $1.3 billion in 2005. That's despite a $36.4 million drop in Tupperware North America revenues. The company made up for it with strong gains in international markets like Europe, Latin America, and Asia. Brownie Wise never made a go of selling cosmetics, but her old employer has. By one estimate, Tupperware's storage containers comprise less than $1 billion in Latin American sales compared to $20 billion in beauty products. Thanks to that kind of product diversity, Tupperware Corp. turned a profit of $85.4 million in 2005. After the departure of Tupper and Wise, Justin Dart's vision in 1958 of taking the company international was the best thing to happen to Tupperware.

The next year, Tupperware profits spiked 10 percent to almost $95 million. In 2006, Tupperware rang up a whopping $1.74 billion in sales, trumping 2005 by almost a half billion dollars. The early buzz in 2007 revolved around an Oscar-winning screenwriter/director preparing to launch *Tupperware*, the major motion picture. If only Hibiscus were still around to stake her claim as leading Tupperware Lady.

Over the years, environmentalists have criticized Tupperware for being so enduring, a plastic scourge clogging the world's landfills. We have "thumped it, sealed it, burped it and stored it."[15] Earl Tupper's Poly-T baby has become a part of the American landscape. For those most responsible for Tupperware's success, its story is the stuff of family lore—the memories of moving to new places, setting up an extended family of dealers and customers, sitting on top of the old station wagon on a steamy Florida July Fourth watching twinkling fireworks reflected in Poly Pond, going to sales rallies, hatching promotional gimmicks, inspiring others to try things they never thought possible, one small piece, one dealer, one order, one customer at a time, each becoming part of an ever-growing mosaic that is Tupperware's uniquely American success story.

○ ○ ○

To appreciate how ahead of her time Brownie Wise was, consider how many ways she could have parlayed her Tupperware know-how and notoriety today. She would have been a natural to host her own syndicated talk show or write a national newspaper column or Web-based feature. Wise could have hit the lecture circuit fetching big money as a motivational speaker; a New York publishing house likely would have been willing to pay her a handsome advance on a book about her ascent in the home-party sales world; she could have launched an Internet-based consulting and sales business; or she could have written her own memoir and sold it to the movies. Today, an executive like Wise would have written into her contract a generous severance package and a whole Wonder Bowl full of stock options, and any one of a number of competitor companies would have snapped her up. With her personality, communication skills, and proven leadership ability, Brownie Wise could have had a shot at political office if she were so inclined.

After parting ways with Tupperware in 1958, Brownie Wise lived out most of her remaining thirty-four years in a more modest, ranch-style home she had built on the west side of Lake Toho, a view of her miracle island off in the distance. The new place was situated next to a small Cracker house built by a pioneer family in the late 1800s, the Laniers. Wise lived a quiet country life, feeding her horse carrots or apples right out the kitchen window. She belonged to a sorority in Kissimmee, stayed active in her church, and participated in contests and craft fairs through area art associations.

She continued efforts to make a new mark in the business world, and from a distance, the principals from her Tupperware past took notice. In compliance with Tupper's wishes, her name was no longer spoken or even written within the walls of Tupperware. "For your information," Hamer Wilson wrote to Tupper in July 1961, "I heard yesterday that the president of Viviane Woodard Cosmetics was relieved of her duties. I hope you are enjoying yourself and that sometime you will give us a ring or a visit."[16]

Wise spent a lot of time on creative projects, whiling away the hours in her pottery studio with Sinatra or one of his contemporaries playing in the background. Colored glazes, not unlike what might go into making Tupperware's trademark pastels, lined the walls of her studio so she could add them by hand to her creations. "Clay is joyous," Wise wrote like a mantra for those in her studio to read. "Clay is here to stay!"

As is often the potter's practice, she kept a bowl at her workspace containing wet clay—for the next project she was inspired to take on. That was another Brownie Wise mantra: progress, moving on, concentrating on what's around the bend. Besides her beloved pottery, Wise made fabric wall hangings and collected fine wicker baskets. She hand-carved tiles and made tools out of chicken bones.

On the east side of the lake—like the other side of her life—Water's Edge sat empty after Brownie and Jerry were forced to vacate. For thirty-one years, the stone mansion at the end of Aultman Road absorbed punishment from the unrelenting central Florida summers, shotgun blasts from hunters, decades of neglect. Trespassers spray-painted graffiti on the bedroom walls Wise had painted pink, left trash in her customized dressing room and the breakfast nook she had constructed over the pool, defaced the carved fireplace and terrazzo tile floors. The sweeping views of Lake Tohopekaliga out of the home's Roman windows were obscured. The lawn had grown junglelike, a haven for the alligators that almost drove Wise away before she ever took up occupancy.

If Brownie Wise ever had occasion to go by the old place, seeing it in such a state of disrepair had to hurt.

A spokesman said the company never felt a compelling need to do anything about the place: "It was just one of a group of assets and there was neither a desire to do anything with it nor a need."[17] At the end of 1989, they finally got around to tearing it down. The same year, Wise was finally invited back to Tupperware to give a fifteen- to twenty-minute speech to distributors on "commitment, quality, and goals."[18]

"You think I ought to go out?" Wise asked her son.

"No I don't," Jerry replied. "They didn't want you—say, '*Tough shit.*'"

"*I don't like that word.*"

"Tell them, '*Stick it up their ass.*'"

"Oh, I'm not gonna tell 'em *that.*"[19]

Brownie Wise may not have been selling Tupperware anymore, but she never relinquished being a *lady.*

Wise sidestepped the invitation, but from time to time gave interviews about the early days. In 1987, she spoke with writer Charles Fishman about turning down *I Love Lucy* and the show producer's plan to have a madcap Tupperware party. "I won't allow it. It won't help us," was her reaction. "I could just see how it would end," Wise recalled, "with Ricky with a Tupperware bowl upside down on his head."[20]

Three decades from the turmoil of her departure, Wise could reflect on the battles with Tupper, often over misguided product ideas like his design for a flour sifter. "I said, 'I will not sell this. It's hard to clean and the holes are too large to do a good job of sifting,'" she recalled.[21] To help make the case, Wise summoned Elsie Mortland. In front of Tupper and all the other executives, she handed Mortland the sifter. "Elsie, what would you do with this if I give it to you?"

"Whoever made this didn't know about sifting flour, that's for sure," Mortland responded quickly.

Trumped again, Earl Tupper wore a familiar red face.

When Charles Fishman in an interview asked Wise about why she left Tupperware in 1958, her answer was neither bitter nor critical: "Just say the company was changing hands and I decided not to go along."[22]

Wise died in 1992 at age seventy-nine, her body riddled with cancer. The central Florida newspapers explained just who this mostly long-forgotten woman was. "Some folks thought Brownie was just a sophisticated huckster who psyched up housewives," wrote Don Boyett. "They never knew her. She had more business sense than a Harvard MBA. She knew people."[23]

"Most of all though," read the September 29, 1992, obituary, "she demonstrated that success in business, as it is in all other aspects of life, is causing people to do better than they think they can. Yes, sir, she was some lady."[24]

Brownie Wise left Tupperware and found lower-key success and fulfillment in the cow town she called home until the day she died.

○ ○ ○

It wasn't easy to find the tranquil place Brownie Wise called home during those final decades. On an uncommonly cold December day, with the morning moon lingering, a pensive fog hovered low over the teardrop ponds that border a newly opened toll road west of town. It's so far out that you still see working citrus groves and only a smattering of new construction, but the toll road will change that. The circuitous route eventually ended up on the Orange Blossom Trail, or U.S. 441 if you prefer. Running 939 miles from Lake City, Tennessee, to Miami, this was the old Mother Road for tourists and settlers intent on living Florida sunshine dreams.

Off another road with cars speeding by as if on a race track, the route headed east. Along a rifle-barrel-straight stretch of blacktop bordering the lake, to one side you could still catch glimpses of the cattle country where barons like Irlo Bronson had lived and made their fortunes. On the other side sat a typical new subdivision bordered by a painted cinder-block wall that defined the neighborhood, separating it from the rural flavor of Kissimmee's southern reaches. Generations of some of the area's oldest families had homesteaded along this side of Lake Toho. You'd have a hard time finding anyone with the ability or inclination to feed horses out of their kitchen windows any more. The central Florida sprawl has infected the area with a suburban sameness. Besides, people drive by so damn fast it's doubtful they have *time* to notice anything.

If you didn't look hard over your right shoulder from the road, you'd just blow by the home and end up in a fancy gated community. Down a short, rutted, dirt-and-grass driveway, past dense overgrowth and discarded bric-a-brac, time had slowed down considerably. An old Nash Rambler sat forgotten in the overgrown yard. One of the first things you noticed about the clapboard house was all kinds of wicker baskets hanging from the screen-porch roof. It could have been a cigar maker's shotgun shack that you'd find in Key West or Ybor City. It was the old Lanier place next to which Brownie Wise built her last home.

In the older, smaller house, Jerry Wise had ridden out a howling, category-three, hell-on-earth hurricane. It had blown away his nursery business. Both he and the house had paid a considerable price; Jerry's home and health were also left in a state of disrepair. It was all he could do to walk a few shuffling steps at a time. During those terrifying August hours, a tree had crashed right through the front-room ceiling; water had poured in. Wise hadn't known if the house would stand up, or if he would live or die. Doctors later informed him he had suffered a heart attack and a stroke. As a result, the only things left agile about him were his mind and caustic wit. His friend Joy, a member of the Lanier family, explained that Brownie's house was too big for Jerry to manage alone, so he moved into the smaller place.

It took several tries to finally convince Jerry to take some time and remember the old days, and the two women who had shaped his life: Brownie Wise and Rose Humphrey. Some of his memories of Tupperware were warm and wonderful, while others brought back pain that past decades could not erase. He spoke of Earl Tupper, Brownie Wise, and some of the other early founders as if they were not long gone; their personalities were too strong to have faded. Sadly, time had taken a considerable toll on the young man who'd ridden horses, raised cattle, played music and practical jokes. As a result, his friend Joy popped in from time to time to check on him, or to add a little extra context to the conversation.

On that frosty December morning, sipping the drink that was always his mother's favorite, coffee and half-and-half, Wise sat in front of a small, flickering television, a PBS children's show barely visible. A long, dusty brown extension chord powered it and a portable heater. Wise wore a knit cap with a ball on the end, like you might see on a little kid in suburban Detroit coming down a snowy hill on his toboggan. He wore a beard that was more salt than pepper, and he spoke in a low register, sometimes involuntarily slurring words, giving sentences a halting cadence. He sometimes referred to "Mother," but more often he called his mother "Brownie." He also spoke of his father as "Bob" or "Bobby" Wise. In the 1960s, Jerry said his mother and father attempted a reconciliation of sorts. She was no longer the maven of Tupperware and he was in Miami, making a serious go of sobriety and success.

"Yeah, he was kind of neat to be around. And my mother said, 'What do you think of your Dad?' I said, 'Well, I've never seen this side of him,'" Jerry recalled. "We went down to see him and Bob was just as sober as could be and looked great."[25] In Miami, Robert Wise was making hydraulic steering wheels for outboard boats and doing quite well. He and Brownie went into business together on a prepaid college tuition idea, a forerunner of a very popular program run by the State of Florida today. That's as far as the fairy-tale ending went.

"He drank it," said his son of the business venture. "Brownie was pissed—oh, she was pissed. She said 'We're gonna clean out his building before his creditors show up.'" Like a broken record, Robert Wise again ended up in trouble with his family and the law. After that last sour experience, Jerry's parents never had any substantive contact. Jerry said his father was around sixty-four years old when he died.

Jerry took strong exception to his mother being painted as virtually penniless and friendless after the Tupperware days. She owned and developed land and had numerous hobbies to pass the time. Jerry admitted that his mother was always "a wallflower" when it came to socializing and that she "didn't get out much." After all the problems with her ex, she seemed to be done with men, with a possible exception of one. "In later life, she wanted her clay, her son, and her horse," said Jerry. About her legacy as a trailblazing independent businesswoman, Brownie would not put up with being called a feminist or a forerunner of the women's liberation movement. Adopting a tone as if he had repeated this many times, Jerry proclaimed: "Brownie just said, 'I needed the money for me and my kid. So I got out there and made it.'" If talk ever turned to why she left Tupperware, Brownie told her son the patent was about to run out and she wanted to move on to new challenges.

With his mother's memory so close, and some good caffeinated coffee in his system, Jerry contemplated something he hadn't done in some time: getting up and making his way to his mother's favorite place in the world. Having reentered the house, his friend Joy told Jerry it would be therapeutic to get up and move around. "You can do it," she urged him. After she retrieved his walker, Joy put it in front of him, and Jerry haltingly came to his feet. "I have a fear of falling," he said.

He slowly shuffled through a storage room containing one of his mother's trademark peacock wicker chairs. He labored out the side door and squinted in the warming, midmorning sunlight. Slowly, down one, two, and three perilous stairs, Jerry made it across the adjoining courtyard and up to a locked door, "If I could get somebody to build a pair of handrails I'd be in here every day. I love it." As the door swung open and the lights went on, Jerry announced, "Here's the world of Brownie Wise."

It was very much a working potter's studio complete with a half-dozen kilns. Adding to the rustic atmosphere, it seemed as if the Tupperware fairy had come through and sprinkled everything with a fine layer of pixie dust. But there was much more—multiple rows of mason jars containing a smorgasbord of colored powders took up the entire far wall. At the other end, a stack of old records featuring crooners of bygone days gathered dust, not having been played in years.

Jerry chimed in, "That wall where all those chemicals are—it's not a meth lab."

It was nice to hear laughter fill a place that had once been vibrant but was in serious need of upkeep. A storage locker had been used as a repository for Jerry's mementos after the storm had come through: in an oval-shaped frame, a dusty black-and-white photograph of Brownie holding the baby she called "Tiny Hands," an autograph from one of the many jubilee guest speakers, rare photos of Brownie later in life, showing her measuring colored glaze for one of her projects. Along another row of shelves sat all of the pottery pieces Brownie made but then didn't know what to do with. "All award winners," her son said with obvious pride. On a high shelf, a dusty cardboard box contained reams of contest ribbons to prove it. Some of the pieces had a special marking, signifying the ones she and Jerry worked on together.

Seated on a small chair with wheels on the bottom, Jerry reflected on a whimsical piece his mother had made that bore a strong resemblance to him: "She said, 'Well, what are you going to do with it?' I said, 'I'm gonna keep it and look at him for the rest of my life.' And she said, 'That's not making progress. Throw that thing out or sell it to somebody. MAKE another one.' I said, 'I don't

Brownie's trademark peacock chair.

Jerry Wise in his mother's pottery studio holding her whimsical statue of him, December 2005.

know where you're getting this from. Are you conversing with a dead great-grandmother?' She said, 'I might be.'"

Jerry never got used to the idea that his mother felt she could actually converse with the departed. "I said, 'How do you do this?' and she said, 'I don't know, but if you practice enough you'll learn. . . . Don't converse with them silently.' I said, 'What if people see me there talking to myself?' She said, 'To HELL with what people think! Do it! Get on with it!'"

Joy headed over to the heart of the room: the area Brownie had used for years as her work space. As Joy lifted the lid off a bowl, she told Jerry, "Oh, it's probably dry by now; you haven't added water to it lately."

"Keep it wet," was all he replied.

With a hint of surprise, Joy said, "No, it's still wet, she was gonna make something with it."

"Yep, she was. I'll end up using it." In that bowl was the last piece of clay Brownie Wise was planning to use, or perhaps, planning to leave behind as an enduring symbol of the bond between a mother and son, sealed not in plastic, but joyous clay. Tears welled up in Jerry's eyes. "She said a potter always kept their clay wet for their son. I'm the son. Sorry about the crying, sometimes I just can't hold it."

Jerry Wise died two years later. On a sunny January afternoon, he was laid to rest next to his mother. "Tiny Hands" was 70. He was never able to give his mother the epigraph Brownie wanted on her headstone: "She made a damn good pot."

○　○　○

The legacy of Brownie Wise begins with the love she had for her only son. In business, she could have let the gender stereotypes, poor southern upbringing, limited education, and abusive spouse confine her in a safe cocoon of excuses and self-pity. But for Brownie Wise—as for many of the so-called greatest generation—those limitations simply steeled her ambition. It was the desire for glamour and fame and for the approval of the famous, as well as the feeling of invincibility of her alter ego, Hibiscus, that took control and brought about the demise of Brownie Wise at Tupperware.

But there were other factors at work. Earl Tupper was also suffering from the stress of trying to grow the phenomenon that Tupperware became. He created his masterwork in Poly-T, built an enormous machine to churn out Tupperware to the masses, and then withdrew from the world with his millions. But in later life he also created a considerable legacy of philanthropy for which he will always be remembered. Both he and Wise had given their all and sacrificed much in the way of their personal lives to raise Tupper's plastic brainchild and to bring the company to the point it had reached in 1958. Then the likes of Justin Dart, Hamer Wilson, Gary McDonald, Elsie Mortland, John Ansley, Joe Hara, and many, many others provided the energy and ideas to take Tupperware worldwide, ushering in a new era of prosperity that continues to evolve today.

Earl Tupper owned the product, the stock, and his company. He had a right to reap the riches of success that only his brilliant, innovative mind had the perseverance to achieve. But he never owned the history, and it was wrong to try to erase Brownie Wise from it. Sure, Wise may have let her ego get away from her, but in the face of such widespread adoration, success, and acclaim, who wouldn't have? Even at her autocratic worst, the people above, below, and around Wise profited. Her detractors argue that it was the collective hard work of the thousands of Tupperware foot soldiers that was the real key to this success story, as well as the efforts of the strong team of young executives who were every bit as willing to put in the long hours necessary to build the Tupperware revolution—and then take it to even greater heights after Wise's exit.

Maybe they're right. But no one can deny how much the program that Brownie Wise put in place, the publicity she attracted, her genius for communication, and the esprit de corps she traveled the world to build accelerated that success—and made Earl Tupper a very rich man. To say she was ahead of her time is an understatement. Brownie Wise was the real chief executive of an international sales company when only a handful of women could be counted as the heads of industry. And this was not in New York or Los Angeles; Brownie Wise did it in the Deep South, where racism, sexism, and ignorance could bury the most ambitious of dreams. Before Walt Disney, before NASA, Apollo, Alan Shepherd, and John Glenn, Brownie Wise put Orlando and Kissimmee on the map when all they were known for was sunshine, citrus, sportfishing, cattle, and cockfighting.

Now hindsight compresses all that happened during the early days of Tupperware. She may have been a reticent feminist, but Brownie Wise is recognized for helping throw open the doors to executive success through which many women have followed. She took the lead role in mapping out a party-plan system that became the gold standard for the company that turned its back on her. While Wise was still at the helm, Peter and Elsie Block were accorded the same kind of unceremonious ouster. It took decades for the legacy of Brownie Wise to rise, not like a phoenix from the ashes, but more like a hidden gem that had sunk way down in the marshy, central Florida soil. Most of those who tried to keep that legacy buried never lived to see the day that America's First Lady of Tupperware again earned what fuels every salesperson's soul: recognition.

Notes

Chapter 1. The Brownie Wise Problem

Epigraph source: "How Brownie Wise Whoops Up Sales," *Business Week*, April 17, 1954, 62.

1. Gary McDonald, interview by the author, The Villages, Florida, September 15, 2005 (hereafter cited as McDonald interview). McDonald introduced Tupperware to Brownie Wise and is the last living executive who was involved in the formation of Tupperware Home Parties.

2. Ibid.

3. Charles Fishman, "Is the Party Over?" *Orlando Sentinel*, March 15, 1987. Fishman spoke at length with Wise for this article.

Chapter 2. Going It Alone

Epigraph source: Earl Tupper, "Advice for Aspirants to Business Careers" (hereafter cited as Tupper Advice), handwritten note from the Earl Tupper Papers, Smithsonian Institution, National Museum of American History (hereafter cited as Tupper Papers).

1. *The Graduate*, directed by Mike Nichols and Lawrence Turman (Metro Goldwyn Mayer, 1967).

2. Brownie Wise to W. Chandler Marshall, July 18, 1946, in Brownie Wise Papers, 1928–1968, Smithsonian Institution, National Museum of American History (hereafter cited as Wise Papers).

3. Jerry Wise, interview by the author, Kissimmee, Fla., December 23, 2005 (hereafter cited as Jerry Wise interview). Wise is the only son of Brownie and Robert Wise.

4. One-page child-support agreement, Wayne County District Court, entered into the record on September 17, 1941, Wise Papers.

5. Earl Tupper invention book, Tupper Papers.

6. McDonald interview.

7. "Fascinating Facts about Earl Tupper," www.Ideafinder.com.

8. Neil Osterweil, "Tupper Biography," typescript, chap. 6, "A Real Education," Tupper Papers.

9. Ibid.

10. Jerry Wise interview.

11. Brownie Wise, undated notebook, Wise Papers.

12. Brownie Wise, undated letter written under the pen name Hibiscus, Wise Papers.

13. Ibid.

14. Ibid.

15. Ibid.

16. Brownie Wise to W. Chandler Marshall, July 18, 1946, Wise Papers.

17. Ibid.

18. Wise, undated letter written under the pen name Hibiscus, Wise Papers.

19. Ed Creiger, "Earl Silas Tupper: The Plastic Years 1945 to 1958," typescript, Tupper Papers.

20. Ibid.

21. Ibid.

22. Ibid.

23. Ibid.

24. Ibid.

25. Ibid.

26. Osterweil, "Tupper Biography," chap. 7.

Chapter 3. The Product and the Plan

Epigraph source: Brownie Wise, *Triangle Unit News*, August 2, 1948, Wise Papers.

1. Jerry Wise interview.

2. "Biography of Frank Stanley Beveridge." www.Stanley.com.

3. McDonald interview.

4. Elmer Nyberg to Brownie Wise, June 13, 1947, Wise Papers, ser. 2. Nyberg was Stanley's education director and an important mentor to Wise.

5. Stanley order form, Wise Papers, ser. 2.

6. Frank Stanley Beveridge, undated unit-manager training materials, Wise Papers.

7. Elmer Nyberg to Brownie Wise, October 9, 1948, Wise Papers.

8. Ibid.

9. Ibid.

10. Elmer Nyberg, "How to Develop Resourcefulness," memo, Wise Papers.

11. Brownie Wise, *Go-Getter*, July 20, 1948, Wise Papers.

12. Ibid.

13. Elmer Nyberg to Brownie Wise, September 13, 1948, Wise Papers.

14. Brownie Wise, *Triangle Unit News*, August 2, 1948, Wise Papers.

15. Ibid.

16. Ibid.

17. Ibid.

18. Ibid.

19. McDonald interview.

20. Ibid.

21. Earl Tupper to J. C. Healy, memorandum, September 14, 1949, Tupper Papers. Healy was one of the Tupper Corporation's first advertising/public relations executives.

22. Ibid.

23. Osterweil, "Tupper Biography," chap. 7.

24. Ibid.

25. McDonald interview.

26. "Earl S. Tupper of Upton Granted Valuable Patent," *Milford (Mass.) Daily News*, undated clipping, Tupper Papers; Tupper Corp. memorandum, November 9, 1949.

27. Ibid.

28. "Tupperware," *Time*, September 8, 1947.

29. Alison J. Clarke, *Tupperware: The Promise of Plastic in 1950s America* (Washington, D.C.: Smithsonian Institution Press, 1999), 42.

30. "Tupperware," *Time*, September 8, 1947.

31. Ibid.

32. Tupper to Healy, memorandum, September 14, 1949, Tupper Papers.

33. Ibid.

34. Early Tupperware full-page magazine ad, "Tupperware Canister Sets, Cereal Bowls, Wonder Bowls, refrigerator bowls, tumblers, headlining a great line of Housewares fashioned from Tupper "material of the future," 1948, Tupper Papers.

35. McDonald interview.

36. Vivian Balch, "How J. L. Hudson Changed the Way We Shop," *Detroit News*, January 26, 2006.

37. Kristin Palm, "One Building's Struggle," *Metropolis Magazine*, June 1998.

38. McDonald interview.

39. "Necessity Became the Parent of Adventure," *Our World*, July 1981. This article marked the thirtieth anniversary with Tupperware of early distributors Ann and Tom Damigella.

40. McDonald interview.

41. Liz Doup, "Tupper, The Man and His Women," *South Florida Sun-Sentinel*, April, 11, 1989.

42. Frank Stanley Beveridge, quoted in the *Stanley Pilgrim*, August 22–25, 1948, Wise Papers.

43. Ibid.

44. Ibid.

45. Ibid.

46. Brownie Wise, *Go-Getter*, November 25, 1950, Wise Papers.

47. Jerry Wise interview.

48. Ibid.

Chapter 4. Filling In the Gaps

Epigraph source: Tupper Advice, Tupper Papers.

1. Earl Tupper to J. C. Healy, memorandum, "He Likes the Ladies," March 8, 1949.

2. Ibid.

3. Ibid.

4. "Formal Notice," Tupper Corporation *Modern Plastics*, November 9, 1949, Tupper Papers.

5. Ibid.

6. Creiger, "Earl Silas Tupper," Tupper Papers.

7. Elsie Block, *My Tupperware Party Was Over and I Sat Down and Cried* (Authorhouse, Bloomington, Ind., 2004), 58.

8. Earl Tupper to J. C. Healy, memorandum, September 19, 1949, Tupper Papers.

9. McDonald interview.

10. Ibid.

11. Ibid.

12. Ibid.

13. Ibid.

14. Brownie Wise, *Go-Getter*, August 19, 1949.

15. Tupperware order form, 1949, Wise Papers.

16. McDonald interview.

17. Jerry Wise interview.

18. Ibid.

19. Ibid.

20. Ibid.

21. *Our World*, July 1981.

22. Ibid.

23. Earl Tupper, "Chart for Blending Tupperware Pastel Colors," n.d., Tupper Papers.

24. *Our World*, July 1981.

25. McDonald interview.

26. Jerry Wise interview.

Chapter 5. A Turbulent New Home

Epigraph source: Brownie Wise to V. Collamore, May 30, 1950, Wise Papers. Collamore was the first person from the Tupperware Corporation to meet Wise in person. He became her company contact when she switched from Stanley to Tupperware.

1. Brownie Wise, "Round Robin" letter to a group of former dealers, May 9, 1950, Wise Papers (hereafter cited as Round Robin letter). This letter gave important details about her move to Florida and first days there.

2. Ibid.

3. Ibid.

4. Ibid.

5. Ibid.

6. Ibid.

7. Ibid.

8. Ibid.

9. Ibid.

10. Ibid.

11. Brownie Wise, foreword to *Patio Parties Training Manual*, May 1950. It was in this early manual that Wise started the "feminization" of Stanley dealer-training techniques.

12. Ibid.

13. Ibid.

14. Brownie Wise, Round Robin letter.

15. Ibid.

16. Ibid.

17. Jerry Wise interview.

18. Brownie Wise to V. Collamore, May 30, 1950.

19. Ibid.

20. Ibid.

21. Jayne and Bob Boltz (Tampa, Fla.) to Brownie Wise, June 8, 1950, Wise Papers.

22. Brownie Wise to Jayne and Bob Boltz, June 10, 1950, Wise Papers.

23. Ibid.

24. Brownie Wise to V. Collamore, July 21, 1950, Wise Papers.

25. Gwen Lord (Orlando, Fla.) to Brownie Wise, July 29, 1950.

26. Brownie Wise to V. Collamore, July 21, 1950, Wise Papers.

27. Brownie Wise to V. Collamore, August 1, 1950, Wise Papers.

28. Ibid.

29. Block, *My Tupperware Party*, 60.

30. Ibid.

31. Norman Squires to Brownie Wise, November 3, 1950, Wise Papers. Squires was the head of Tupper's short-lived Hostess Division.

32. Block, *My Tupperware Party*, 65.

33. Ibid.

34. Ibid., 66.

35. B. M. Cant to Brownie Wise, September 3, 1950, Wise Papers. Cant was the executive secretary to Squires at Hostess.

36. Ibid.

37. Brownie Wise, *Go-Getter*, November 25, 1950, Wise Papers.

38. Ibid.

39. Brownie Wise to Norman Squires, January 13, 1951, Wise Papers.

40. T. L. Coffman to Brownie Wise, February 18, 1951, Wise Papers. Coffman was an early unit manager in Florida who resigned over unpaid commissions. This foreshadowed later problems with Hostess.

41. Brownie Wise to Norman Squires, January 13, 1951, Wise Papers.

42. Brownie Wise, "welcome speech," dated 1951, Wise Papers.

43. Osterweil, written transcript of taped interview with Glenn Tupper, Tupper Papers.

44. Ibid.

45. Ibid.

46. Ibid.

47. Brownie Wise to Norman Squires, January 13, 1951, Wise Papers.

48. Ibid.

49. Brownie Wise to Norman Squires, February 14, 1951, Wise Papers.

50. Ibid.

51. Ibid.

52. Brownie Wise to Squires, March 16, 1951, Wise Papers.

53. Ibid.

Chapter 6. The Confluence of Genius

Epigraph source: Tupper Advice, Tupper Papers.

1. Fishman, "Is the Party Over?"

2. Ibid.

3. Clarke, *Tupperware: The Power of Plastic*, 93. Multiple sources confirm the allegation of Squires's embezzlement.

4. Ibid.

5. Fishman, "Is the Party Over?"

6. Ibid.

7. Brownie Wise, "welcome speech," Wise Papers. In this speech, Wise recounts that the first meeting between her, Tupper, and other early distributors was at the Garden City Hotel, not in Worcester, Massachusetts.

8. Brownie Wise to Norman Squires, February 14, 1951, Wise Papers.

9. Fishman, "Is the Party Over?"

10. Earl Tupper to Tupperware dealers, memorandum, May 3, 1951, Tupper Papers.

11. McDonald interview.

12. Ibid.

13. Ibid.

14. Ibid.

15. Block, *My Tupperware Party*, 68.

16. Ibid.

17. Fishman, "Is the Party Over?"

18. Brownie Wise, "The Story of Poly," undated typescript, Wise Papers.

19. Ibid.

20. Ibid.

21. Ibid.

22. Brownie Wise, speech to Tupperware dealers in Detroit, 1951, Wise Papers. This is believed to be her first speech in her new managerial role at Tupperware Home Parties.

23. Ibid.

24. Ibid.

25. Ibid.

26. Ibid.

27. Ibid.

28. Ibid.

29. Brownie Wise, "This Is the Story of Tupperware," undated typescript, Wise Papers. This is a lengthy and important document in which Wise writes her own history of THP to that point, likely 1956. (Hereafter cited as "Story of Tupperware.")

30. Tupperware advertisement in *Salesman's Opportunity*, November 1951, Tupper Papers.

31. Wise, "Story of Tupperware."

32. *Tupperware Sparks* 1 (November 1951).

33. McDonald interview.

34. Brownie Wise to Earl Tupper, January 1, 1952, Wise Papers. This important letter details the land that Wise hoped Tupper would purchase for THP. It also indicates that Orlando was not her first choice of locales.

35. Ibid.

36. Fishman, "Is the Party Over?"

37. Brownie Wise to Earl Tupper, January 1, 1952.

38. Hal Boyle, "Glowing Picture of Florida Painted by Hal Boyle," *Orlando Sentinel*, January 28, 1952. Boyle was a Pulitzer Prize–winning war correspondent who noted how many soldiers were setting down roots around their former bases in Florida.

39. Ibid.

40. Ibid.

Chapter 7. Permanent Roots

Epigraph source: Brownie Wise, "Talk for July Conference" (rough draft), 1952, Wise Papers.

1. Brownie Wise to Earl Tupper, January 1, 1952.

2. Ibid.

3. Ibid.

4. Wise, "Story of Tupperware."

5. Block, *My Tupperware Party*, 73.

6. Ibid., 75.

7. Ibid.

8. Ibid.

9. Brownie Wise to Earl Tupper, January 1, 1952.

10. "Million Dollar Plastic Firm to Come Here," *Orlando Morning Sentinel*, January 2, 1952.

11. Ibid.

12. Ibid.

13. "Another Central Florida Triumph," editorial, *Orlando Sunday Sentinel-Star*, January 20, 1952.

14. McDonald interview.

15. Ibid.

16. Ibid.

17. Ibid.

18. Steve Elling, "Swing into History," *Orlando Sentinel*, December 15, 2005.

19. "Plastic Firm Official Spreads City's Fame," *Orlando Evening Star*, January 24, 1952. Brownie Wise established a pattern of seeking publicity before it became the norm of THP's public relations department.

20. Ibid.

21. McDonald interview.

22. Jerry Wise interview.

23. Ibid.

24. *Tupperware Sparks* 1, no. 2 (January 1952).

25. Ibid.

26. Brownie Wise, early Tupperware training materials, Wise Papers.

27. Ibid.

28. Ibid.

29. Ibid.

30. Ibid.

31. Brownie Wise, "Just between YOU and ME," February 27, 1952, Wise Papers.

32. Earl Tupper to Brownie Wise, handwritten note, February 29, 1952, Wise Papers.

33. Brownie Wise to Earl Tupper, memorandum, February 27, 1952, Wise Papers.

34. Brownie Wise to Earl Tupper, memorandum, March 12, 1952, Wise Papers.

35. Ibid.

36. *Tupperware Sparks* 2, no. 4 (April 1952).

37. Earl Tupper to Brownie Wise, handwritten note, April 7, 1952, Wise Papers.

38. *Tupperware Sparks* 2, no. 5 (May 1952).

39. Brownie Wise to Russell Bassett, May 3, 1952, Wise Papers. This letter shows how Wise put the responsibility for an early distributor's struggles entirely on him.

40. Ibid.

41. Brownie Wise to Earl Tupper, memorandum, May 9, 1952, Wise Papers. This memo, subtitled "Frosted Crystal to be Put in the Store Line," shows Wise's willingness to take exception to Tupper's edicts, especially when it came to the sales side.

42. Ibid.

43. Ibid.

44. Earl Tupper to Brownie Wise, sketch, May 4, 1952, Wise Papers.

45. Earl Tupper to Brownie Wise, memorandum, May 15, 1952, Wise Papers.

46. Frank Klein, "Bronson Holdings Are the Largest in Osceola," *Orlando Sentinel-Star*, March 12, 1952.

47. McDonald interview.

48. *Tupperware Sparks* 2, no. 6 (June–July 1952).

49. Ibid.

50. Ibid.

51. Block, *My Tupperware Party*, 78.

52. Ibid.

53. Ibid.

54. *Tupperware Sparks* (June–July 1952).

55. Brownie Wise, "Talk for July Conference," July 1952, Wise Papers.

56. *Tupperware Sparks* 2, no. 6 (June–July 1952).

57. Earl Tupper to Robert Evans, memorandum, August 4, 1952, Tupper Papers. This important memo shows Tupper's confidence in Wise to other distributors, particularly Evans, with whom Wise had clashed early on.

58. Ibid.

59. Ibid.

60. Brownie Wise, "Memo to All Distributors and Sub-distributors," August 15, 1952, Wise Papers.

61. Ibid.

62. Brownie Wise, "Speech to the Orlando Junior Chamber of Commerce," August 1952, Wise Papers.

63. *Tupperware Sparks* 2, no. 9 (September 1952).

64. Ibid.

65. Ibid.

66. Ibid.

67. Block, *My Tupperware Party*, 86.

68. Thomas Damigella (Everett, Mass.) to Earl Tupper, November 10, 1952, Tupper

Papers. The Damigellas were founding distributors in THP and were also credited with pioneering the home-party system. They bought directly from Tupper before the advent of THP.

69. McDonald interview.

70. Jerry Wise interview.

Chapter 8. Groundwork for a Revolution

Epigraph source: Brownie Wise, "Opening talk, January conference," January 1953, Wise Papers.

1. McDonald interview.

2. Brownie Wise, "Opening talk, January conference," January 1953, Wise Papers.

3. "Tupper Purchases Home on Lake," *Kissimmee Gazette*, November 14, 1952.

4. Jerry Wise interview.

5. Ibid.

6. Ibid.

7. "Darden Has Bagged 500 Wildcats in Area," *Kissimmee Gazette*, December 12, 1952.

8. Wise, "Story of Tupperware."

9. Elsie Mortland, interview by the author, Kissimmee, Fla., March 28, 2005 (hereafter cited as Mortland interview). Mortland was the first hostess demonstrator within Tupperware Home Parties.

10. Ibid.

11. Ibid.

12. Ibid.

13. Ibid.

14. Ibid.

15. "How a Typical Homemaker Learned the Secret That Can DOUBLE Your Family's Income," *Salesman's Opportunity*, March 1953.

16. Ibid.

17. Ibid.

18. Ibid.

19. Ibid.

20. Ibid.

21. Ibid.

22. Earl Tupper memorandum to "Fellow Workers," February 3, 1953, Tupper Papers.

23. Ibid.

24. Ibid.

25. Ibid.

26. Ibid.

27. Ibid.

28. *Tupperware Sparks* 2, no. 12 (December 1952–January 1953).

29. *Tupperware Sparks* 3, no. 6 (June 1953).

30. Wise, "Story of Tupperware."

31. *Tupperware Sparks* 3, no. 2 (February 1953).

32. Brownie Wise, "Opening talk for January conference," January 1953, Wise Papers.

33. Ibid.

34. *Tupperware Sparks* 3, no. 3 (March 1953).

35. Ibid.

36. Ibid.

37. Ibid.

38. Ibid.

39. Block, *My Tupperware Party*, 71.

40. Ibid.

41. Ibid.

42. Ibid., 72.

43. Ibid.

44. Ibid.

45. Ibid.

46. "Tupperware Commissions Huge Mural," *Kissimmee Gazette*, May 15, 1953.

47. Brownie Wise, "Art Fund Questionnaire," January 31, 1953, Wise Papers.

48. Earl Tupper birthday card to Brownie Wise, May 25, 1953, Wise Papers.

49. Jerry Wise interview.

50. Ibid.

51. Ibid.

52. Ibid.

53. Ibid.

54. Ibid.

55. Wise, "Story of Tupperware."

56. "Tupperware Distributors in Conference Here," *Kissimmee Gazette*, June 30, 1953.

57. *Tupperware Sparks* 3, no. 7 (July 1953).

58. Ibid.

59. Brownie Wise to Earl Tupper, memorandum, November 21, 1953, Wise Papers.

60. Ibid.

61. Ibid.

62. Brownie Wise to Earl Tupper, memorandum, October 27, 1953, Wise Papers.

Chapter 9. Success and Jubilation

Epigraph source: McDonald interview.

1. Brownie Wise to Earl Tupper, memorandum, October 27, 1953, Wise Papers.

2. Press party invitation, Wise Papers.

3. "Dorothy Shea at the Maisonette," www.Craigsbigbandsandbignames.com.

4. Ibid.

5. Brownie Wise to Earl Tupper, memorandum, October 27, 1953, Wise Papers.

6. Ibid.

7. Ibid.

8. McDonald interview.

9. Ibid.

10. Ibid.

11. Ibid.

12. Brownie Wise to Earl Tupper, memorandum, November 21, 1953, Wise Papers.

13. Ibid

14. Ibid.

15. Ibid.

16. Ibid.

17. Ibid.

18. Ibid.

19. Don Fuhr, in *Tupperware!* PBS documentary, produced, written, and directed by Laurie Kahn-Leavitt (Public Broadcasting, 2004).

20. *Business Week*, April 17, 1954.

21. Block, *My Tupperware Party*, 118.

22. Wise, "Story of Tupperware."

23. Earl Tupper, handwritten year-by-year sales analysis, Tupper Papers.

24. *Tupperware Sparks* 3, nos. 15–16 (April–May 1954).

25. Ibid.

26. Block, *My Tupperware Party*, 118.

27. Ibid.

28. Ibid.

29. Wise, "Story of Tupperware."

30. "Tupperware Ends Homecoming Here," *Kissimmee Gazette*, April 16, 1954.

31. Fishman, "Is the Party Over?"

32. Brownie Wise to Rose Humphrey, January 19, 1954, Wise Papers. Wise does not mention that distributor Humphrey is her mother.

33. Wise, "Story of Tupperware."

34. Ibid.

35. McDonald interview.

36. Ibid.

37. Ibid.

38. Ibid.

39. "Tupperware Set for Big Celebration," *Kissimmee Gazette*, April 2, 1954.

40. Ibid.

41. Brownie Wise, "Welcome" speech, 1954, Wise Papers.

42. "Life Goes on a Big Dig," *Life*, May 3, 1954, 172.

43. Ibid, 174.

44. McDonald interview.

45. "Life Goes on a Big Dig," *Life*, May 3, 1954, 174.

46. "Tupperware Makes Life," editorial, *Kissimmee Gazette*, April 30, 1954.

47. Ibid.

48. *Business Week*, April 17, 1954.

49. Ibid.

50. Ibid.

51. Ibid.

52. Ibid.

53. Ibid.

54. Ibid.

55. Ibid.

56. Ibid.

57. Ibid.

58. Brownie Wise, "Ad Astra," Wise Papers.

59. Ibid.

60. Ibid.

61. Ibid.

62. *Business Week*, April 17, 1954.

63. Ibid.

64. McDonald Interview.

Chapter 10. Explosive Growth

Epigraph source: Tupperware Sparks 3, nos. 21–22 (October–November 1954).

1. *Business Week*, April 17, 1954.

2. McDonald interview.

3. Earl Tupper to Brownie Wise, memorandum, June 1, 1954, Tupper Papers.

4. "5,000 Attend Tupper Open House Sunday," *Kissimmee Gazette*, May 7, 1954.

5. *Tupperware Sparks* 3, nos. 17–18 (June–July 1954).

6. McDonald interview.

7. Wise, "Story of Tupperware."

8. Mortland interview.

9. Former secretary to Brownie Wise, telephone interview by the author, July 18, 2005 (hereafter cited as Wise former secretary interview). This former employee asked not to be named.

10. *Tupperware Sparks* 3, no. 20 (September 1954).

11. Ibid.

12. Wise, "Story of Tupperware."

13. Jerry Wise interview.

14. Ibid.

15. *Tupperware Sparks* 3, nos. 21–22 (October–November 1954).

16. Wise, "Story of Tupperware."

17. Ibid.

18. Ibid.

19. Earl Tupper to Brownie Wise, memorandum, November 8, 1954, Tupper Papers.

20. Wise, "Story of Tupperware."

21. *Tupperware Sparks* 3, no. 23 (December 1954).

22. Ibid.

23. McDonald interview.

Chapter 11. A Revolt from Within

Epigraph source: Jerry Wise interview.

1. Ibid.

2. Ibid.

3. Ibid.

4. Ibid.

5. Ibid.

6. Ibid.

7. Tony Ponticelli, interview by author, Maitland, Fla., September 29, 2005 (hereafter cited as Ponticelli interview). Ponticelli was former special events director of THP.

8. Ibid.

9. Ibid.

10. Ibid.

11. Ibid.

12. Ibid.

13. Ibid.

14. Jerry Wise interview.

15. Ibid.

16. Ibid.

17. Hinton interview.

18. Ibid.

19. Jerry Wise interview.

20. Marguerite Obermeyer, "What a Woman!" *Orlando Sentinel Florida Magazine*, January 9, 1955.

21. Ibid.

22. Ibid.

23. Hinton interview.

24. Wise, "Story of Tupperware."

25. Ibid.

26. Block, *My Tupperware Party*, 88.

27. Ibid.

28. Ibid.

29. Brownie Wise, "An Open Letter to Tupperware Distributors and Dealers," August 21, 1955, Wise Papers.

30. McDonald interview.

31. Ibid.

32. Ibid.

33. Earl Tupper to Brownie Wise, confidential memorandum, September 21, 1955, Wise Papers.

34. Brownie Wise letter to distributors and dealers, August 21, 1955.

35. McDonald interview.

36. Ibid.

37. Hinton interview. Both Hinton and McDonald confirm the bugging efforts to determine which distributors were trying to unionize.

38. Ibid.

39. McDonald interview.

40. Ibid.

41. Ibid.

42. Block, *My Tupperware Party*, 22. In her book, Elsie Block never admits to any plan on the part of herself or her husband to unionize distributors. She claims not to know why their Tupperware distributorship was taken away.

43. Ibid.

44. Ibid.

45. Ibid.

46. Ibid., 26.

47. Brownie Wise to Earl Tupper, memorandum, May 27, 1957, Wise Papers.

48. Ibid.

49. Ibid.

50. Ibid.

51. McDonald interview.

52. Ibid.

53. Kay Tilden, San Diego, Calif., dealer, to Brownie Wise, March 1, 1958, Wise Papers.

54. Notie Baumgardner, Evansville, Ind., dealer, to Brownie Wise, December 2, 1957, Wise Papers.

55. Ibid.

56. Irene Swan, dealer, to Brownie Wise, December 22 (year unknown), Wise Papers.

57. Ibid.

58. "Tupperware Article in March Coronet," *Kissimmee Gazette*, February 25, 1955.

59. Brownie Wise, "Welcome Address," April 1955, Wise Papers.

60. "Dr. Peale is Speaker at Tupperware Jubilee, *Kissimmee Gazette*, April 22, 1955.

61. *Tupperware Sparks* 5, no. 28 (May 1955).

62. Wise, "Story of Tupperware."

63. "Tupperware Plans Larger Museum," *Kissimmee Gazette*, May 20, 1955.

64. Earl Tupper, "Dear Fellow Worker and Family," memorandum, August 9, 1955, Tupper Papers.

65. Ibid.

66. Ibid.

67. Brownie Wise to Earl Tupper, memorandum, May 27, 1957, Wise Papers.

68. Ibid.

69. Ibid.

Chapter 12. New Players in Place

Epigraph source: Pat Jordan, interview by the author, Orlando, Florida, April 4, 2005 (hereafter cited as Jordan interview). Jordan was an early South Florida dealer who went on to distributorships in Norfolk and Orlando.

1. Ibid.

2. Ibid.

3. Ibid.

4. Ibid.

5. Ibid.

6. Ibid.

7. Ibid.

8. Ibid.

9. Ibid.

10. Ibid.

11. Ibid.

12. Mortland interview.

13. Ibid.

14. Ibid.

15. Ibid.

16. Ponticelli interview.

17. McDonald interview.

18. Jordan interview.

19. McDonald interview.

20. Ibid.

21. Ponticelli interview.

22. Hinton interview.

23. McDonald interview.

Chapter 13. The Foundations Shaken

Epigraph source: Brownie Wise, *Best Wishes, Brownie Wise* (Orlando: Podium, 1957), 164.

1. Eleanor Pollack, "Mrs. Carmony Goes to an All-Girl Convention," *McCall's*, January 1956.

2. *Tupperware Sparks* 5, no. 1 (January 1956).

3. *Tupperware Sparks* 5, no. 2 (February 1956).

4. "Women at Work, Business Finds They're People Too," *Newsweek*, February 27, 1956.

5. Wise former secretary interview.

6. Ponticelli interview.

7. Jerry Wise interview.

8. Ibid.

9. Marilyn Mennello, telephone interview by the author, Winter Park, Fla., January 27, 2006. Mennello was Hamer Wilson's ex-wife.

10. Ponticelli interview.

11. McDonald interview.

12. Wise, *Best Wishes*, 164.

13. Ibid. 168.

14. Ibid.

15. *Business Week*, April 17, 1954.

16. Wise, *Best Wishes*, 169.

17. "50 Most Important Floridians of the 20th Century," *Lakeland Ledger*, copyright 1998.

18. *Tupperware Sparks* 5, no. 5 (May 1956).

19. Ibid.

20. Jerry Wise interview.

21. Ibid.

22. Ibid.

23. Wise, *Best Wishes*, 164.

24. Napoleon Hill, "Women Now Coming into Own in Business World," *Houston Post*, November 6, 1956.

25. Jerry Wise interview.

26. "Mrs. Wise Endorses Reserve Plan: Giving Two Sons to Army," *Kissimmee Gazette*, June 22, 1956.

27. Mariellen Kauch, "Brownie Creates Magic with Treasurama," *Orlando Sentinel*, July 1, 1956.

28. Ibid.

29. Brownie Wise, "Welcome Home" speech, July 1956, Wise Papers.

30. "Kaltenborn, Rudy Vallee Entertain at Tupperware Jubilee, *Kissimmee Gazette*, July 6, 1956.

31. Jerry Wise interview.

32. Jordan interview.

33. "Tupperware Homecoming Jubilee Extra," *Kissimmee Gazette* Supplement, July 1956.

34. McDonald interview.

35. Ibid.

36. Osterweil, "Tupper Biography," chap. 10.

37. McDonald interview.

38. Osterweil, "Tupper Biography," chap. 10.

39. *Tupperware Sparks* 5, no. 7 (July 1956).

40. Lavon Weber, Wichita, Kans., dealer, to Brownie Wise, December 6, 1957, Wise Papers.

41. Jordan interview.

42. *Tupperware Sparks* 5, no. 7(July 1956).

43. *Tupperware Sparks* 5, no. 9 (September 1956).

44. Ibid.

45. Don Hinton, "Mrs. Brownie Wise Is Extended High Honor," *Kissimmee Gazette*, October 26, 1956.

46. Ibid.

47. Ibid.

48. Ibid.

49. McDonald interview.

50. Brownie Wise to Earl Tupper, memorandum, May 27, 1957, Wise Papers.

51. Ibid.

52. Ibid.

53. Ibid.

54. Ibid.

55. Ibid.

56. Ibid.

57. Brownie Wise to Earl Tupper, memorandum, November 21, 1953, Wise Papers.

58. Brownie Wise to Earl Tupper, memorandum, May 27, 1957, Wise Papers.

Chapter 14. Hibiscus, the Sunshine Cinderella

Epigraph source: Brownie Wise to Earl Tupper, memorandum, May 27, 1957, Wise Papers.

1. Gary McDonald to Brownie Wise, memorandum, January 7, 1958, Wise Papers.

2. Brownie Wise to Earl Tupper, memorandum, May 27, 1957, Wise Papers.

3. "Publishing Company Formed in Orlando," *Orlando Sentinel*, January 19, 1957.

4. Jon Whitcomb, Darien, Conn., to Brownie Wise, January 28, 1957, Wise Papers. Whitcomb was a magazine writer who struck up a friendship with Wise while working on an article.

5. Brownie Wise to Earl Tupper, memorandum, May 27, 1957, Wise Papers.

6. Ibid.

7. Ibid.

8. Max Norris, "Culture Comes to City, but City Won't Come to Culture," *Kissimmee Gazette*, January 25, 1957.

9. *Tupperware Sparks* 6, no. 1 (January 1957).

10. Fred DeWitt, interview by the author, Winter Park, Fla., August 15, 2005 (hereafter cited as DeWitt interview). DeWitt was a freelance photographer who did a number of jobs for Wise and Tupperware.

11. Ibid.

12. Jon Whitcomb, "Sunshine Cinderella," *Cosmopolitan*, April 1957.

13. Ibid.

14. Ibid.

15. Ibid.

16. Ibid.

17. Ibid

18. "April Cosmopolitan Has Local Features," *Kissimmee Gazette*, undated clipping, Wise Papers.

19. "Brownie Gives Royalties to Heart Fund," *Kissimmee Gazette*, undated clipping, Wise Papers.

20. "Brownie's Book Is Proving Popular," *Kissimmee Gazette*, undated clipping, Wise Papers.

21. Ibid.

22. Earl Tupper to Brownie Wise, memorandum, April 29, 1957, Wise Papers.

23. Brownie Wise to Earl Tupper, memorandum, May 26, 1957, Wise Papers.

24. Ibid.

25. Ibid.

26. Legal settlement document detailing settlement between Wise and writer Robert Froman, Wise Papers.

27. Brownie Wise to Earl Tupper, memorandum, May 26, 1957, Wise Papers.

28. Ibid.

29. Ibid.

30. Mrs. Franklin D. Roosevelt (New York, N.Y.), to Brownie Wise, May 20, 1957. Wise sent copies of her book to many famous people. Roosevelt sent a thank-you note.

31. Wise, *Best Wishes*, 17.

32. Ibid.

33. Dr. Norman Vincent Peale, foreword to *Best Wishes*, by Wise, 7.

34. Brownie Wise to Lawrence Rogers, May 30, 1958, Wise Papers.

35. Mortland interview.

36. Ponticelli interview.

37. Brownie Wise to Earl Tupper, memorandum, May 27, 1957, Wise Papers.

38. Ibid.

39. Ibid.

40. Ibid.

41. Ibid.

42. Brownie Wise, handwritten note to mark her son's nineteenth birthday, Wise Papers.

43. McDonald interview.

44. Ponticelli interview.

Chapter 15. Jubilee Nightmare

Epigraph source: McDonald interview.

1. Brownie Wise to Earl Tupper, memorandum, May 27, 1957, Wise Papers.

2. Ibid.

3. Ibid.

4. "Tupperware Turned into World in Miniature," *Kissimmee Gazette*, June 28, 1957.

5. Ibid.

6. "Hawaiian Luau is Highlight of Party," *Kissimmee Gazette*, July 4, 1957.

7. Ibid.

8. Ibid.

9. Deposition of Hamer Wilson, September 15, 1959, *Croxton, Boyd, Boyd and Rector vs. Tupper, Rexall, Tupper Corp. Tupperware Home Parties, Richard Fletcher and William Herrin*, Ninth Judicial Circuit, Osceola County, Fla. Hereafter, depositions in this case will be cited by the name of the person deposed.

10. "Hawaiian Luau Is Highlight of Party," *Kissimmee Gazette*, July 4, 1957.

11. Jack McCollum, interview by the author, Saint Cloud, Fla., July 17, 2005 (hereafter cited as McCollum interview). McCollum was Tupperware's unofficial photographer for years and photographed many key events and people.

12. Wilson deposition.

13. Gary McDonald deposition, September 11, 1959.

14. McCollum interview.

15. William Boyd deposition, September 11, 1959. Boyd was one of the boat drivers during the luau.

16. Glen Bump deposition, September 15, 1959. Bump was another member of the Tupperware public relations department.

17. Thelma Croxton deposition, September 8, 1959. Croxton's husband was a boat driver seriously hurt in a collision on Lake Toho.

18. Gerald Croxton deposition, September 8, 1959. Croxton was a victim of the boat collision.

19. Ibid.

20. Ibid.

21. Boyd deposition.

22. Ibid.

23. Dr. M. L. Jewell deposition, October 7, 1960. Jewell triaged boat-accident victims at the city dock. He also attended the luau.

24. Jerry Wise interview.

25. McDonald interview.

26. Ponticelli interview.

27. Jerry Wise interview.

28. Ponticelli interview.

29. Mortland interview.

30. McDonald interview.

31. "Hawaiian Luau Is Highlight of Party," *Kissimmee Gazette*, July 4, 1957.

32. McDonald interview.

33. Mortland interview.

Chapter 16. The Breaking Point

Epigraph source: Creiger, handwritten memoir, Tupper Papers.

1. Ibid.

2. Hinton interview.

3. Earl Tupper to Brownie Wise, memorandum, November 25, 1957, Tupper Papers.

4. Earl Tupper, "History of Tupperware," 3, Tupper Papers. This typescript offers Earl Tupper's own brief account of his company's history. There is no mention of Wise.

5. Ibid.

6. Brownie Wise to Lawrence Rogers, May 31, 1958.

7. Ibid.

8. McDonald interview.

9. *Croxton vs. Tupper et al.*, At law no. 2328, Circuit Court of the Ninth Judicial Circuit for Osceola County. Three lawsuits were filed individually and later joined as a single case. Hereafter, citations will include the individual case name and the case number).

10. *Boyd vs. Tupper et al.*, At law no. 2329.

11. Ibid.

12. Brownie Wise to Lawrence Rogers, May 31, 1958, Wise Papers.

13. Ibid.

14. Ibid.

15. Ibid.

16. Earl Tupper to Brownie Wise, memorandum, November 12, 1957, Wise Papers.

17. Earl Tupper to Brownie Wise, memorandum, November 8, 1957, Wise Papers.

18. Brownie Wise to Earl Tupper, memorandum, November 16, 1957, Wise Papers.

19. Ibid.

20. Ibid.

21. Brownie Wise to Earl Tupper, memorandum, December 20, 1957, Wise Papers.

22. Ibid.

23. Ibid.

24. Ibid.

25. Creiger, handwritten memoir, Tupper Papers.

26. McDonald interview.

27. Brownie Wise to Earl Tupper, memorandum, December 20, 1957, Wise Papers.

28. Ponticelli interview.

29. McDonald interview.

30. Ponticelli interview.

31. Ibid.

32. Earl Silas Tupper, "Renunciation," typescript, 1967, Tupper Papers.

33. Earl Tupper to Brownie Wise, memorandum, December 31, 1957, Wise Papers.

34. Ibid.

35. Ibid.

36. Ibid.

37. Brownie Wise to Earl Tupper, memorandum, January 3, 1958, Wise Papers.

38. Ibid.

39. Ibid.

40. Ibid.

41. Ibid.

Chapter 17. Pictures of Despair

Epigraph source: Brownie Wise to Earl Tupper, memorandum, May 27, 1957, Wise Papers.

1. Earl Tupper to Brownie Wise, undated telegram (likely early January 1958), Wise Papers.

2. Ibid.

3. Brownie Wise to Lawrence Rogers, May 31, 1958, Wise Papers.

4. Ibid.

5. Ibid.

6. Ibid.

7. Ibid.

8. Creiger, handwritten memoir, Tupper Papers.

9. McDonald interview.

10. Ibid.

11. Ibid.

12. Ibid.

13. Brownie Wise to Earl Tupper, February 25, 1958, Wise Papers. This letter, detail-

ing the meeting where the contract was discussed, is believed to be the last written correspondence from Wise to Tupper.

14. Ibid.

15. Osterweil, handwritten notes detailing the timeline of events regarding Wise's dismissal, Tupper Papers.

16. Kahn-Leavitt, *Tupperware!*

17. Earl Tupper to Brownie Wise, January 30, 1958. This letter, detailing Wise's removal, is believed to be the last letter from Tupper to Wise.

18. Creiger, handwritten memoir, Tupper Papers.

19. Hinton interview.

20. Ibid.

21. Mortland interview.

22. McDonald interview.

23. Wise, *Tupperware Spark-O-Gram*, February 1, 1958, Wise Papers.

24. Tupperware press release, February 3, 1958, Tupper Papers.

25. "Employment Contract," page 2, section 2, subsection c., Wise Papers (hereafter cited as Contract). The dispute over this agreement led to Brownie Wise being entirely let go from Tupperware.

26. Contract, page 3, sec. d.

27. Ibid., page 4, sec. 4.

28. Ibid., page 5, sec. 5.

29. Brownie Wise to Earl Tupper, February 25, 1958, Wise Papers.

30. Wise response to Seraphine audit, Wise Papers.

31. Ibid.

32. Ponticelli interview.

33. Murray Overstreet, Kissimmee, Fla., to Lawrence Rogers, March 7, 1958, Wise Papers. This letter documented the official end of Brownie Wise's employment with Tupperware.

34. Jerry Wise interview.

35. *Wise vs. Tupper et al.*, case number 5701, Circuit Court for the Ninth Judicial Circuit of Florida, Osceola County (hereafter cited as Wise lawsuit). This was the $1.6-million lawsuit filed against Tupper and other members of THP's executive staff including Wilson and McDonald.

36. Ibid.

37. Typed timeline of events leading up to Brownie Wise's dismissal, signed by George Reynolds, Wise Papers. Reynolds explains that Wise had a list of dealer names but willingly returned it, and that Tupper seemed satisfied.

38. Earl Tupper to Don Hinton at al., memorandum, June 7, 1958, Tupper Papers.

39. Brownie Wise to Lawrence Rogers, May 17, 1958, Wise Papers.

40. McDonald interview.

41. Hinton interview.

42. Earl Tupper to Hamer Wilson and Gary McDonald, memorandum, Tupper Papers.

43. Ibid.

44. Nellie Stewart, Jasonville, Ind., Tupperware dealer, to Brownie Wise, August 21, 1958, Wise Papers.

Chapter 18. Moving on, Selling Out

Epigraph source: Tupper Advice.

1. Rita Hunt, "Brownie Wise Sees Future Here," *Kissimmee Gazette,* February 7, 1958.

2. "First New Home Is Sold at Brownie Wise Developments," *Kissimmee Gazette,* February 7, 1958.

3. Ibid.

4. Mary Frances Babb to Frank Lightbown, memorandum, May 8, 1958, Tupper Papers. Babb was secretary to Brownie Wise and continued on after Wise's ouster.

5. McDonald interview.

6. Ibid.

7. Mortland interview.

8. Ibid.

9. Wise, "Tupperware is the way," undated speech, Wise Papers.

10. Mortland interview.

11. McDonald interview.

12. Ibid.

13. "Justin Whitlock Dart," biography, www.Answers.com.

14. Creiger, handwritten memoir, Tupper Papers.

15. McDonald interview.

16. Fishman, "Is the Party Over?"

17. Tupperware press release, September 30, 1958, Tupper Papers.

18. Ibid.

19. Tupper, "History of Tupperware."

20. Ibid.

21. "Cinderella Shows Very Rapid Growth, *Kissimmee Gazette,* November 21, 1958.

22. "Executives Fly to Sales Meetings," *Kissimmee Gazette,* August 1, 1958.

23. Jerry Wise interview.

24. Ibid.

25. Tupper, "History of Tupperware."

26. Creiger, handwritten memoir, Tupper Papers.

27. Tupper, "Renunciation."

28. McDonald interview.

29. Ibid.

30. Treaster, "Earl Tupper, the Father of Home Parties, Dies," *New York Times,* October 7, 1983.

31. Jordan interview.

32. "Tupperware, a Company Built in the 50s," *Orlando Sentinel,* February 20, 2000.

33. Ponticelli interview.

Chapter 19. Legacies

Epigraph source: "Tupperware, a Company Built in the 50s," *Orlando Sentinel*, February 20, 2000.

1. Jordan interview.
2. Mortland interview.
3. McCollum interview.
4. Ponticelli interview.
5. McDonald and Ponticelli interviews.
6. Ponticelli interview.
7. Ibid.
8. Hinton interview.
9. Wise, "Story of Tupperware."
10. www.Tupperware.com
11. Ibid.
12. Dave Barry, "Bang the Tupperware Drum Slowly," *Miami Herald*, February 15, 1987.
13. Gina Kaufmann, "Appetite for Destruction," *Pitch*, February 7, 2006.
14. "Victims Find Unlikely Survival Tools," *Knight Ridder Newspapers*, MyrtleBeach Online.com, September 12, 2005.
15. www.Tupperware.com
16. Hamer Wilson to Earl Tupper, memorandum, July 1961, Tupper Papers.
17. "Tupperware Home to be Demolished," *Orlando Sentinel*, September 16, 1989.
18. "Fran," Tupperware executive, to Wise, handwritten letter, 1989, Wise Papers. This letter was written in anticipation of Wise giving a fifteen-minute speech in 1989. She decided not to attend.
19. Jerry Wise interview.
20. Fishman, "Is the Party Over?"
21. Ibid.
22. Ibid.
23. Boyett, "The Lady Who Built Tupperware," *Orlando Sentinel*, September 29, 1992.
24. Ibid.
25. Jerry Wise interview. All subsequent quotations are taken from this interview.

SELECTED BIBLIOGRAPHY

Block, Elsie. *My Tupperware Party Was Over and I Sat Down and Cried*. Bloomington, Ind.: Authorhouse, 2004.

Boyd, Valerie. *Wrapped in Rainbows: The Life of Zora Neale Hurston*. New York: Scribner, 2003.

Clarke, Alison J. *Tupperware: The Promise of Plastic in 1950s America*. Washington, D.C.: Smithsonian Institution Press, 1999.

Dickinson, Joy Wallace. *Orlando, City of Dreams*. Mount Pleasant, S.C.: Arcadia, 2003.

Fishman, Charles. "Is the Party Over?" *Orlando Sentinel*, March 15, 1987.

Green, Ben. *Before His Time: The Untold Story of Harry T. Moore, America's First Civil Rights Martyr*. New York: Free Press, 1999.

Halberstam, David. *The Fifties*. New York: Random House, 1996.

Hetherington, Alma. *The River of the Long Water*. Chuluota, Fla.: Mickler House, 1980.

Kwolek-Folland, Angel. *Incorporating Women: A History of Women and Business in the United States*. New York: Twayne, 1998.

Mormino, Gary. *Land of Sunshine, State of Dreams*. Gainesville: University Press of Florida, 2005.

Wise, Brownie. *Best Wishes*. Orlando: Podium, 1957.

Index

Angebilt Hotel, 1–3, 122, 189, 190
Ansley, John, 142, 201, 219

Babb, Mary Frances, 144, 161, 169, 188, 190, 199
Bakelite, 16
Barry, Dave, 209
Bassett, Russell, 52, 74
Bendix, 12, 13, 18
Best, Bob, 175, 178
Best Wishes, 148, 159, 162–66
Beveridge, Frank Stanley, 17–19, 26, 27
Blackstone, R.I., plant, 103, 133
Block, Peter, and Elsie Block, 20, 43, 44, 55, 58, 63, 65, 77–78, 80, 90, 102; ouster from Tupperware, 125–29, 135, 220
Boca Raton, Fla., 60, 64
Boltz, Jayne, and Bob Boltz, 33, 40, 42
Boston, Mass., 25, 32, 91, 154, 203
Boyd, Jon, and Sylvia Boyd, 142
Boyd, William (Bill), 174, 175, 181
Branch River Lab, R.I., 152, 179
Bronson, Irlo, 76, 99, 171, 214
Brownie Wise Developments, 198
Bump, Glen, 113, 116, 146, 172, 174

Canada, expansion into, 47, 57
Carmony, Margaret, 143
Cinderella International Corporation, 199–202
Collamore, Victor, 33, 40, 42, 43
Collins, LeRoy, 146
Conlogue, Jack, 137, 139, 156
Conlogue, Jean, 137, 138, 139, 156, 203
Costa Rica, Earl Tupper's home in, 203

Creiger, Ed, 14–15, 59, 179, 183, 188, 189, 191, 195, 200, 202
Croxton, Gerald (Gerry), 174–76, 178, 180–81
Cuba, 111
Cuero, Tex., 29, 47–48, 60

Dallas, Tex., 9
Damigella, Ann, and Tom Damigella, 25, 30, 32, 44, 52, 56, 71, 80, 91, 161
Dart, Justin Whitlock, Sr., 200–201, 203, 211, 219
Dearborn, Mich., 11, 17, 26, 35
Deland, Fla., 85, 140
Detroit, Mich., 7–9, 11, 12, 20, 21, 23, 25, 33, 40, 42, 43, 58, 73, 75, 85
DeWitt, Fred, 160, 173
Dubsdread Country Club, 68, 77
DuPont, 10, 16, 56

Evans, James B., 40, 42, 43, 65, 78, 80

Farnumsville, Mass., 11, 23, 25, 32, 33, 44, 53, 56, 57, 67, 88, 90, 103, 104, 119, 133
Feinberg, Harold, 110
Fiene, Ernest, 133
Fisherville, Mass., 53, 55, 61, 66, 103
Footwear Plastics Corporation, 180
Fortier, Ann, 73
Fort Lauderdale, Fla., 36, 49
Froman, Robert, 148, 164, 194
Fuhr, Don, 100–101, 116, 125
Fuller Brush Company, 17

Go-Getter newsletter, 19, 45

Hara, Joe, 142, 159, 203, 219
Hawaii, 94, 95
Henry, Dot, and Bill Henry, 126
Hibiscus (pen name of Brownie Wise),
 12–14, 31, 36, 47, 93, 148, 219
Hibiscus Sales, 103, 115
Hinton, Don, 122, 124, 127, 129, 142, 153,
 154, 176, 179, 189, 191, 196, 208
Homestead, Fla., 137
Hostess Division, Tupperware, 44–46,
 49, 52–54
Humphrey, Rose (Brownie Wise's
 mother), 9, 11, 33, 36, 185, 198, 202;
 as Stanley manager: 20–21; as
 Tupperware distributor, 46, 68, 77, 80,
 102–3, 110, 115, 125, 134, 137, 200

I Love Lucy, 167, 213
Isla Milagra (Makinson Island), 145, 159,
 162, 167, 172, 198, 205

J. L. Hudson Department Store, 23, 25,
 33, 75, 204
Jordan, Pat, 136–39, 141, 152, 156, 166, 203,
 206
Jordan, Phil, 156, 206
Jubilee (Tupperware tradition), 1, 101,
 118, 120, 141, 159, 194; first annual,
 104–11; 1955 annual, 131–32; 1956 annual, 147, 148, 150–53; 1957 annual, 159,
 167, 170–77; 1958 annual, 197, 199

Kissimmee, Fla., 46, 61, 76, 81, 82–84,
 106–8, 112, 120, 146, 148, 172, 175, 177,
 178, 189, 195, 198–202, 206, 212, 214,
 220
Kissimmee Gazette, 76, 83, 84, 91, 105, 107,
 114, 154, 163, 170, 177, 198, 202
Korean War, 45, 55

Lake Tohopekaliga, 2, 81, 83, 84, 145, 172,
 179, 205, 212, 214
Levitt, Corliss, 88, 91, 116, 134
Long Island, N.Y., 44, 52
Lord, Gwen, 43

McBurney, Charles, 103, 113, 115, 116, 124,
 140, 159, 172, 177, 191, 199, 202
McCall, Jack, 100, 108, 159
McCollum, Jack, 91, 123, 147, 173, 174, 176,
 206, 208
McDonald, Gary, 1, 210; association with
 Stanley, 20–21, 25–26; character and
 personality, 2, 31, 142; as marine recruit, 35, 55; move to Florida, 67; recol-
 lections of, 5, 30, 60, 69, 97, 99, 103,
 104, 107, 110, 113, 126–28, 130, 161, 169,
 172–77, 184, 190, 196, 199, 200–201,
 208; relationship with Brownie Wise,
 31, 33, 191–92; role in THP, 55, 56,
 68, 91, 96, 189, 191, 204; view of Earl
 Tupper, 76, 152, 154, 203
Makinson, Dick, 146, 172, 177
Makinson Island, 205
Mann, Jack, 171, 208
Marshall, Jack, 27, 85, 91, 94, 99, 108, 116,
 125, 127, 128, 145, 159, 208
Martin Aircraft Company, 159
Mennello, Marilyn, 203
Miami, Fla., 37, 45, 49, 60, 61, 64, 66, 68,
 77, 117, 138, 159, 214, 215
Moore, Harry T., and Harriette Moore,
 62
Mortland, Elsie, 85, 113, 140, 142, 153, 166,
 176, 178, 191, 199, 200, 204, 206, 207,
 213
Museum of Modern Art, 22

New York City, 22, 29, 96, 97, 114, 116, 120
Norfolk, Va., 139, 206
North Smithfield, R.I., plant 133
Nyberg, Elmer, 19–20

Orange Blossom Trail, 2, 76, 82, 89, 150,
 159, 205, 214
Orlando, Fla., 1, 2, 3, 43, 45, 76, 102,
 103, 131, 133, 177, 202, 206, 207, 220;
 Brownie Wise's home in, 68, 77; site
 of Hibiscus Sales, 102–3; temporary
 home of THP, 61–62, 66–69, 72, 79–80
Orlando Evening Star, 68

Orlando municipal airport, 60, 61, 66, 67
Orlando Sentinel-Star, 66, 163

Paris, France, 101, 102, 114, 143
Pasadena, Calif., 43, 59, 77, 88, 125, 128
Patio Parties, 37–40, 42, 45, 103
Peale, Norman Vincent, 131, 148, 166
Plastics Hall of Fame, 203
Polyethylene, 16, 21, 22, 32, 86, 97, 107,
    108, 201
Poly-T, 22, 23, 25, 30, 31, 32, 39, 52, 62, 95,
    140, 184, 203, 219
Ponticelli, Tony, 120, 121, 136, 141, 142,
    144, 145, 166, 168, 173, 176, 184, 194,
    204, 207, 209

Rexall Drug Company, 200–203
Reynolds, George, 113, 116, 132, 152, 167,
    172, 176, 184, 191, 195
Rogers, Marge, 58, 74
Roosevelt, Eleanor, 164
Ruder and Finn, 95–99

Saint Augustine, Fla., 36
Saint Petersburg, Fla., 40, 42, 78, 80
Sanford, Fla., 2, 46
Sara Lee Corporation, 210
Schofield, Eli, 77, 80, 125
Segregation, 62, 84, 146
Seraphine, Dave, 116, 180, 191, 194, 195,
    207
Shannon, Dorothy, 20, 21, 35, 63
Shirley, Mass., 10
Smithell, John, 148, 149
Smithfield, R.I., 133, 152
Squires, Norman, 44, 45, 47, 49, 50, 52, 53
Stanley Home Products, 17–21, 26, 27,
    30, 44
Starke, Fla., 60
Sterhan, Eleanor, 86–87

Tampa, Fla., 35, 40, 42, 113
Tifton, Ga., 31
Tourism, 61, 76, 105, 132, 205, 207
Tupper, Earl Silas: characterization, 1, 3,
5, 15, 48, 67, 76, 77, 79, 119, 152, 181, 203;
    early life, 9–10; management style,
    28, 87, 100, 103, 118, 127, 133–34, 157;
    marriage and family, 10–11, 185, 202;
    philanthropy, 219; relationship with
    Brownie Wise, 52, 71–73, 92, 99, 112,
    119, 142, 163, 168, 169, 178, 179, 180,
    183–85; retirement, 202–3; death, 203
—career: Tupper Tree Doctors, 10;
    Viscoloid, 10–11; founding of Tupper
    Plastics, 11; early business plans, 14–16;
    research and invention, 21–22; mar-
    keting strategy, 29–30, 44, 56, 74–75,
    95; expansion of Tupper Corporation,
    47–48, 60–61, 88, 101, 103–4, 116–17,
    133; role as company president, 99,
    106, 112, 124, 163, 179, 182, 186; firing of
    Brownie Wise, 5, 189–96; chairman of
    Tupper board, 201
Tupper, Glenn, 48, 185
Tupper, Marie Whitcomb, 10, 11, 185, 202
Tupper, Mark, 185
Tupper, Myles, 10, 21, 185
Tupper, Ronald, 10, 185
Tupper, Starr, 11, 185
Tupperware (product), 7, 26, 29–31,
    52–53, 58, 78, 85, 93, 101, 108, 137, 140,
    161, 182; invention of, 22; manufacture
    of, 32, 56–57, 201; merchandising of,
    56, 74–75, 88, 100, 154; "Millionaire
    Line," 23–25; origin of parties, 31, 32,
    44; popularity of, 23, 73, 99, 125, 140,
    166, 200, 211
Tupperware Art Fund, 91, 133, 160
Tupperware Brands Corporation, 210–11
Tupper Corporation, 25, 33, 66, 67, 83,
    183; global market, 29; organization of,
    44–45, 59, 179; sale of, 200–201
Tupperware Home Parties Division
    (THP), 53, 55, 58, 101; move to Florida,
    67–69; first birthday, 73; purchase of
    land for, 76; new headquarters, 82–83,
    89–91, 94; second birthday, 91; press
    party, 96, 97–98; relationship with
    distributors, 126–35; growth, 142

Tupperware Sparks newsletter, 59, 69, 71, 78, 80, 89, 91, 93, 102, 143, 147

Whitcomb, Jon, 159–62

Wilson, Hamer, 1, 2, 5, 113, 125, 128, 137, 144, 183, 184, 189, 191, 195, 206, 212; characterization, 139, 142, 145, 208; president of THP, 201, 203; recollections, 172, 174–75

Wise, Brownie Humphrey: autocratic style, 74, 125, 144, 166, 219; characterization, 3–5, 14, 27, 39, 79, 85, 94, 160, 206, 219; childhood, 12, 31; health problems, 47, 49, 123, 184; image, 93, 95, 98–99, 118–19, 121, 123, 129, 154, 163, 171, 190; marriage, 9, 122; motherhood, 7–9, 11–12, 167; move to Florida, 35–37; relationship with Earl Tupper, 4, 51–52, 75–77, 100, 119, 142, 157, 178, 180, 184, 186–87, 189; as speaker, 18, 58, 98, 109–10; values, 12, 62, 146, 149, 165; Water's Edge home, 81, 83–84, 93, 189, 193, 195; as writer, 12–13, 59, 70, 148; death, 213–14

—career: Bendix executive secretary, 12–13; Stanley dealer, 17–18, 20, 26–27; Tupperware dealer and distributor, 30, 33–34, 45–46, 49–51; Tupper Corporation general sales manager, 53, 55–58; Tupper Corporation vice president, 59, 80, 99–100, 124, 155–56; termination with THP, 190–96; Cinderella International Corporation president, 199–202

Wise, Jerry: author's interview of, 214–19; birth, 8; childhood and teen years, 9, 11–12, 26, 33, 35, 36, 40, 60, 69, 81, 83, 92, 93, 148–50, 161, 172, 175, 185, 191, 194–95; relationship with Brownie Wise, 41, 123, 124, 147, 167, 199; relationship with Robert Wise, 122; view of Brownie Wise, 119, 144, 145, 146, 176, 213, death, 219

Wise, Robert (Bobby), 9, 11, 122, 215, 216

Workforce, women in, 7, 11, 12, 27, 28, 33, 53, 87, 144, 154

World War II, 9, 11, 18, 22, 30, 53, 69, 87

Young, Herbert, 89, 73, 171

Zewicky, Florence, 20, 33

Bob Kealing is an Emmy Award–winning reporter for NBC's WESH-TV in Orlando and the author of *Kerouac in Florida: Where the Road Ends.*